MW00781154

Dear Kelly:

I hope you enjoy reading this book as much as I enjoyed writing it.

Brian J. "Doc" Shelley

9/10/08

# Have You Lost Your Mind?

*Honoring God with Your
Thinking and Decisions*

## BRIAN J. SHELLEY

GlobalEdAdvancePress
37321-7635 USA

Have You Lost Your Mind?
Honoring God With Your Thinking and Decisions

Copyright © 2008
Brian J. Shelley

Printed in the United States of America
ISBN 978-0-9801674-1-2

Published by

GlobalEdAdvancePress
37321-7635 USA

# Dedication

**To my wife, Sharon,**
**For her help and support.**
**God blessed me with her.**

# TABLE OF CONTENTS

# AUTHOR'S PREFACE

People are usually surprised to learn that the Bible does not teach that

- Money is the root of all evil
- Spare the rod and spoil the child
- God helps those who help themselves.

If you do not believe me, get a Bible concordance and look up the words to search for each reference. I'll wait. . .

. . .Welcome back. Find them? I didn't think so. You found something similar to the first two statements (the "love" of money is the root of all evil, and if you spare your rod, you hate your son), but nothing remotely close to "God helps those who help themselves," and it is no surprise since this is actually a pagan teaching, not a Christian doctrine. Aesop, c. 550 B.C. said, "The gods help them that help themselves." The true God of the Bible does the opposite—He helps those who cannot help themselves.

These are somewhat trivial statements; they probably have not had a profound influence upon how you have lived or will live your life. However, there are other subjects you may incorrectly believe the Bible teaches that can result in a lack of power, joy, spiritual growth, and effectiveness in your Christian life.

You, like everyone, have many questions about how to live the Christian life. Many questions get answered correctly, but some do not. How would you know if what you were told was accurate or an error? This book will provide you with tools to help you distinguish the true from the false.

We will also examine some questions Christians have that are not usually addressed like:

- How can God be the sovereign, absolute ruler of the universe, and yet we seem to have a free will that can thwart His plans?

- Does God determine, or cause, everything that happens, or do some things "just happen?"

- Why does God allow bad things to happen to good people, like hurricanes and tornadoes?

- You have probably been taught that when you're making a decision, to seek a sign from the Lord or a feeling of peace about what you should do. Have you ever investigated whether people in the New Testament sought signs, revelation, a peaceful feeling, or leading or guiding of the Holy Spirit when they made decisions?

- Have you wondered if God really commands abstinence from alcohol (the story of Jesus turning water into wine has perhaps made you wonder about this)?

- If terrorists stormed your home, murdered one of your two children, asked if you have another child, and you said, "No," would you later have to repent to God and ask the terrorists for forgiveness for lying?

- Does God see all nudity and sexuality in art as pornography?

- Are faith and logic compatible?  How do you reconcile the two?

- You became a Christian.  Have you lost your mind? One of the fears some people have about becoming a Christian is that once they get saved, they will have to leave their brain at the church door.  Is that true?

The biblical answers to these questions may surprise you. If these are questions you have asked or to which you would like to find answers, keep reading. Jesus said you are to love the Lord your God with all your mind. Investigate with me how to do that.

Yet ah!  Why should they know their fate?

Since sorrow never comes too late,

And happiness too swiftly flies.

Thought would destroy their paradise.

No more; where ignorance is bliss,

'Tis folly to be wise.


Thomas Gray

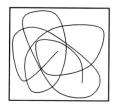

# CHAPTER ONE

# Combining Logic and Faith

## Introduction

### Brain Teaser

Jael, the Jewish wife of Heber the Kenite, was a great thinker and a woman of faith. Her story is tucked inside the account of Judge Deborah and General Barak's fight against King Jabin of Canaan and his general Sisera in Judges 4 (if you cannot find Judges 4, look closer at the non-dog-eared portion of your Bible). Jabin and Sisera cruelly oppressed the Israelites for twenty years. They had 900 iron chariots (the nuclear weapons of the day), and Israel was chariotless.

Under the leadership of Deborah and Barak, the out-manned Israeli army rebelled against Sisera's army. Sisera positioned his chariots for battle in the normally dry Kishon Creek bed. God sent a gully washer that flooded the creek, immobilizing Sisera's army and neutralizing his advantage. Chariots do not work in mud or in a flood. Sisera and his charioteers were up the creek. Israel conquered the Canaanites, but General Sisera escaped. He sought refuge in Heber's tent since they had a peace treaty with one another, but Heber was not home. However, Jael was home, and she had signed no treaty. Deborah had prophesied in verse nine the honor of killing Sisera would go to a woman—and he just entered a woman's tent.

Jael evidently considered herself part of the Israeli army. She did not wait long to execute her critically-thought plan—let Sisera go to sleep and then permanently put him to sleep. Jael offered Sisera milk and hid him under a blanket, cultural signs that she would protect his life. Sisera felt protected and safe, ordering Jael not to tell anyone he was there. Verse 21 says, "But Jael, Heber's wife, picked up a tent peg and a hammer and went quietly to him while he lay fast asleep, exhausted. She drove the peg through his temple into the ground, and he died." Now that is being tired! Since Bedouin women were responsible to pitch the tents, swinging mallets and driving stakes were part of her regular routine.[1] She had no trouble using her thinking and hammering abilities to the glory of God.

What a smashing story. Point taken. She nailed him.[2] He pegged her wrong, but she certainly pegged him right. Sisera was the first man to get hammered after drinking just milk. The milk was not spiked, but he was. Yesterday Sisera was beating his brains to try to figure out how to defeat Barak; today Jael was beating his brains. Jael demonstrated that women really do know how to get inside a man's head. You have to wonder what was going through his mind. This verse contains the understatement of the Bible—"and he died." No kidding! He not only died, he decided to stick around.[3]

Jael exhibited great thinking ability and displayed great faith in God. She knew how to make a decision and flesh it out. Our decision-making process does not always seem to work as well as Jael's did because we often do not see the connection between logic and faith. What does logic have to do with faith?

## Decision Difficulties

"Lord, what do you want me to do? I have to make this decision; I need your wisdom." You pray...and pray... and pray some more, but the heavens are hushed. You beg God for a sign, a feeling, something, anything—but nothing. Other Christians tell you "the Lord led me" or "God told me." If you're honest with yourself (although you, too, may even use that Christian jargon), you are not sure what God wants or if God tells you anything. In the darkness of the night, tossing and turning in your bed, you wonder if the Lord is ignoring you. You question why God tells every other Christian what to do, but He does not tell you. You wonder if there is sin in your life, but you confess your sins, and still the Lord is silent. What does God want you to do in desperate times like these?

So, you look into Scripture; you cannot find even one person in the Bible who said the phrase "the Lord led me." The closest verse you can find is John 16:13 where Jesus promised the Holy Spirit would guide the apostles as they wrote Scripture. That gives you assurance about the veracity of Scripture but no help with the vagueness of decision-making. When the Bible was being written, God spoke to a few people audibly and through dreams and visions, but it was clear, direct revelation, unlike the fuzzy feelings associated with the popularly taught, everyday decision-making process guided by the phrase, "the Lord led me."

You read what theologians, preachers, and commentators say. You find that often these authors do not agree on what particular passages of Scripture mean. If they do not agree, can they possibly all be right? If there is such a concept as truth, and if God had a point He was trying to make when He inspired the writings of Scripture, then, at best, only one of the writers or preachers can be right, which also leaves the possibility that all of them could be wrong. How can you tell which person, if any, is right? How can you tell which ones are wrong? What does God want you to do in desperate times like these?

## So That's What That Means

The Lord wants you to use a form of logic He designed; we call it critical thinking. Logic is the science of correct reasoning, or reasoned thinking that discovers truth. Logic must, therefore, be the driving force of decision-making and interpreting Scripture.

Critical thinking, a form of logic, is a branch of the philosophical category known as epistemology, which answers the questions "What is real?" and "What is truth?" We must, therefore, not only use the principles of logic to guide our decision-making and how we interpret Scripture, but we must also use the principles of critical thinking as well.

When most people hear the word "critical," they think of something negative, like a parent or teacher who is quick to find fault, a crisis resulting from a water shortage, or a person in an unstable condition in the hospital.

However, critical also means crucial, important, and indispensable. I will use critical in the latter sense.

Critical thinking has been defined in various ways. Critical thinking means "carefully considering a problem, claim, question, or situation to determine the best solution....you take time to consider all sides of an issue [and] evaluate evidence."[4] Richard Paul and Linda Elder from the Center for Critical Thinking defined critical thinking as "thinking that displays mastery of intellectual skills and abilities. [It is] the art of thinking about your thinking while you are thinking in order to make your thinking better: more clear, more accurate, more defensible."[5] They added that critical thinking is "that mode of thinking in which the thinker improves the quality of his or her thinking by skillfully taking charge of the structures inherent in thinking and imposing intellectual standards."[6] Nosich said:

> Critical thinking involves having my thinking measure up to criteria. I can think about something accurately or inaccurately. I can use evidence that is relevant to an issue or irrelevant, or somewhere in between . . .

> Accuracy, relevance, and depth are examples of *standards* or *criteria*. The words "critical" and "criteria" come from the same root, meaning "judgment." For my thinking to be *critical* thinking, I have to make judgments that meet criteria of reasonableness[7] (author's emphasis).

Reichenbach said critical thinking involves analyzing, creatively working with, and evaluating what you read and hear so you can decide whether to believe or do something.  To become a critical thinker, you must separate truth from falsehood and judge whether the author or speaker has adequately defended his ideas. A critical thinker is a reflective, persistent questioner who asks *why* something should be believed or done and investigates the reasons in support of an idea. "Because they have reasoned and reflected carefully, critical thinkers ultimately have better grounds than most people for deciding what to believe and how to act reasonably.  In a sense, critical thinkers are skeptics."[8]

Reichenbach did not mean critical thinkers are skeptics in the philosophical sense, but that critical thinkers question what they are taught, even when the teacher is their spiritual authority.  God says the Bereans were more noble-minded because they challenged what Paul said, "examining the Scriptures daily to see whether these things [what Paul was telling them] were so" (Acts 17:11). God was not angry with the Bereans for being critical thinkers. He calls them "noble-minded." The Lord did not tell them, or us, to blindly believe what we are told.  We are to critically think through what everyone tells us.  God wants us to not only be in charge of what we think about, which is usually the emphasis in Christian teaching, but also of *how* we think—the process of thinking.

M. Carroll Tama defined critical thinking as, "A way of reasoning that demands adequate support for one's beliefs and an unwillingness to be persuaded unless support is forthcoming."[9] "They say. . ." is not good enough for a critical thinker. The correct critical thinking response is, "They who say?" So is, "How do you know this?" and, "Where did you get your information?" Couple these with, "How do you know what your source said is true?"

Critical thinkers, therefore, control their own thinking. They use logic to investigate what preachers proclaim and writers write. Critical thinkers analyze what they hear and read to determine whether what is being articulated is accurate. Critical thinkers are restless until they are certain they have uncovered the truth. They skeptically question information that others present to them. Critical thinkers are not afraid to challenge what religious authorities say. Their purpose is not to be belligerent, but to better understand what is being taught by getting clarification and documentation from the teacher and to ensure that the instructor has critically thought through the issue or passage under consideration. Martin Luther's purpose was not to start a protest movement. He tacked his 95 Theses to the door of Wittenberg Church calling for a debate and to get clarification. Unfortunately, as Luther discovered, and as you may find, people in positions of authority, including religious authority, do not always welcome the challenges.

Critical-thinking Christians ask "Why?" and want their teachers to give evidence to support a position they have taken. Critical-thinking Christians are open-minded when they hear a new interpretation of a passage of Scripture or when someone questions a theological view that may be popular. Critical-thinking Christians do not quickly dismiss what they are hearing or reading simply because it does not agree with what they were previously taught. They recognize that all humans are fallible and that what someone told them, or even what they discovered on their own, may be wrong. They are not "carried about by every wind of doctrine" (Ephesians 4:14-15).

Critical-thinking Christians are not passive listeners but active participants in the learning process. They take notes when listening to teachers and preachers and later investigate whether what they have been told is true.

Critical-thinking Christians grow in the grace and the knowledge of the Lord Jesus (2 Peter 3:18) and recognize that they cannot grow spiritually if what they are hearing or reading is not true. Critical thinkers combine the truth they learn with the principles of logic to become able decision-makers. Critical thinkers are in charge of their thinking and their lives. They please God, who designed their minds to think critically.

## Does Critical Thinking Eliminate Emotions?

One of the first objections people offer when I talk about critical thinking is that I am trying to remove emotion from Christianity. Nothing could be farther from the truth. Thinking about God generates emotions of awe, wonder, and humility. Thinking about God leads to praise and expression of deep emotion in worship. If we truly love God, Jesus said we love Him not only with all of our heart, but also with all of our mind (Matthew 22:37). To say that critical thinking eliminates emotions indicates the person does not understand critical thinking. Thinking leads to emotions. Critical thinking and emotions are inseparable—they are two sides of the same brain. Gerald Nosich, in <u>Learning to Think Through Things: A Guide to Critical Thinking Across the Curriculum</u>, said, "Some emotions can interfere with critical thinking. On the other hand, certain other emotion-laden states help with critical thinking: the love of truth is an example. So are the joy of discovery, anger at biased presentations of information, and fear of making an unreasonable decision when something very important hangs in the balance."[10] Eric Jensen said, "Our emotions help us to focus our reason and logic. . . .Our thinking is not 'contaminated' by emotions: rather, our emotions are an integral aspect of our neural operating system. Emotions speed our thinking."[11] When Jesus was in the Garden of Gethsemane the night Judas betrayed Him, He agonized over going to the cross to the point that His sweat was the size of blood droplets. Yet Christ's decision to go to the cross was made in response to His love for us and His obedience to His Father's will. His emotion correlated with His thinking. Thinking cannot be separated from emotions.

## Thinking About Thinking

How many statues can you name or recognize? Most readers probably know the <u>Statue of Liberty</u>, Michelangelo's <u>David</u>, and <u>Venus De Milo</u>. There are few other statues most people can name, except one. This statue features a naked man sitting on a stump, his left hand clasping his right knee, his right elbow resting on his right thigh, his chin resting on top of his closed fist, which is turned parallel to his neck, while staring at the ground. You may not know the sculptor was Rodin, but, without even seeing it, you know the statue is <u>The</u>

Thinker. Why, of the tens of thousands of statues in the world, has The Thinker captured our attention? The best way to answer that question may be to mimic the position of the statue's subject as described above (you do not need to get naked). Do not move from that position for 30 seconds. Come on. Do it. I am. What are you experiencing?

Your back and arm may be hurting; you feel uncomfortable and think you are wasting precious time. This statue is an apt representation of logic and critical thinking. Since it is uncomfortable and time consuming, most people rarely, if ever, engage in critical thinking. It is much easier to think about issues at the surface level or just believe what other people tell you.

The Thinker statue is popular because, deep within each of us, we long to have time to stop and think. With our fast-paced lifestyles, we have little time or energy to think deeply, to use our minds to reason about or reflect upon important issues. Additionally, I believe there is a more basic reason for our lack of critical thinking—we have never been taught how to do it. Have you ever had a course in critical thinking? Is such a class important? After all, aren't Christians supposed to emphasize faith instead of thinking?

## Are Faith and Logic Compatible?

In the evangelical tradition in which I was reared, some pastors seemed proud that they were uneducated. It was a badge of honor to say in the middle of a sermon, "I know I'm a dumb preacher, but I believe this by faith," as if knowledge and faith are unconnected.

I remember one instance when a guest speaker made a good point and quickly said, "I know I'm a dumb preacher, but..." A man we kids called "Amen Bob" yelled "Amen!" celebrating the preacher's good point just prior to the preacher's self-deprecating comment of being a dumb preacher. The church erupted into laughter. The speaker, evidently being somewhat insecure and not connecting the complimentary "amen" with the previous good point, was offended and chastised Amen Bob: "Brother that was the wrong time to say amen." In reality, the wrong words being said were "I know I'm a dumb preacher." I assume it was a veiled way to have people tell him "No, you're a smart man." Of course, there is always the possibility we cannot rule out—maybe he was a dumb preacher. After all, he inappropriately chastised Bob in front of the congregation, and Bob did not deserve that public humiliation.

The writer to the Hebrews disagrees with the error that "dumb" preachers should teach Scripture or that there is some spiritual advantage or reward for being uneducated. Hebrews 11:1 says, "Now faith is being sure of what we hope for and certain of what we do not see." Faith is being sure; faith is being certain. Faith is not wishful thinking or blind belief. Faith is rooted in the promises and Person of God, who wants us to know Him.

We must use our mind to think about the promises of God and the Person of God before we can have faith. However, we must be theologically correct in our understanding of God and His promises. For example, Christians should not tell people who are sick that if they have faith, they will get better. That is wishful thinking. The advice givers have good intentions, perhaps, but they cause needless pain nonetheless. Pain-causing Christians have often said this untruth to my wheelchair-bound mother. God has made no such promise to us. Just because you can find a description in the Bible of God healing someone does not provide a prescription from God guaranteeing to heal someone today. Not everyone in the Bible was healed (2 Timothy 2:20). Good Christians get sick and even die from sickness. Sometimes God heals; sometimes He does not. There are no promises God will heal.

However, I can tell someone who has trusted Christ as Savior that one day she will be in Heaven. That is not wishful thinking. Belief in living with God in Heaven is based on the promises of God. It is based on facts and truth. It is sure; it is certain. Believing those promises requires faith, but it is not blind faith. True faith is based in the evidence God supplied in His inerrant Word.

God's Word is inerrant. The original manuscripts, the autographs, were without error. The International Council on Inerrancy stated it well:

**We affirm** that any pre-understandings that the interpreter brings to Scripture should be in harmony with scriptural teaching and subject to correction by it.

**We deny** that Scripture should be required to fit alien pre-understandings, inconsistent with itself, such as naturalism, evolutionism, scientism, secular humanism, and relativism.

**We affirm** that since God is the author of all truth, all truths, biblical and extra-biblical, are consistent and cohere, and that the Bible speaks truth when it touches on matters pertaining to nature, history, or anything else. We further affirm that in some cases extra-biblical data have value for clarifying what Scripture teaches, and for prompting correction of faulty interpretations.

**We deny** that extra-biblical views ever disprove the teaching of Scripture or hold priority over it.

**We affirm** the harmony of special with general revelation and therefore of biblical teaching with the facts of nature.

**We deny** that any genuine scientific facts are inconsistent with the true meaning of any passage of Scripture.

**We affirm** that Genesis 1-11 is factual, as is the rest of the book.

**We deny** that the teachings of Genesis 1-11 are mythical and that scientific hypotheses about Earth history or the origin of humanity may be invoked to overthrow what Scripture teaches about creation.[12]

Outside the New Testament, the word translated "certain" in Hebrews 11:1 was translated as "evidence" or "proof." The word was objective, not subjective. It was not used in connection with wishes or feelings but with known facts. In Hebrews 11:3, God tells us we know by faith that He created the world because He told us that in Genesis 1:1.

It is sure; it is certain. That our almighty God created the world and the universe is an objective fact, not a subjective wish. On the other hand, to declare that the universe resulted from natural selection and macroevolution is a subjective wish of materialistic atheists.

Relishing in being stupid or dumb is not a biblical idea. God wants us to think, to know, because thinking and knowing lead to faith. You cannot be stupid and have faith. The Christian mind is a product in flux. "It is being hewed from a Christian's growing grasp of Scripture in the context of a recalcitrant culture [and] . . . a growing understanding of what Scripture really teaches."[13]

The Lord wants us to "be transformed by the renewing of our minds" (Romans 12:1-2). To be transformed means that we allow God to change the way we think and act so we think and act like Jesus Christ. The word "transformed" is a present passive imperative in the original Greek. It is best translated as "allowing an outside influence to continually change you." That outside influence is God and His Word changing the way we think. The new thinking precedes growth in faith and action. We must change the way we think so we can change the way we act. We cannot renew our minds if we do not think correctly. Faith is not just a responsive act of the soul; it is first an understanding in the mind. We must eschew the false dichotomy between faith and thinking. Nosich (not writing from a Christian perspective) said, "Critical thinking, in the fullest sense, results in belief. It even results in action."[14]

For centuries, many Christians, including some of the Church Fathers, have not believed that thinking precedes and then leads to faith.  Augustine of Hippo (A.D. 354-430) said, "Understanding is the reward of faith. Therefore seek not to understand that you may believe, but believe that you may understand."  Augustine believed that faith preceded knowledge.   Duns Scotus (1265? - 1308) echoed Augustine, saying, "Faith is before reason. Without faith, reason cannot arrive at the truths of Christianity."[15] The influence of Augustine upon Christian teaching is unmistakable, but was he infallible?  Like everyone else, Augustine made incorrect interpretations, particularly since much of what he said about the Bible was first filtered through his beliefs in Plato's teachings.  His view of logic and faith is one example of his errors.

John Stewart Mill, in his 1869 treatise "On Liberty" said:

> "No one can be a great thinker who does not recognize that as a great thinker it is his first duty to follow his intellect to whatever conclusions it may lead. Truth gains more even by the error of one who, with due study and preparation, thinks for himself than by the opinions of those who only hold them because they do not suffer themselves to think."[16]

Christians would do well to listen to Mill's counsel.  Mill was saying that what we believe may be wrong.  Since none of us is perfect, we are all wrong about something, even what we think we know about the Bible.  I know I am wrong about some of my interpretations of passages in the Bible.  My problem is that I do not know when I am wrong. Since knowledge is necessary for my spiritual maturity, my ignorance hinders my faith in God.  I have had to re-preach sermons because I discovered what I taught was wrong.

Admitting I am not perfect and may be wrong is what Richard Paul and Linda Elder called intellectual humility. They said you can determine if you manifest the opposite characteristic—intellectual arrogance—by asking yourself some questions.  Consider these: "Do you ever argue for or against views when you have little evidence upon which to base your judgment?", and "Do you ever assume your group is correct (when it is in conflict with others) even though you have not looked at the situation from the point of view of the others with which you disagree?"[17]  I find it much easier to be intellectually arrogant than to be intellectually humble because intellectual arrogance does not require critical thinking.

If you are wrong, admit it.  A police officer stopped a man in his car after he ran a stop sign.  The officer said, "Sir, you did not stop at that stop sign back there; you just slowed down and drove through it."  The guilty driver protested, "Slow down or stop, what's the difference?"  The police officer then took out his nightstick and began whacking the driver on the side of the head.  After several blows to the brains, the officer asked, "Now, sir, do you want me to slow down or to stop?"  If you are wrong, admit it.

Former atheist Antony Flew changed his mind about evolution and the existence of God.  Flew, a famous British atheist, writer, professor, and lecturer said his current ideas, arrived at after examining DNA research findings, have some similarity with American "intelligent design" theorists. He now doubts Darwinian evolution can explain the origins of life.  Flew said if his belief upsets people, "Well, that's too bad.  My whole life has been guided by the principle of Plato's Socrates: Follow the evidence, wherever it leads." Although Flew does not yet embrace the God of the Bible, his view of God is similar, he said, to Thomas Jefferson's deist god.[18] Flew exhibited intellectual humility, admitting he was wrong.

Additionally, John Stuart Mill proposed that many people find it easier to listen to others than to think for themselves. Christians have told me they do not like my sermons because they make them think. They just wanted to go to church and have someone tell them what to believe. How terrible and how spiritually dangerous! Another Jim Jones may have a glass of Kool-Aid with their name on it. God gave us minds to think about Him and His Word, which increases our faith. To have someone else do our spiritual thinking for us is to undermine the faith and spiritual maturity that God wants to build in us. It also makes us susceptible to being blown about by every wind of doctrine.

Mill also asserted that many people do not develop their intellect. Many Christians are not in charge of their ideas and thoughts about biblical issues. They believe other people's ideas and rarely investigate whether what they were taught is true. They engage in wishful thinking, hoping, or even worse—not caring, if what other Christians told them is true. Truth is not driven by wishful thinking or apathy. As a result, many Christians are not as mature as the Lord desires.

Truth is not determined by anyone's beliefs. Believing something does not make it true. Because your pastor believes something does not make it true. Because Augustine believed something does not make it true. I tire of hearing Christians say, "What this verse means to me is…" The question is not what the verse mean to you or me, but what does the verse to mean to God. When we interpret the passage, either we are right or wrong.

We do not determine the meaning of Scripture—God does. We only discover the meaning of Scripture. If we were dead, what would the verse mean? The interpretation of a passage of Scripture is not dependent upon us; it is dependent upon God and His intent. What we believe about the Bible must be based in evidence and in truth. Which of your biblical beliefs are based in evidence and truth? How can you tell?

Critical thinkers analyze and evaluate what they hear or read for the purposes of interpretation and understanding. Our goal is to get inside the heads of the writers of Scripture to find out exactly what they meant. It does not matter what a Bible text means to me. When we understand what the writers of Scripture intended and what God intended the passage to mean, we believe it or exercise faith in it. We know that what we believe is true. The caveat at all times is that I may not have had enough information when I decided what the passage meant, and I may need to change my position if further information makes my previous interpretation untenable. Critical thinkers attempt to reach a conclusion by being intellectually humble and evaluating their position and the opposing position based upon the available evidence and arguments. When interpreting Scripture, we use critical thinking principles to determine the best possible interpretation of the passage being studied. We ask questions, research to get answers, and then ask more questions about the answers we reach.

Critical thinking may result in us not agreeing with the way our church, our friends, or our small group interprets a passage. Now what do we do? We develop a backbone and a voice. We use the power of the Spirit of God to overcome the fear of ridicule or rejection by our peers. We argue our position with grace, ever mindful that we could be wrong, but in the end standing for what we believe is right. We must jettison any belief that does not jive with an accurate interpretation of Scripture.

If we want to please God, we must live by faith because the just shall live by faith (Romans 1:17). The Christian does not have the option to not live by faith. The great news is that we can live by faith. That means, however, that we must apply the principles of logic and critical thinking to our study of the Bible and to the ideas we believe. We must admit we do not know everything, and that some of what we believe may be in error. We must take nothing we believe for granted and examine everything. Critical thinking is hard work. Stand out in the crowd; think critically and stand for and know the truth. Believers in Jesus Christ should welcome the challenge. However, how do we know what is true? We will investigate that in the next chapter.

## For Review and Discussion

- Describe a time when you had to make an important decision but you were unsure what God wanted you to do.

- Define logic.

- Define critical thinking.

- What role do emotions play in critical thinking?

- Why is faith not blind belief?

- What can Christians glean from John Stewart Mill's statements about being a great thinker?

## ENDNOTES

1. Campbell, Donald K. Judges: Leaders in Crisis Times. Wheaton, IL: Victor Books, 1989, p. 55.

2. Davies, Paul. God and the New Physics. London: J. M. Dent & Sons, Ltd., 1983, p. 69.

3. Some of the groans in this paragraph were provided by my wife Sharon and my daughters Amy and Lisa.

4. Chesla, Elizabeth. Critical Thinking and Logic Skills for College Students: The Tools You Need to Succeed. Upper Saddle River, NJ: Prentice Hall, 1999, p. 18.

5.  Paul, Richard W. and Linda Elder. <u>Critical Thinking:
    Tools for Taking Charge of Your Professional and
    Personal Life</u>. Upper Saddle River, NJ: Prentice Hall,
    2002, p. 316.

6.  Ibid, p. 15.

7.  Nosich, Gerald M. <u>Learning to Think Through Things:
    A Guide to Critical Thinking Across the Curriculum</u>.
    Upper Saddle River, NJ: Prentice Hall, 2005, p. 3.

8.  Reichenbach, Bruce R.    <u>Introduction to Critical
    Thinking</u>. Boston: McGraw-Hill Higher Education,
    2001, pp. 13 and 19.

9.  Tama, M. Carrol.  "Critical Thinking: Promoting It in
    the Classroom." Learn2Study May 1989. <http://
    learn2study.org/teachers/critical.htm>.

10. Nosich, p. 18.

11. Jensen, Eric.  <u>Brain-Based Learning</u>. San Diego: The
    Brain Store, 2000, pp. 199 and 201.

12. Rusbult, Craig. "Inerrancy and Science."  American
    Science Affiliation: Science Education.<http://www.
    asa3.org/ASA/education/origins/icbi.htm>.

13. Sire, James W. <u>Discipleship of the Mind: Learning
    to Love God in the Ways We Think</u>. Downers Grove,
    IL: InterVarsity Press, 1990, p. 23. Nosich, p. 10.

14. Nosich, p. 10.

15. Edelstein, Melvin. "Reason and Revelation in the Middle Ages." William Paterson University. <http://www.wpunj.edu/~history/study/edelciv13.htm>.

16. Mill, John Stewart. On Liberty. Indianapolis: Hackett Publishing Company Inc., 1978, p. 32.

17. Paul and Elder, pp. 22-23.

18. Fox News. "Leading Atheist Philosopher Concludes God's Real." 9 December 2004. <http://www.foxnews.com/story/0,2933,141061,00.html >.

Freedom had been hunted round the globe;
Reason was considered as rebellion; and
The slavery of fear had made men afraid to think.
But such is the irresistible nature of truth,
That all it asks, and all it wants,
Is the liberty of appearing.

Thomas Paine

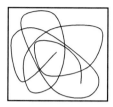

CHAPTER TWO

# Thinking is for Christians

## Going in Circles

Draw a circle on a piece of paper. Let this circle represent everything God knows. Now, color in the portion of the circle identifying the amount of knowledge you possess. No matter how small of a dot you colored, you are being generous with yourself. You cannot make a dot small enough to represent your lack of knowledge. Are you admitting you are ignorant? Actually, you are. Does that offend you? Admitting you are ignorant is a good thing. Ignorance means a lack of knowledge. Admitting ignorance is acknowledging your lack of knowledge. Ignorance drives studying subjects, research, and scientific investigation.

Look at the colored area—your measly mark. You are more ignorant than you are intelligent. Humbling, isn't it? We are experts at being ignorant. Hopefully, you are not stupid. Stupid means you cannot learn or that you do not care to learn. You are stupid if you uncritically believe whatever any authority figure, religious or otherwise, tells you, whether in a sermon, book, Sunday School class, school or college class, or small group.

We are born ignorant; stupidity is an acquired taste. Aristophenes, a fifth century B. C. poet said, "Youth ages, immaturity is outgrown, ignorance can be educated, and drunkenness sobered, but stupid lasts forever."[1] Following on that theme, Albert Einstein said, "Only two things are infinite, the universe and human stupidity, and I am not sure about the former."[2]

This book is a celebration of ignorance. In fact, we will start a new 12-step program called Ignorants Anonymous. "Hello. My name is Brian and I am ignorant. My goal in life is to claim as much of the white space in my circle as I can, particularly when it comes to knowing God and His Word." Now it is your turn. "Hello, my name is..."

Look closer at the dot you colored in the circle. See how small it is. The dot represents what you think you know, but how much of what you think you know is not true? How much of what you think you know about the Bible is not true? I will show you a plethora of popular Christian cultural misbeliefs. For example, you know the Christmas story inside out, right? You have heard it over and over again. You probably believe three kings named Melchior, Bathasar, and Caspar, journeyed from the Orient following a star that eventually led them to Jesus' manger on the night of His birth, a few minutes after the shepherds arrived. What percentage of that story is true? 100%? 75%? 50%? Less?

The answer is 0%. In the account in Matthew 2, Magi traveled to Jerusalem. We are not told how many Magi there were, much less their names. People assume there were three Magi because there were three gifts given to the Christ child. Two Magi could have brought three gifts, or fifty Magi could have brought three gifts.

Magi are not kings. "Magi" is a Medo-Persian word. Magi were priests in the Zoroastrian religion in Persia, modern-day Iran. So, Iranian priests traveled to Israel to celebrate the birth of a Jewish King—how times have changed. (How did they know about Jesus? Daniel, A former magi, prophesied the time of Jesus' birth—Daniel 9:24-27. Iranians believed Daniel; the Jews did not.) Matthew 2:2 says the Magi asked King Herod, "Where is the one who has been born king of the Jews? We *saw* his star in the east" (emphasis added). If the Magi had followed the star from Persia, they would not have had to stop to ask directions (some may conclude the Magi had to be women because they asked for directions, but they were men). If the Magi had followed the star from Persia, they would not have said they "saw His star," but they would have said, "We followed His star here." If they followed the star, why did it take the Magi to Jerusalem instead of Bethlehem where Jesus was living? If you had no other information, where else would you go to find the birthplace of a king but to the capital city and to the king himself? The Jewish religious leaders told Herod the Messiah was to be born in Bethlehem, a small town about seven miles south of Jerusalem. King Herod sent the Magi on their way, asking them to return to him when they found the Child so he could go and "worship" the new King.

Verse nine says, "They went on their way, and the star they had seen in the east went ahead of them until it stopped over the place where the child was." The Magi again see the star they had not seen since they were in Persia. The star points out the exact location of Jesus and His parents. Verse 11 tells us that Jesus was not then in a manger, but in a house. The Magi did not arrive the night of Jesus' birth. It probably took them anywhere from two months to two years to get to Bethlehem. Notice King Herod inquired of the Magi when they had seen the star (verse seven). King Herod does not kill the two-day-old babies. He kills (i.e., "worships") all of the Bethlehem babies "two years of age and under, in accordance with the time he had learned from the Magi" (verse 16). So, the next time you see a nativity scene with Jesus in the manger and the Magi present, kick them out. In celebration of the Magi's arrival, build a house in your front yard about February, and have the Magi knocking on the door.

The version of the Magi story most people believe comes not from the Bible, but from the Christmas carol "We Three Kings." How much of what you think you know about the Bible is based on culture and tradition and not Scripture itself? How much of what you think you know about the Bible is not true? How much of the colored space in your circle represent things you think you know but are not true?

We are ignorant, but we do desire to learn, to use our minds. Jesus said we are to love the Lord our God with all our mind (Matthew 22:37). Those who live by faith use their mind. Logic and critical thinking precede faith. Scripture commands us to think deeply. One of Jesus' favorite questions to his disciples was, "What do you think?"

Paul commands us to think about what is true, noble, right, pure, lovely, excellent, and admirable (Philippians. 4:8). YHWH, Jehovah God, invites us to reason with Him (Isaiah 1:18). God builds arguments with reasons. Many times an argument is concluded with the phrase "for this reason" (e.g. Ephesians 3:14). Peter commanded us to be able to give a reasoned argument for what we believe (1 Peter 3:15). God invited Job to consider His wonders in creation (Job 37:14).

The blessed man meditates upon God's Word day and night (Psalm 1:1-2). The wise consider the great love of God (Psalm 107:43). Solomon instructs us to consider, to think deeply about, what God has done (Ecclesiastes 7:13). Jesus said we are to consider how the lilies grow (Luke 12:27). The Lord wants us to think about how to spur one another on toward love and good deeds (Hebrews 10:24). When our faith is tested, God wants us to stop and think about it as a wonderful thing; we are to consider it all joy when we are tempted (James 1:2). David invited the Lord not only to examine his heart, but also to examine his mind (Psalm 26:2). The result of Solomon using his mind to investigate life led to the faith conclusion, "Remember your Creator" (Ecclesiastes 12:1). Deciding what elements of culture to participate in is not a result of the Lord leading us to certain decisions, but of being "fully convinced in one's own mind" (Romans 14:5).

Faith is not incompatible with logic and critical thinking. The great Renaissance astronomer and critical thinker Galileo said it well, "I do not feel obliged to believe that the same God who has endowed us with sense, reason, and intellect has intended us to forgo their use."[3] Use your mind and think—it will increase your faith.

## What is a Fact?

This is a fact: it is difficult to get people to agree upon the definition of a fact. What makes a fact a fact? Give a man some facts and he will draw his own confusions.

## Does Democracy Determine Facts?

Is a fact a fact because of the fact that most people believe it is a fact? Most people believe doing good works will earn Heaven for them. Can they get to Heaven by their good works? No. Therefore the statement that doing good works will earn Heaven is not a fact, even if most people believe it.

In July, what color are most leaves? A majority of people believe most leaves are green in July. However, most leaves are not green in July; most leaves are brown. Green leaves constitute one season's growth. Leaves on the ground are brown and represent two-to-four years of growth. Besides, in July in the Southern Hemisphere, there is nothing but brown leaves since the Southern Hemisphere is experiencing winter. Not only that, leaves are not really green; their true color is revealed in the fall when they show their red or yellow hue. The green color in the leaves in July is not the leaf color, but chlorophyll, which captures sunlight for photosynthesis during the spring and summer months. Chlorophyll leaves the leaf in the fall. Depending on how you view it, in July, only 0% to 20% of leaves are green, regardless of what most people believe.

Most people believing something does not make it a fact. Most people believe Christopher Columbus sailed west from Europe because he was one of the few people in the ancient world who believed the Earth was round. However, few educated people in the history of Western Civilization from the third century B.C. onward believed the Earth was flat. Of course, the oldest reference to the Earth being a sphere is from the eighth century B.C., recorded in Isaiah 40:22 where we learn that the Lord "sits enthroned above the sphere of the Earth."

I was erroneously told, and I erroneously repeated to others, that Isaiah 40:22 motivated Columbus to sail around the world and to argue against the flat-headed, flat-Earth believing people of his day. Columbus is, therefore, presented as a great Christian thinker. However, Pythagoras, in the sixth century B.C., postulated a round Earth. Aristotle concluded the Earth was round after seeing that the shadow of the Earth on the moon during an eclipse was round and observing that the North Star was directly overhead in the northern part of the planet but was at the horizon when standing at the equator. Euclid and other Greek philosophers agreed. Thousands of Christian theologians and other scholars embraced the spherical view throughout the early and medieval Church.[4]

C. S. Lewis, the Oxford University scholar and Christian said, "Physically considered, the Earth is a globe; all the authors of the high Middle Ages are agreed on this." Lewis next detailed some minor exceptions that believed in a flat Earth. He then said, "The implications of a spherical Earth were fully grasped."[5]

So, where did the flat Earth story come from? Washington Irving fabricated the tale that medieval people believed the Earth was flat like a squashed bug. In 1828, Irving, using "creative license" animated by his animosity toward Christianity, crafted the story of Columbus arguing for a spherical planet before an evil pack of theologians at a council in Salamanca, all of whom believed, according to Irving, that the Earth was not round, but flat. Columbus, scientists, and theologians did meet at Salamanca in 1491, but Irving's caricature is a lie. Columbus believed the circumference of the Earth was about 7000 miles. Remember, Columbus thought it was faster to sail west to get to India ("India" referred to the land masses of India through China and Japan) than to sail around the Horn of Africa (which was about 4,000 miles). The land route was dangerous to travel because Muslims had conquered Constantinople. Columbus believed the distance west was less than 4,000 miles, hence the 7,000 mile circumference of the Earth.

The ancient Greek philosopher Eratosthenes (third century B.C.) estimated the circumference of the Earth to be 25,000 miles, and most educated people of the fifteenth century A.D. believed Eratosthenes' number. The Council at Salamanca, believing the circumference of the round Earth was 25,000 miles, opposed Columbus because his calculations were wrong, not because he was the only believer in a round Earth. If Columbus had not stumbled on the Americas, he would have perished at sea because of his stupidity. He did not take enough provisions to feed himself and his crew on a seagoing voyage of more than 10,000 miles from Europe to China.

Columbus incorrectly thought he landed in India, not the Caribbean. He did not know where he was going or where he was (even though he and his crew believed they knew where they were). Most people think Christopher Columbus was a genius. Columbus Day? I think not. It should be called Columbus Day. Most Americans believe the tale that Columbus was smarter than everyone else of his day. They were taught this nonsense in elementary school and have believed it ever since. Think again about the question of fact. Regardless of where the information comes from, the majority of people believing something does not make it right.

When the twelve Jewish spies went into the land of Canaan following the Exodus from Egypt, 83% said the Israelites could not take the land. All the Jews except Moses, Aaron, Joshua, and Caleb agreed with the nay sayers. Since God told them He would give them the land of Canaan, the majority was wrong. In the Gospels, the Pharisees and Sadducees views were the majority position of religious belief. The Jewish people lived in fear of violating one of the religious leaders' man-made rules. The religious leaders were wrong. John the Baptist called them a brood of vipers; Jesus called them hypocrites and white-washed tombs. Truth is not determined by majority vote.

## Beyond a Reasonable Doubt

Another disputed definition of a "fact" is "something that can be supported beyond a reasonable doubt." Supporting beyond a reasonable doubt means you supply all the evidence you can muster to persuade a reasonable person to agree with your position. This is the definition that best fits into apologetics, which is explaining Christian beliefs to pre-Christians and answering their questions about God and the Bible.  This is also the system used in our courts of law.  Notice the definition does not include the word "prove," but support.  We cannot prove anything to anyone; we especially cannot prove the reality of God to an unbeliever.  What we can do is support our argument with evidence.  Proof is subjective; evidence is objective. For example, I can give the same evidence to two pre-Christians; this is objective.  One will believe; one will not.  For the new believer, the evidence rose to the level of proof, and thus faith, but the same evidence did not rise to the level of proof and faith for the one who did not believe. Therefore, proof is subjective. (Did I prove it to you?)  Our goal should never be to prove anything to anyone; our goal should be to provide evidence and then give the person the opportunity, without any coercion or manipulation, to accept or reject the evidence as proof. The hearer determines proof.  Our job is just to offer information and evidence.

A fact being something supported beyond a reasonable doubt is also the best way to give evidence for historical documents.  For example, no one living today knew Julius Caesar or even knew anyone who knew him.  Yet few educated people would deny his existence.  By faith, we assume that historians of his day were trying to tell the truth, and by the preponderance of the evidence, we believe Julius Caesar lived.  We believe his existence is a fact beyond a reasonable doubt.  However, we must assume that Julius Caesar lived.  The best we can do with historical documents (except the Bible) is to believe them beyond a reasonable doubt, but never with absolute certainty. Nothing we believe that we have not personally experienced can be accepted as fact without making some assumptions. Everything we have not personally experienced we believe by faith through what others say or write. We believe these sources of information are reliable beyond a reasonable doubt.

Is this a fact? When you see the sun, you are looking 8 minutes, 16 seconds into the past. We can calculate the answer. Light travels at 186,000 miles per second, or 11,160,000 miles per minute. On average, the sun is 93 million miles from Earth. Do the math and find that the sunlight we now see left the surface of the sun 8 minutes, 16 seconds ago. What assumptions did we make? We assume we cannot see the sun at any given moment in real time because there is always a delay due to the speed of light and the distance of the sun from the Earth. We assume, by faith, that light travels at a certain speed, and the sun is a certain distance from the Earth.

Probably none of us has done the scientific studies to determine these facts. Most of us have never measured the speed of light or the distance to the sun. We trust the people who made those measurements are telling us the truth. We also assume that NASA has not yet implemented its plan to stop global warming—move the Earth farther away from the sun. NASA's plan is to maneuver a comet close to the Earth so the comet's gravitational pull would increase Earth's orbital speed, resulting in a further orbit away from the sun. "Engineers would then direct their comet so that it passed close to

Jupiter or Saturn, where the reverse process would occur. It would pick up energy from one of these giant planets. Later its orbit would bring it back to Earth, and the process would be repeated."[6] (NASA will receive a lot of tax money to research this project, but I am sure NASA scientists do not promote global warming as a reality because of the money they can make from "fixing" the problem.)

Other tales are foisted on us as facts. David Quammen said this about evolution:

> Evolution is both a beautiful concept and an important one, more crucial nowadays to human welfare, to medical science, and to our understanding of the world than ever before. It is also deeply persuasive—a theory you can take to the bank. The essential points are slightly more complicated than most people assume, but not so complicated that they cannot be comprehended by any attentive person. Furthermore, the supporting evidence is abundant, various, ever increasing, solidly interconnected, and easily available in museums, popular books, text-books, and a mountainous accumulation of peer-reviewed scientific studies. No one needs to, and no one should, accept evolution merely as a matter of faith.[7]

However, if you rigorously investigate the evidence supporting evolution, critical thinking will cause you to conclude you do not have that much faith to believe such nonsense. To extrapolate from being able to crossbreed pigeons (micro-evolution), as Darwin did, that all life on planet Earth evolved from amoeba (macroevolution), takes a tremendous quantum leap of faith. Faith must be based in evidence, something macroevolution cannot produce. Conversely, Columbus did not have faith in the mileage he was told about the circumference of the Earth. Those who have measured these distances have faith that their measuring instruments, calculations, and conclusions are correct. The people who made the measuring instruments had to have faith that their work was accurate and the tools they used to calibrate their measuring instruments were accurate. So, when we say by faith that light now hitting the Earth left the sun 8.3 minutes ago, we are exercising faith in the work of the scientist, who exercised faith in his education and his instruments made by people who exercised faith in the tools they used to manufacture and calibrate the instruments the scientist used. Yet people say they do not believe anything they cannot experience with their five senses. We assume what we were told is true, by faith, beyond a reasonable doubt for nearly everything in life.

## Is it True?

A third disputed definition of a "fact" is something that is true. As we saw in the previous examples, what is true is not always easy to determine. This definition does not easily solve our dilemma about the nature of a fact because there is little agreement about what truth is.

## What is Truth?

What is truth? Simple enough question; complex enough answer. John Hospers, retired former chair of the Philosophy Department at the University of Southern California, raised questions about defining truth. "A true statement is one that states a *fact*. But the word 'fact' is ambiguous" (author's emphasis) . . . A true proposition is one that asserts the existence of some actual state-of-affairs (or any fact about the world). . . A statement is true if it corresponds with the facts."[8] But how do we discover what is true? How do we know if something occurs or did occur?

There are four basic theories about the nature of truth: the correspondence, the coherence, the relativistic or pragmatic, and the absolute theories of truth. Each theory is fraught with strengths and weaknesses.

## The Correspondence Theory

The correspondence theory of truth says that truth must relate to reality in the world. Propositions are true if they correspond with the facts.[9] The correspondence theory is empirical, meaning it can be tested. The statement, "Water boils at $212^0$ F at sea level" is true because water boils at $212^0$ F at sea level. Although we can test it, I never have; I accept it by faith. "Bush beat Kerry in the 2004 electoral election" corresponds with a fact. We can verify the statement with voluminous amounts of data. "Kerry beat Bush in the 2004 electoral election" does not correspond with a fact, even though the same words are used. "Bush beat Kerry in the 2004 electoral election" is therefore true, while "Kerry beat Bush" is false.

It sounds simple enough, but how much of a correspondence does there have to be? How do we know the facts this current proposition must correspond to are true? What if we have newly discovered information that does not correspond to anything, or that we cannot test? Does that mean the discovery is not true? No. This theory of truth is insufficient, so we need another definition of truth.

## The Coherence Theory

The coherence theory says a statement is true if it is consistent with other statements that are regarded as true. If it is consistent, that automatically makes it true. The question is, "Does it fit?" Mathematics is based on this theory,[10] but if your starting point is wrong, your answer and conclusion will be wrong. For centuries people believed in spontaneous generation—if you let beef sit out, it will spontaneously produce maggots. If you see pork with a maggot infestation, the maggots must have spontaneously erupted. This statement about the pork coheres, or fits, with the statement about the beef, but the statement about the beef was not true. Neither beef nor pork produces maggots. They are housefly eggs. (I hope you are not eating a burger right now. As an aside, if you have mushrooms on it, the FDA allows 20 maggots per 100 grams.[11] If you are eating a hot dog—there is a maggot allowance in hot dog production.)

It is difficult to know if what I already know is fact. For example, it is a fact that my eldest brother's name is Stuart, but he only knows that is true by corresponding what my parents called him (Stuart, or when he was in trouble, Stuart Harold Shelley!) with his birth certificate. Although it is not something he worries about, he has to assume that his birth certificate is accurate. He has never seen the official, original document in the state capital; he only has a copy of it. Likewise, my father has always spelled his own name "Stuart Robert Shelley." This cohered with what his parents called him and how they taught him to spell his name. When my dad was making his will, the attorney told him, to my father's surprise, that his birth certificate said his name is "Stuart Robert Feiser Shelley." What we believe as fact may not correspond to other facts because what we know as "fact" may be wrong. This theory of truth is undependable; we need another definition of truth.

## The Pragmatic Theory

The pragmatic theory, or relativism, says truth is dynamic and changing, subjective and relative depending on one's culture or circumstances. Relativism says two opposing or contradictory belief systems are both correct and acceptable. Ironically, the statement itself cannot, therefore, even be analyzed, because if everything is relative, I cannot determine whether the definition is true. If we accept the pragmatic position, no one can say that the position itself is right or wrong.

A bumper sticker said, "A closed mind is a wonderful thing to lose." Isn't that a closed-minded statement? Do you think the promoter of that thought will change his mind about this sentiment? Pragmatists hypocritically accept an absolute—pragmatism, or relativism, as true. The only absolute permitted by pragmatists, and often expressed by my students, is there are no absolutes. I ask them, "Are you absolutely sure?" Harry Blamires observed, "The post-Christian mental world is not a world of structures but a world of fluidity. What issues from the mind bereft of divine affiliation is passing opinion, transient feeling, today's or tomorrow's capricious preference. The universal language of reason and morality gives place to a wholly relativistic vocabulary of emotive predilections."[12]

Pragmatists believe all people have the right to believe whatever they desire (another absolute statement), or "first amendment relativism,"[13] as if it is a God-given right to personally determine truth. I agree everyone has the right to believe anything, but that does not mean that everyone's view is equally true. I will defend everybody's right to believe whatever the individual wants to believe; but if I believe someone is wrong, I will say so and try to persuade that person to my position.

Pragmatists have little time for critical thinking or the concept of truth. Truth is what the individual wants it to be.

Pragmatism is exhibited through the popular belief in tolerance. Tolerance contends that all beliefs are equal and valid. Even though I say something is blue and you say it is white, we are both right in the realm of relativism. Tolerance also says you must give your approval and endorsement to other people's views.[14] If someone believes homosexuality is a positive lifestyle, tolerance says you must agree with that person.

The United Nations' Declaration of Principles on Tolerance, signed by the Member States of UNESCO on 16 November 1995 said, "Tolerance is the responsibility that upholds human rights, pluralism (including cultural pluralism), democracy and the rule of law. It involves the rejection of dogmatism and absolutism and affirms the standards set out in international human rights instruments."[15] The United Nations' definition puts Christians in the crosshairs, as does its Declaration on the Elimination of All Forms of Intolerance and of Discrimination Based on Religion or Belief that said:

- Concerned by manifestations of intolerance and by the existence of discrimination in matters of religion or belief still in evidence in some areas of the world,

- Resolved to adopt all necessary measures for the speedy elimination of such intolerance in all its forms and manifestations and to prevent and combat discrimination on the ground of religion or belief,

- Proclaims this Declaration on the Elimination of All Forms of Intolerance and of Discrimination Based on Religion or Belief.[16]

The United Nations declared they are intolerant of intolerance. We Christians believe our message is the only way to Heaven, and if you are going to Heaven, you must go through Jesus Christ (John 14:6). We are guilty of intolerance according to the United Nations.

Pragmatism is an unsuccessful, incoherent theory that turns its proponents into hypocrites. We need to find a better theory to explain truth.

## The Absolute Theory
The absolute theory says truth is complete; it is perfect and the final authority. Truth is not open to change or

modification.  God and His Word are the only sources of absolute truth.  What God says in His Word is the only information that can be trusted absolutely since God is the only One without flaws, weaknesses, and errors. Douglas Groothius said, "God's truth is invariant.  It is true without exception or exemption.  Neither is God's truth relative, shifting, or revisable.  The weather may change, but God will not."[17]  God's truth is absolute because God is immutable.  God, by His very nature, is incapable of changing.  Numbers 23:19 says, "God is not a man, that He should lie, nor a son of man, that He should change His mind.  Does He speak and then not act?  Does He promise and not fulfill?"  David adds, "Your Word, O LORD, is eternal; it stands firm in the heavens."  God's Word is absolute and immutable like He is.

God's absolute truth does not change because of cultural beliefs.  The same sin is sin in Indore, India as it is in Indramayu, Indonesia and in Indianapolis, Indiana.  God's truth applies "everywhere, to engage everything, and exclude nothing."[18]  God's Word does not change over time. What God declared as sin during the Roman Empire was still sin during the Holy Roman Empire, is still sin today, and will be sin forever.  God's Word is absolutely true and unalterable.  "The grass withers and the flowers fall, but the Word of our God stands forever (Isaiah 40:8).

## Putting the Four Theories to Work

All truth ultimately comes from God.  However, does God tell us all truth?  No.  The Bible is revealed, absolute truth, but there are millions of times more truth than is found in the Bible.  It is true that it is 68° in my office as

I write this sentence.  You will not find that in the Bible, but it is nonetheless true (the correspondence theory supports this—I can test it with a thermometer—applying many assumptions).  Not only does God provide absolute truth in His Word, He also has created truth that must be discovered, like what my father's name is or what the temperature is.

Some people object to the Bible being called absolute truth.  How do we know that it is?  We can construct an argument for the Bible being absolute truth.  The Bible is the absolute truth because Jesus said to His Father it was in John 17:17, "Your Word is truth."  Either Jesus is right or He is wrong.  Since Jesus is God, unable to lie or be wrong, Jesus is right and God's Word is absolutely true.  The Bible is the very expiration (Greek *theopneustos*, or the breathing out) of God (we use the word inspiration because it does not sound right to say the Bible is expired— it does not curdle like expired milk).  God determined and controlled the writing of Scripture.  He assured that all that was written therein were the exact words He wanted communicated to us (2 Peter 1:19-21).

The writers of Scripture claimed to be giving eyewitness accounts of what they saw and heard.  In the 2 Peter passage, verses 16-18, Peter said, "We did not follow cleverly invented stories when we told you about the power and coming of our Lord Jesus Christ, but we were eyewitnesses of his majesty [on the Mount of Transfiguration in Matthew 17].  For He received honor and glory from God the Father when the voice came to Him from the Majestic Glory, saying, 'This is my Son, whom

I love; with Him I am well pleased.' We ourselves heard this voice that came from heaven when we were with Him on the sacred mountain." Peter claimed He heard the Father say he was to listen to the Son. The Son later said the Word of God is truth. Listen to Him.19

The Apostle John also said in 1 John 1:1-3 he was an eyewitness to Jesus, "That which was from the beginning, which we have heard, which we have seen with our eyes, which we have looked at and our hands have touched— this we proclaim concerning the Word of life. The life appeared; we have seen it and testify to it, and we proclaim to you the eternal life, which was with the Father and has appeared to us. We proclaim to you what we have seen and heard, so that you also may have fellowship with us. And our fellowship is with the Father and with his Son, Jesus Christ."

We have an absolute, authoritative Word from Heaven providing everything we need pertaining to life and godliness (2 Peter 1:3).We can absolutely trust everything the Bible says because the Bible is absolutely true.

Some critics say using the Bible to prove itself as absolute truth uses circular reasoning, a logical fallacy, but that charge is a straw man argument (another logical fallacy— see chapter 4). Letting the Bible speak for itself is self-testimony, just like anyone could use in his own defense in a court of law. My goal in presenting the Bible's testimony was not to prove anything to anyone; I cannot prove anything. My goal was to present evidence that others can evaluate and let them decide for themselves whether or not the evidence rises to level of proof for them. "To confess the absolute truth of Christ does not entail that one must be able to prove it absolutely to anyone on command. The nature of truth and its verification are two different matters."[20]

Some people in our culture condemn Christians for being narrow-minded, in their opinion, because we make the Bible our authority. However, using the Bible as our authority is not being narrow-minded. It is weighing the evidence and making a reasoned decision based on truth. Truth is narrow. I hope the person driving in the oncoming lane of traffic believes truth is narrow. I want the air traffic controller who is controlling the course and glide path of the descending airplane headed for touchdown to believe truth is narrow. Belief in the Bible is not being narrow-minded; it is allowing truth to limit what I believe. The Bible is the highest level of truth. How then do we use the other three theories to determine truth?

Besides revealed truth in the Bible, there is truth that needs to be discovered. The Coherence Theory provides our next level of support for truth. If the information I have agrees with the Bible, or does not contradict the Bible, I can assume it is true, but not with the absolute certainty I can have with what the Bible says. For example, biologists tell us that plant life preceded animal life on planet Earth. This agrees with Genesis 1, so I take it as fact. Anthropologists tell us that humans and apes descended from a common ancestor. This contradicts Genesis 1 and 2, which says that humans are the special creation of God, so the anthropologists' statement is false. If the information before me agrees with the Bible, I believe it. If it does not agree, I check my understanding of the Bible. If I am convinced my interpretation of the Bible is correct, I reject the information as false.

Information that agrees with the Bible is easy to evaluate for its truth, but what about information the Bible does not talk about in any sense, like the circumference of the Earth? Columbus could have learned from the Bible that the Earth was spherical, but not how large a sphere it was. The Correspondence Theory provides our next level of support for truth. This theory allows for scientific investigation of the universe to discover new information.

Newtonian physics works well to help us understand the movement of planets and the affects of gravity. Albert Einstein theorized that Newton's views were insufficient to explain all phenomena in our space-time continuum, so he postulated his two theories of relativity. No philosophical systems or information were available at the time to which his theory could cohere, but that did not make $E=MC^2$ untrue. Because Einstein's theories can be supported by scientific research, they are believed to be true. Niels Bohrs reasoned that, although Einstein's theories worked well, they did not work at the sub-atomic level. So he postulated quantum theory, much of which, like string theory, can never be tested, and which Einstein objected to on theological grounds (see chapter 11). Truth at the Correspondence level is much more tenuous to believe.

It is wise to hold a certain amount of skepticism about truth claims because what is "true" today may not be true tomorrow. This is where the pragmatic theory comes into play. If something seems reasonable, I believe it, but I must be willing to abandon "truth" from the Correspondence Theory realm if more evidence (like the fact that maggots come from housefly eggs, not beef and pork) becomes available.

## Conclusion

Being ignorant is a good thing (aren't you glad about that?), as long as we seek after knowledge, facts, and truth. As the colored area in our circle grows larger, so will our faith in the God who created the truth we learn. Once we have procured facts and truth, we can use them to win arguments and persuade others to our beliefs. We will examine how to do that in the next chapter.

## For Review and Discussion

- Describe a time when you disagreed with your group and boldly stated your views. Why did you do that? How did the group react?

- Describe a time when you disagreed with your group, but kept quiet. Why did you do that?

- Explain why most people believing something does not make it true.

- Explain what it means to support something as being true beyond a reasonable doubt.

- Why cannot you prove anything?

- What is your definition of truth?

- Explain the difference between revealed truth and discovered truth.

## ENDNOTES

1. Aristophenes. "Quote of the Week." Busymind. <http://users.adelphia.net/~sentry/quote.htm >.

2. Einstein, Albert. "Albert Einstein Quotes." Brainy Quotes. <http://www.brainyquote.com/quotes/ quotes/a/alberteins100015.html>.

3. Galilei, Galileo. The Little Red School House. <http:// suzyred.com/quotesense.html>.

4. Russell, Jeffrey Burton. Inventing the Flat Earth: Columbus and Modern Historians. Westport, CT: Greenwood Publishing Group, Incorporated, 1997, p. 45.

5. Lewis, C. S. The Discarded Image: An Introduction to Medieval and Renaissance Literature. Cambridge, MA: Cambridge University Press, 1964, pp. 140-141.

6.  McKie, Robin. "NASA Aims to Move Earth." <u>Guardian Newspapers Limited</u>., 2004.   10 June 2001. <http://observer.guardian.co.uk/international/ story/0,6903,504486,00.html>.

7.  Quammen, David.   "Darwin's Big Idea."   <u>National Geographic</u>. 206.5 (2004), p. 8.

8.  Hospers, John.   <u>An Introduction to Philosophical Analysis</u>, 3<sup>rd</sup> ed.   Englewood Cliffs, NJ: Prentice Hall, 1988, p. 9.

9.  Marian, David.   "The Correspondence Theory of Truth."   Stanford Encyclopedia of Philosophy.   10 May 2002. <http://plato.stanford.edu/entries/truth-correspondence>.

10. Young, James O.  "The Coherence Theory of Truth." Stanford Encyclopedia of Philosophy. 31 May 2002.<http://plato.stanford.edu/entries/truth-coherence>.

11. Bailey, Stephanie.   "Bugs as Food!?!"   <u>University of Kentucky Department of Entomology</u>.   20 January 1999.<http://www.uky.edu/Agriculture/Entomology/ ythfacts/bugfood/bugfood2.htm>.

12. Blamires, Harry. <u>The Post-Christian Mind.</u>. Ann Arbor, MI: Vine books, 1999, p. 13

13. Evans, C. Stephen.   Why Believe?: Reasons and Mystery as Pointers to God.  Grand Rapids, MI: Wm. B. Eerdmans Publishing Co., 1996, p. 11.

14. McDowell, Josh and Bob Hostetler. The New Tolerance: How a Cultural Movement Threatens to Destroy You, Your Faith, and Your Children.  Wheaton, IL: Tyndale House Publishers, 1998, p. 22.

15. "Declaration of Principles on Tolerance."
United Nations Educational, Scientific and Cultural Organization.   <http://www.unesco.org/tolerance/declaeng.htm>.

16. "Declaration on the Elimination of All Forms of Intolerance and of Discrimination Based on Religion or Belief."  United Nations.  <http://www.un.org/documents/ga/res/36/a36r055.htm>.

17. Groothius, Douglas. Truth Decay: Defending Christianity Against the Challenges of Postmodernism.  Downers Grove, IL: InterVarsity Press, 2000, p. 69. Ibid, p. 72.

18. Ibid, p. 72.

19. For a helpful discussion of the reliability of the Bible see I am Glad You Asked: In-Depth Answers to Difficult Questions About Christianity by Boa and Moody.

20. Groothius, p. 70.

Every Sabbath he (Paul) reasoned in the synagogue,
Trying to persuade Jews and Greeks.

Acts 18:4

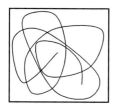

CHAPTER THREE

# Crafting and Winning Arguments

## I Cannot Argue with That

People generally think of an argument in a negative sense. We picture two people screaming in each other's face, but that is quarreling, not arguing. G. K. Chesterson, whose work *The Everlasting Man* contributed to the conversion to Christianity of a young atheist named C. S. Lewis, said, "People generally quarrel because they cannot argue."[1] "Properly channeled, argument can be a substitute for violence rather than an incitement to it."[2] The Apostle Peter (1 Peter 3:15) commanded Christians to be ready to make a defense (Greek—*apologia,* from which we get our word "apologetics"), or a reasoned argument, telling unbelievers what we believe. The ability to argue is not antithetical to being a Christian; the ability to argue is at the heart of what it means to be a Christian. Peter adds that we are to argue with gentleness and meekness. This does not mean we cannot be aggressive; it means we are not to quarrel with unbelievers.

We learned to argue at an early age. Our youthful arguments ranged from a desire to stay up later at night to getting a candy bar in the checkout line at the grocery store. We argue about the quality of a movie or a book. Men are convinced there are two theories to arguing with women—neither one works.

An argument is any form of communication that offers one or more reasons in support of a claim. An argument has a logical sequence that supplies supporting evidence or an explanation of a conclusion.[3] An argument has structure and order. In the terminology of logic, the claim an argument attempts to support is called the conclusion of the argument.[4] The reasons offered in support of the argument are called premises. The simplest arguments have only one premise, as in the following example:

**Premise:** Thinking logically is an important skill.
**Conclusion:** All Bible students should study the fundamentals of logic.

When someone presents an argument to us, it is important we are aware of the arguer's intentions. The primary purpose of an argument is to convince someone that a claim is true or false, or that a proposed course of action is or is not the right action to take. Convincing someone requires giving reasons for what we believe. The claim, along with the reasons for it, comprise an argument.

A husband and his wife woke up one Sunday morning, and the wife dressed for church. It was just about time for the service when she noticed her husband had not moved a finger toward getting dressed. Perplexed, she asked, "Why aren't you getting dressed for church?"

He said, "'Cause I do not want to go." She asked, "Do you have any reasons?" He said, "Yes, I have three good reasons. First, the congregation is cold. Second, no one likes me. And third, I just do not want to go."

The wife replied, "Well, honey, I have three reasons why you should go. First, the congregation is warm. Second, there are a few people there who like you. And third, you're the pastor!"[5] As usual, the wife won.

## Opinions are Like Asphalt—They are Everywhere

A conclusion differs from an opinion, although the two words are used interchangeably. People often use the term "opinion" to refer to an argument they are making in which they hope to persuade you, but an opinion is nothing more than a vague idea in which you place some confidence. Technically, an opinion is a claim without supporting evidence. Opinions lack objective evidence and facts. Opinions are ideas someone believes but cannot support with evidence. Opinions are ideas you have about something or someone that are based mainly on your feelings and beliefs. The person holds a certain position about something, but over time has forgotten the premises or has just adopted someone else's idea.

A mother and daughter were making a Christmas ham. When the mother cut off both ends of the ham, the daughter was puzzled. She asked her mother why she cut off the ham ends. "I do not know," the mother replied. "Your grandmother always did that. I'll call her and ask why she does this." The mother calls her mother and asks the same question. "I don't know," the grandmother replied. "Your grandmother always did that. I'll call her and ask why she does this." The grandmother calls her mother and asks the same question. "Mom, why did you cut both ends off the ham?" Her mother replied, "Because the pan I had was too small; it is the only way I could get the ham to fit." Expediency evolved into a meaningless tradition and opinion.

In contrast, a conclusion is a finalized decision based on an exhaustive review of available data, facts, assumptions, and interpretations. Conclusions are the decisions you reach after doing all your study, research, and thinking. Conclusions vary greatly in degree of truth depending on the strength of the supporting factual evidence. During the research and thinking process, some evidence may be missing. Further study and data revealed at a later date might make you change your conclusion (but that is all right because you are ignorant and getting over it—your dot is swallowing more of the circle).

A Pennsylvania Dutch farmer was on the witness stand, suing a man for the pain and suffering he experienced from the other driver hitting his horse-drawn buggy. The defendant's attorney said to him, "The police report says when the officer asked you if you were all right at the scene of the accident, your response was, 'I feel great. I never felt better in my life.'"

The farmer said, "Yes, I said, 'I feel great. I never felt better in my life,' but you have to understand the context of my statement. I was riding in my horse-drawn buggy with my dog tied to the back. The dog was following the buggy down the lane. We came to the stop sign at Kramer Road. No one was coming, so I pulled out onto Kramer Road. Suddenly, your client approached me at break-neck speed and crashed into my wagon, seriously injuring my horse, my dog, and me. The police officer walked around to the front of the buggy, took one look at the terrible condition of my horse, and shot him, putting him out of his misery. The officer walked around to the back of the buggy, took one look at the terrible condition of my dog, and shot him, putting him out of his misery. The officer approached me and said, 'Sir, how are you feeling? Are you all right?'" Some evidence may be missing that, when found, may change your conclusion.

Is this an opinion or a conclusion: Abortion is murder because the baby is human? It is an opinion, even if stated by a medical doctor or a theologian. I am not saying the statement is false; it is only an opinion because no evidence was given that the baby is human or that killing a human is murder. Conclusions can be formed only after evidence is given. Conclusions are the final part of an argument. The statement, "Abortion is murder because the baby is human" would become a conclusion after facts and premises were added about when human life begins and what constitutes murder. To say that the statement without facts is just an opinion does not mean it is not true. The statement lacks evidence, and therefore has little value since it is not an argument. Opinions cannot persuade others to our beliefs. If you only said to a pro-abortionist, "Abortion is murder because the baby is human," he would not change his mind and agree with you. He would want facts and evidence to support your statement that he would analyze before he changed his mind. So, do not try to persuade people with your opinion; persuade them with evidence that leads to a logical conclusion.

Arguments come in two forms—deductive and inductive. Understanding the structure of arguments will help us craft better arguments.

## Deductive Arguments

Deductive reasoning is reasoning in the form "If A, then B." If you know that a bulb's filament must be intact for it to light, and the filament is broken (if A), then the bulb will not light (then B). This is deduction. The conclusion is a mathematical certainty. A deductive argument offers two or more assertions that lead automatically to a conclusion. Deductive arguments can usually be phrased as *syllogisms*, or as brief, mathematical statements in which the premises automatically lead to the conclusion.

A deductive argument has three parts: a *major premise*, a minor premise, and a conclusion. The major premise is a statement   of general truth dealing with categories rather than individual examples.  Some examples of a major premise are:

- *All of Jacob's children were males.*
- *The existence of historical figures must be believed in by faith.*
- *God promises that all who put their faith in Jesus have eternal life.*

The <u>minor premise</u> is a statement of particular truth dealing with a specific case governed by the *major premise:*

- <u>Ephraim was one of Jacob's children.</u>
- <u>Martin Luther was a historical figure.</u>
- <u>Bill put his faith in Jesus.</u>

The conclusion is the statement resulting from the <u>minor premise's</u> correlation to the *major premise.* It does not mean the conclusion is correct; it is the logical deduction that follows from the premises:

- *All of Jacob's children were males.*
- <u>Ephraim was one of Jacob's children.</u>
- Ephraim was a male.

- *The existence of historical figures must be believed in by faith.*
- <u>Martin Luther was a historical figure.</u>
- Martin Luther must be believed in by faith.

- *God promises that all who put their faith in Jesus have eternal life.*
- <u>Bill put his faith in Jesus.</u>
- Bill has eternal life.

There are no other possible conclusions to these premises. Each of the three conclusions is a mathematical certainty. The conclusion follows automatically from the major and minor premises.

Deductive arguments are not referred to as "true" or "false," but as "sound" or "unsound." While a deductive argument may be both true and sound, like those discussed already, a deductive argument can also be true but not sound.

- *All of the Galilean disciples at Pentecost had a cloven tongue of fire resting on their head.*
- <u>Peter was a Galilean.</u>
- Peter had a cloven tongue of fire resting on his head at Pentecost.

True, but unsound. Why? The syllogism never demonstrated that Peter was a disciple. You cannot skip what may seem like an obvious step. What is obvious to you might not be obvious to someone else. We cannot allow gaps in our logic. Someone reading this may not know that Peter was a disciple. The argument misses a logical step because the speaker probably thought, "Everyone knows Peter was a disciple." Not everyone does know Peter was a disciple.

Conversely, a deduction can be sound, yet demonstrably untrue:

- *No Gentiles at Pentecost had a cloven tongue of fire resting on their head.*
- <u>The Apostle Peter was a Gentile.</u>
- <u>Peter was present at Pentecost.</u>
- The Apostle Peter did not have a cloven tongue of fire resting on his head at Pentecost.

The syllogism works, but it is untrue—Peter was not a Gentile. If you get on the wrong airplane, regardless of whether or not you had a smooth take-off and landing or a turbulence-free flight, you will land at the wrong airport. Many of the conclusions we reach in interpreting the Scriptures may come from deductively sound arguments, but they will not be true if one of the premises is not true. Making no errors in the premises is vital to correct biblical interpretation. Many arguments against the existence of God are deductive arguments:

- *Nothing exists that I cannot see, hear, or touch.*
- <u>I cannot see, hear, or touch God.</u>
- God does not exist.

It is pointless to argue the conclusion. "God exists; God does not exist." That is bantering. Bantering back and forth is quarreling, and quarreling leads nowhere. To be productive, you have to argue the major premise. The syllogism is sound, but untrue. People do believe in things they cannot see, hear, or touch—atoms, molecules, solar systems, and historical figures. They believe there are chairs in the next room, and they even ask the proverbial question, "If a man is walking in the woods, and there is no woman present to hear him, is he still wrong?" So, argue the major premise, not the minor premise or the conclusion.

Until the people we are arguing with change their beliefs about the major premise, in this case that things exist that they cannot see, hear, or touch, they will not begin to contemplate the possibility of God's existence. We will only quarrel with them, not argue with them. We will not persuade them to consider our conclusion until they agree with our premises and agree that at least one of their premises is wrong. I have to give evidence that things exist that cannot be seen, heard, or touched. "I always admired atheists. I think it takes a lot of faith."[6]

Deductive reasoning is reasoning in the form "If A, then B." Deductive arguments have major and minor premises and a conclusion. Correct deductive arguments are both sound and true. Unfortunately, not all arguments are constructed in such a neat package, which contributes to difficult decision-making.

## Inductive Arguments

Unlike deductive reasoning, inductive reasoning does not produce mathematical certainty. Induction involves collecting pieces of information and adding it to our own knowledge and experience in order to make an interpretation about what is *probably* true. Inductive reasoning does not use syllogisms, but a series of observations with the purpose of reaching a conclusion. Inductive arguments contain enthymemes: parts of the equation are not known for certain.[7] For example

- Observation: The Trout's were not in church today.
- Prior Experience: The Trout's do not miss church without telling me.

## Conclusion: Someone in the Trout family must be sick.

The enthymeme in this scenario is the actual reason the Trout's were not in church today. You do not know if the Trout's were sick. It is a reasonable assumption based on the evidence and your prior experience with the Trout's. However, the Trout's may have overslept, someone close to them may have died, they may just be playing "hooky," or they may have gone away for the weekend and not told you. You do not know for certain; you just know something smells a little fishy about the Trout's. Inductive reasoning yields conclusions that are, at best, highly probable. The evidence only offers strong support for the conclusion with the reservation that you may be wrong.

Inductive logic can produce great faith as evidenced by the inductive logic Abraham used on Mt. Moriah in Genesis 22. God commanded Abraham to sacrifice his son, Isaac. Abraham obeyed the Lord based on inductive logic. God promised Abraham in the previous chapter (Genesis 21:12) that his descendants would come through Isaac. God is testing Abraham's faith about this promise. In Genesis 22:5, we find Abraham believed that he and Isaac would return after the sacrifice, although Abraham also believed he would first kill Isaac. Abraham had never heard about resurrection, but based on what he had learned about God (among them, his 90-year-old wife conceiving Isaac), Abraham inductively reasoned:

God promised that my descendants will come through Isaac;

- God told me to kill Isaac;
- I will obey God and kill Isaac;
- God can do anything, including raise the dead;
- God will raise Isaac from the dead.

Hebrews 11:19 says, "Abraham reasoned that God could raise the dead, and figuratively speaking, he did receive Isaac back from death." Faith and reasoning are integral partners.

You make inductive arguments when you use facts or research findings to make generalizations like, "Men do not ask for directions," or "Women always say men are wrong." Inductive arguments are assessed on the basis of their strength. A strong inductive argument does not guarantee the truth of the conclusion; rather, it provides strong support for the conclusion. When we offer evidence that gives weight to a conclusion, but not complete certainty, we are reasoning inductively. Deductive arguments offer certainty; inductive arguments offer strength.

Most biblical interpretation is based on inductive reasoning. We examine the context of the passage and its historical context, do word studies, and then combine that information with other truths that we know about the Bible to reach a reasoned conclusion (see chapter 6). We are either right or wrong. We do well to investigate other people's interpretations because someone may have better information than we do, or they may have reasoned better than we have. Unfortunately, we easily ignore information that contradicts what we think. Espousing the attitude that I can ignore information I do not like (that, in essence, is saying that I cannot be wrong) may seriously impede my spiritual growth. Bible passages not only merit my study, but also merit my further study if someone offers a different interpretation. The other person may not be right; then again, I may not be right, either. Since both of us are fallible, one of us is wrong at best, and both of us are wrong at worst. Only one of us can possibly be right.

Most of the decisions we make in life are arrived at inductively, which is why they are often so difficult to make.

We make observations about a situation and combine that information with other truths we know about the Bible and our life experiences to make a decision. Since most of the decisions we make do not have mathematical certainty because of the limited information we possess, the Bible tells us to seek the counsel and wisdom of others (Proverbs 15:22 and 19:20). Since we do not have absolute certainty that we gathered all the information we need to make a decision, our decisions cause us anxiety. We pray, "Lord, what should I do?" Would it not be much easier if God just phoned us and told us what decision to make so we could know what to do with absolute certainty? Sure, but our experience tells us that life and God do not work that way.

## Compare and Contrast

There is one main difference between an inductive and a deductive argument. Inductive arguments make a projection about what *could* occur, going beyond the information contained in the premises. Deductive arguments draw conclusions from the premises, and do not exceed the boundaries of those premises.[8] Deductive arguments have more authority than inductive arguments.

How Hot is it in Hell? (Purportedly a true story portraying inductive logic):

A thermodynamics professor prepared a written take-home exam for his graduate students. It had one question: Is Hell exothermic (gives off heat) or endothermic (absorbs heat)? Support your answer with a proof.

Most of his students wrote proofs of their beliefs using Boyle's Law (gas cools off when it expands and heats up when compressed) or some variant of that law. One student, however, wrote the following:

"First, we need to know how the mass of Hell is changing in time. So we need to know both the rate at which souls are moving into Hell, and the rate at which they are leaving. I think we can safely assume that once a soul gets to Hell, it will not leave. Therefore, no souls are leaving.

As for how many souls are entering Hell, let's look at the different religions that exist in the world today. Some of these religions state that if you are not a member of their religion, you will go to Hell.

Since there are more than one of these religions and since people do not belong to more than one religion, we can project that all people and all souls go to Hell. With birth and death rates as they are, we can expect the number of souls in Hell to increase exponentially.

Now, we must examine the rate of change of the volume of Hell. Because Boyle's Law states that in order for the temperature and pressure in Hell to stay the same, the volume of Hell has to expand as souls are added. This provides two possibilities:

1. If Hell is expanding at a slower rate than the rate at which souls enter Hell, then the temperature and pressure in Hell will increase until all Hell breaks loose.

2. Of course, if Hell is expanding at a rate faster than the increase of souls in Hell, then the temperature and pressure will drop until Hell freezes over.

So which is it? If we accept the postulate given to me by Ms. Therese Banyan during my Freshman year, 'that it will be a cold night in Hell before I date you', and take into account the fact I still have not succeeded in having dated her, then number 2 cannot be true, and so Hell is Exothermic." The student got the only A![9]

## Conclusion

As we have seen, a good argument, per this chapter's definition, is not something negative. We make arguments to others about what we believe. We make arguments as we study the Bible, and we make arguments to ourselves when we go through the decision-making process. Being able to make well-reasoned arguments is a valuable tool for a Christian to possess.

God wants us to exercise logic and exhibit faith like Jael, who made sure Sisera was out of his mind. Critical thinking-induced faith and decisions please the Father.

Are there biblical examples of people using critical thinking in the Bible? We will examine this in the next chapter.

## For Review and Discussion

- Define "argument" and create one for this statement: Christopher Columbus was not one of the wisest men of his day.

- Distinguish between a conclusion and an opinion.

- Define deductive argument and create one for the existence of God, positive and negative.

- Define inductive argument and create one.

## ENDNOTES

1. Chesterton, Gilbert K.  "Quarrels Quotations." Nonstopenglish.  <http://www.nonstopenglish.com/ reading/quotations/k_Quarrels.asp>.

2. Graff, Gerald. Clueless in Academe: How Schooling Obscures the Life of the Mind. New Haven, CT: Yale University Press, 2003, p. 156.  See pp. 155-172 for helpful about information building an argument.

3. Thomas, Stephen Naylor.  Practical Reasoning in Natural Language, 4th edition.  Upper Saddle River, NJ: Prentice Hall, 1997, p. 8.

4. Ibid, p. 10.

5. Case, Dan. "Pastor Appreciation . . . Month?" <u>Case Studies</u>.2004.<http://www.case-studies.com/articles/pastor_appreciation_month.htm>.

6. Frolov, Diane and Andrew Schneider. "Atheism." <u>The Quotations Page</u>. <http://www.quotationspage.com/subjects/atheism/>.

7. Fearnside, W. Ward. <u>About Thinking</u>, 2nd edition. Upper Saddle River, NJ: Prentice Hall, 1997, pp. 154-155.

8. Waller, Bruce N. <u>Critical Thinking: Consider the Verdict</u>, 5th edition. Upper Saddle River, NJ: Prentice Hall, 2005, p. 15.

9. "How Hot Is It In Hell - A True Story." <u>Social Work Examination Services, Inc.</u> <http://www.swes.net/humor/hell.html>.

Men occasionally stumble over the truth,

But most of them pick themselves up

And hurry off as if nothing had happened.


Sir Winston Churchill

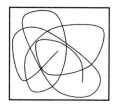

CHAPTER FOUR

# Critical Thinking
# in the Bible

## Introduction

How did believers in Bible times make decisions? "Well," you say, "God gave them revelation. God told them what to do." At times, that was true. For example, God told Adam not to eat from the tree of the knowledge of good and evil. God told Abraham to offer his son Isaac as a burnt offering. The Lord told Jonah to go to Nineveh and preach against that great city. According to the author of Hebrews (1:1), God spoke to people in various ways. The Scriptures reveal God speaking to humans through dreams, visions, angels, spoken word, and even a donkey (God can use any jackass).

Most of the time, however, God did not tell people what to do, just as you experience on a daily basis. God does not tell you which side of the bed to sleep on, the time to set your alarm clock, which side of the bed to get out, which kind of toothpaste to use, how many breaths to take per minute, what to eat for breakfast, what to wear, which way to drive to work, ad infinitum. If we waited to hear from God on the details of everyday living, we would be immobilized, not carrying out our purposes in life.

How do we make decisions? The same way God makes decisions—by using critical thinking. Scripture provides many examples of God being a critical thinker. We will examine a few of them.

## God is a Critical Thinker

### Intelligent Designer
The order of creation reflects God's critical thinking. Water, atmosphere, sun, and land precede plant life to support the survival of the plants. Plant life precedes animal life to support the survival of the animal kingdom, including humans, who were vegetarians before the Flood. The order of creation reflects intelligent design in its Creator, a critical thinker. All of the complexity and purpose in the universe argues for a critical thinking Creator—the God revealed in the Bible.

### God Can Use Any Crack Pot
God used critical thinking to destroy the Midianites. In Judges 6, the Midianites had conquered Israel. Gideon rallied 32,000 soldiers to wage war against the invaders. The Lord whittled the number of warriors to three hundred. At night, God ordered the three hundred Israeli soldiers to surround the Midianite camp from the hills above it. Each Jewish warrior carried only a horn and a lantern in a jar. The warriors blew the horns, smashed the pots, and caused confusion in the Midianite camp. The Midianites did some inductive logic of their own, but their premises were wrong. The Midianites mistook the three hundred soldiers for leaders of three hundred battalions because battalion leaders held lamps. During the panic created by

the horn blowing and pot smashing, the Midianites turned their swords on each other. After the Israelites pursued and slaughtered the remaining Midianites, 120,000 of their mutilated, dead carcasses demonstrated how grisly it is when God decorates a battlefield. God used inductive logic against the Midianites who associated three hundred lanterns with three hundred battalions and delivered Israel through Gideon. Not having all of the facts in an inductive argument can be deadly. God's critical thinking won the day.

## Cross this One Off His List

The cross of Jesus Christ demonstrated God's critical thinking skills. Galatians 3:13-14 says the Lord used the cross to fulfill His promise to Abraham that through him all the nations of the Earth would be blessed. God also used the cross as the way to justify killing Jesus, an Innocent Man.

God the Father requiring the death of Jesus raised an issue of justice. How could God, the Righteous Judge, condemn an Innocent Man to death? The answer is found in the Old Testament in Deuteronomy 21:23, as quoted in Galatians 3, stating God brought anyone who hangs on a tree under the curses of the law. When Jesus was nailed to the tree, i.e., the cross, through no fault of His own, He became a technical violator of the Law, and therefore fell under its curse of death. Jesus remained sinless and the Father remained just (Romans 3:26). Crucifixion was the only way Jesus could have died. Although Jesus would have bled if He had been stoned to death, cut with a sword, or beheaded, the Father would have been unjust in killing Him that way. Jesus would not have been a technical violator of the law. Jesus hanging by a rope or drowning would not have resulted in bleeding or God being just. God demonstrated not only His love toward us on the cross (Romans 5:8), but He also demonstrated His critical thinking abilities in the substitutionary death of Jesus Christ upon the cross. Nothing else would have worked to procure our salvation. Nothing else would have worked for God to remain just. Thank God the Lord is a critical thinker. Following is the deductive syllogism God explained to Paul in making His crucifixion decision:

- God is just and cannot kill an innocent man;
- Jesus is innocent;
- God can only remain just if Christ can become a technical violator of the law;
- Being hung on a cross makes someone a technical violator of the law (if A);
- Christ will die by crucifixion (then B).

God is not the only critical thinker in the Bible. It is logical (inductive logic) to conclude that if God is a critical thinker and humans are created in the image of God, humans will also be critical thinkers. Since that argument uses inductive logic and therefore is not an assured mathematical certainty, we will have to test the hypothesis. The Scriptures are filled with stories of men and women of faith, made in the image of God the critical thinker, who were also logical thinkers. God often rewarded not only His servants for acting in faith, but also their logical, critical thinking. The Old Testament and New Testament are replete with examples.

## Old Testament Examples of Critical Thinking

### This is a Test

Abraham, the father of those who put their faith in God (Galatians 3:7), was a critical thinker, as we discussed last chapter. Hebrews 11:18, which described Abraham as a man of faith, says Abraham reasoned that God could raise the dead. The syllogism was: *if* God's promises are through Isaac and *if* the all-powerful, resurrecting God wants me to sacrifice Isaac, then God will raise Isaac from the dead. In Genesis 22:5 we find that Abraham was so confident in this syllogism that he told his servants to wait with the donkeys as he and Isaac climbed Mt. Moriah, and that he and Isaac would return (a resurrected Isaac would return, from Abraham's perspective).

God rewarded Abraham for employing logic and acting in faith. God said to Abraham, "I will surely bless you" (Genesis 22:17). The blessing extended to God explaining to Abraham how Christ would die on Mt. Moriah two thousand years later and letting him see what would happen to Christ on the cross (John 8:56, Galatians 3:8).

Abraham is a stellar example of the relationship between logic and faith. Whenever we trust the promises of God, as Abraham did when God promised him a son (Galatians 3:6), we are reasoning that God can be trusted and does not lie. God can do what He has promised, so we act upon that promise in faith. Faith is first an act of the mind reasoning about the Person of God; then it is a belief or action that demonstrates our trust in what God has said and who He is.

## Judge Not, Judge

Jethro, father-in-law of Moses, provides an example of critical thinking in Genesis 18:13-27. While Moses was leading the Israelites out of Egypt, Jethro visited him. The next day, Moses served as judge of the people from morning until evening. Jethro rightly reasoned that this was neither good for Moses nor the people. Moses had not been thinking critically. Jethro's critical thinking resulted in a positive solution. He said Moses would better serve the people by being an intermediary with God by teaching the people God's law. He suggested that Moses choose wise (critical thinking), honorable men to preside over groups of a thousand, hundred, fifty, and ten. He told Moses to let these men serve as judges of their groups, with Moses only adjudicating the difficult cases. Moses became the Supreme Court Chief Justice of Israel. Jethro's wise critical thinking skills unchained Moses from the judge's bench to pursue his other, more important, duties. Critical thinker's delegate so all responsibilities are performed more effectively.

## Whiners are not Winners

The team of Joshua and Caleb provide another example of critical thinking. Joshua, Caleb and ten other men were chosen to represent their respective tribes to explore the land of Canaan before the Israelites invaded following the Exodus. Of the twelve spies who entered the Promised Land, only Joshua and Caleb used good critical thinking skills. The other ten spies returned to the Israelites with a report based upon an incorrect major premise—the Canaanites are too big for us (i.e., God is not big enough to defend us), resulting in the conclusion not to enter and subsequently take the land (Numbers 13:26-32). As I said last chapter, if you get on the wrong plane, you get off at the wrong airport. These ten cowards just landed in Faithlessville in the country of Stupid (a highly populated country, I might add).

Joshua and Caleb's report was based on the major premise that God would give the Israelites the land (13:1). Caleb's critical thinking led to faith—"We can certainly take possession of the land" (13:30). Joshua agreed with Caleb. Joshua said God would give the Israelites the land, the Canaanites' protection was gone, and the Lord was with Israel. Joshua's critical thinking also led to faith. Joshua and Caleb used deductive logic—if God promised the land (if A), then we can certainly take possession of it (then B).

God blessed the critical thinking and the resultant faith of Joshua and Caleb. Although they, like all the Israelites, would have to wander in the wilderness for forty years, they would receive the blessing of being the only two people over age twenty-one at the time of the spies' report who would enter the Promised Land. God would later crown Joshua to be Moses' replacement and give Caleb any land he chose.

## Even the French Could Win this Way

In Joshua 17, the Amalekites attacked the Israelites at Rephadim. God gave no orders about what to do. Moses told Joshua to choose some warriors and to fight the Amalekites. As long as Moses held up his hands, the Israelites were winning; when Moses lowered his hands, the Amalekites were winning. Back and forth it went—arms up, Israel was on top—arms down, and the Amalekites had the "upper hand." The critical thinking solution was to figure out a way to keep Moses' arms in the air. Aaron and Hur sat Moses on a rock and held his arms aloft. God blessed their critical thinking skills by allowing the Israelites to win the battle that day. The Israelites won hands down.

## He Left Him Behind

Ehud is a remarkable example of a believer who knew how to make a decision. His story is recounted in Judges 3.

The Israelites failed to drive the Canaanites from the land. According to Judges 3, the Israelites did evil in the sight of the Lord, and God gave them into the hands of Eglon, the king-sized king of Moab. The Israelites cried out to the Lord for a deliverer, and God sent them Ehud, a left-handed man. Left-handedness was rare and seen as a defect at best, or evil at worst. Even today, our language is biased against lefties. For example, "sinister" and "gauche" (lacking social refinement) mean left hand in Latin and French respectively. However, someone who is capable is dexterous, Latin for right hand. Back to the story.

The Israelites chose Ehud to be part of the party that took tax payments to the portly potentate. Remember, Ehud was a left-handed man. Since most people were right-handed then as today, most people kept their swords on their left sides and drew their swords across the front of their bodies with their right hands. It is physically impossible to draw a sword from the right side of the body with the right hand (if you do not believe me, go get your sword and try it). Ehud hid his dagger on his right side, under his cloak. When he approached Eglon's guards, they patted down Ehud's left side looking for a weapon but not his right side where the dandy dagger dangled dapperly. This was a wise, inductive-logic, critical thinking move for Ehud, but a monstrous mistake for the Moabites.

Ehud tells the king he has a message from God. The Atkin's diet defector strained to rise from his throne. Ehud drew his sword with his left hand and plunged the blade into the mammoth majesty's midriff. You can almost hear the "Schlurp!" as the fat wrapped around the sword. The entire blade and handle entered the emperor's entrails, exiting Eglon's anus. Yuck! Ehud dislodged the dagger from Lord Lard and ran from the room. The guards became anxious about King Eglon. Smelling the excrement that exited Eglon's body, the guards thought Eglon was on the "throne," so they did not enter the room, giving Ehud time to escape. Ehud should be the patron saint of proctologists. Ehud said he had a message from God; Eglon got the point.

God blessed Ehud for his faith-induced critical thinking skills by giving the entire Moabite army into his hand, and the land enjoyed peace for eighty years. Ehud used inductive logic regarding guards' method of checking for weapons. He used that information to his, Israel's, and God's advantage.

## Half Off
It should not surprise us that the wisest man to ever live was a critical thinker. People came from near and far

to see Solomon's wisdom in action. Others came to put Solomon to work for them. Such is the case in I Kings 3. Two harlots who lived together were fighting over a baby. One of the women rolled over in bed and smothered her baby. She then swapped her dead child with the other woman's baby. The two were quarreling about who was the baby's mother, and they wanted Solomon to solve the case. Using inductive logic, Solomon asked for a sword and commanded a servant to cut the baby in half. Each woman would receive half of a dead baby. One woman agreed with the solution; the other said she would rather the baby live with the other woman than see it killed. Solomon rightly determined that the latter woman was the rightful mother.

Solomon assumed a mother would protect her young. A threat to the baby's life would draw out those motherly instincts. So, Solomon threatened to slay the child. The true mother tried to protect her baby as Solomon postulated, and he solved the mystery of who was the child's mother. The Israelites saw the critical thinking wisdom of God in Solomon as he administered justice (verse 28).

## The Greatest Miracle in the Book of Jonah

Jonah is an example of critical thinking gone awry. He was one of the few people in history privileged to receive an audible revelation from God. The Lord did not lead him or give him an impression. God spoke to Jonah. "Go to the great city of Nineveh and preach against it, because its wickedness has come up before me" (1:2). Nineveh was located in modern-day Iraq, 500 miles northeast of Israel. In disobedience to the Lord, Jonah jaunted to

Joppa and jumped aboard a junket journeying east for Tarshish in modern-day Spain "away from the presence of the Lord." I have heard preachers declare that Jonah was choosing God's second best. No, Jonah was willfully disobeying a direct order from the very mouth of God. I know it sounds like a whale of a tale, and to some the story smells a little fishy, but Jonah ended up down in the mouth. He repented, the big fish vomited him onto the beach, and "then the word of the LORD came to Jonah a second time: 'Go to the great city of Nineveh and proclaim to it the message I give you'" (3:1-2). Jonah obeyed.

Jonah walked all day from the city gate to the center of town and gave the shortest sermon in history, "Forty more days and Nineveh will be overturned" (3:4). The whole city repented, from the king to the most important person; more than 500,000 people repented and became believers. God decided to spare the city from the coming promised destruction. This was the greatest revival in history, and the greatest miracle in the Book of Jonah, but the prophet Jonah was depressed.

Jonah left Nineveh and built a shelter on a hill overlooking the city. He hoped God would again change His mind and destroy the city. Unlike today, the Ninevites (Iraqis) hated Israelites (yes, it is sarcasm—it comes free of charge). They ruthlessly tortured prisoners of war, even flaying and decapitating them alive. Jonah hated the Ninevites and wanted them dead in Hell, not Heaven-bound. Jonah became angry. He prayed, "O LORD, is this not what I said when I was still at home? That is why I was so quick to flee to Tarshish. I knew that You are a gracious and compassionate God, slow to anger and abounding in love, a God who relents from sending calamity. Now, O LORD, take away my life, for it is better for me to die than to live" (4:1-3). Jonah had his theology right; he just did not like it. Look at the logic in his prayer:

- I want the Ninevites dead.
- God is gracious and compassionate.
- God is slow to anger and abounding in love.
- God relents from sending calamity (if A).
- So, if the Ninevites repent, God will spare their lives (then B).

Jonah so hated the Ninevites that his loathing smothered his critical thinking. Knowing the right thing to do is not enough; we must also do the right thing. Critical thinking is only valuable to us if it leads us to trust in God and His plan and stimulates the will and faith to execute that plan.

## Hang Him High

Women also were critical thinkers in the Old Testament; Esther was among them. In 586 B.C., the Babylonians conquered Israel and carted the Jews into captivity. King Ahasuerus married a Jewish maiden, although he did not know she was Jewish. Ahasuerus' second-in-command, Haman, was incensed that Esther's uncle, Mordecai, would not bow before him (Haman did not know that Mordecai was Esther's uncle). Mordecai said that as a Jew, he could not bow before Haman. Haman was quite impressed with himself and thought everyone should bow before him, so he plotted to kill all the Jews. Haman received King Ahasuerus' blessing to do so, although it does not seem that Ahasuerus was paying close attention to what Haman told him.

Mordecai told his niece Esther, the queen, about Haman's scheme. Esther received no revelation from God. In fact, God is never mentioned in the book, yet the survival of the Jewish race is at stake. Using critical thinking skills and inductive logic, Esther plotted a scheme of her own. Esther decided to use Ahasuerus' love for her and Haman's love for himself to protect the Jewish people in "such a time as this" (4:14). Esther knew God had promised to curse those who curse the Jews (Genesis 12:3).

Esther, risking her own life, approached her husband the king, unbidden, and invited him to a banquet she was preparing the next day because she had a favor to ask him. Esther asked if Haman could also come. Haman's head swelled more than a church parking lot on Christmas and Easter Sunday. He amassed his friends and his wife and recounted the greatness of all he had. Haman also said, "Even Esther the queen let no one but me come with the king to the banquet which she had prepared" (5:12). I can envision Haman strutting like a peacock. Esther had him right where she wanted him.

At the banquet, the king asked Esther to tell him her petition. She explained that someone connived to annihilate her people. Ahasuerus asked who was presuming to do such a thing. Pointing at Haman, she replied, "A foe and an enemy is this wicked Haman!" An ill wind suddenly blew through the room for Haman, and he was soon swaying in its breeze. You might say he was hanging on every word that Esther and Ahasuerus said. Ahasuerus had Haman hanged on gallows that Haman had built, gallows upon which Haman had hoped to hang Mordecai, the queen's uncle, for not bowing before him.

In the absence of revelation, Esther exhibited logic-induced faith, just as the people of God had done for centuries before her throughout the Old Testament. However, logic-induced faith is not just found in the Old Testament .

## Critical Thinking in the New Testament

The Gospels and the Epistles recount many occasions where Jesus and the Apostles used critical thinking and logic. Decision-making in the New Testament centered on logical reasoning that led to acts of faith and courage.

## Our Critical Thinking Christ

If God is a critical thinker, by definition Jesus is a critical thinker, since He is God (If "A," then "B"). Jesus always won arguments with logic. One of the main reasons the Sadducees and the Pharisees wanted to kill the Lord of Heaven and Earth was because He continually humiliated them in public using His critical thinking skills.

## Silencing Satan

Jesus refuted Satan by applying biblical texts to what Satan was tempting Jesus to do (Matthew 4). He logically determined what the Word of God said about each temptation and then argued using the wisdom of God. Jesus dumbfounded the Devil in all three temptations. The

Serpent had no recourse except to surrender and slither from the field of battle. Critical thinkers know the Bible and apply its logic to beat temptation. When we sin we are out of our minds. Paul tells us in 2 Corinthians 10:3-5, "For though we live in the world, we do not wage war as the world does. The weapons we fight with are not the weapons of the world. On the contrary, they have divine power to demolish strongholds. We demolish arguments and every pretension that sets itself up against the knowledge of God, and we take captive every thought to make it obedient to Christ." Critical thinking is a powerful weapon against temptation.

## Centurion Sense

Jesus was not only a critical thinker, but He also admired critical thinking in others. In Matthew 8:5-13, a Roman centurion approached Jesus. The centurion told Jesus about his sick servant. The Lord said He would go to the centurion's home and heal the servant. The centurion politely protested, using a deductive argument. He said he was not worthy to have Jesus visit his home. The centurion knew Jesus could just speak a word and his servant would be healed. The centurion said that he, too, was a man under authority, with soldiers under him. He tells his soldiers what to do, and they do it.

The centurion's implication was that since Jesus has authority over disease (if A), He can tell the disease to leave, even from a distance, and it will do so (then B—deductive logic). The centurion's logic resulted in faith. No one told this to him. There had been no revelation from God about Jesus' authority over disease, especially at a distance. The centurion logically analyzed this by himself.

When Jesus heard the critical thinking reasoning of the centurion, He marveled and said, "Truly I say to you, I have not found such great faith in Israel." Jesus called this man's deductive logic "great faith" (verse 10) and "believing" (verse 13). Critical thinking pleased the Savior and the Savior cured the servant.

## Dogged Faith

The critical thinking of another Gentile, a Canaanite woman, also impressed Jesus (Matthew 15:21-28). She begged Jesus to heal her demon-possessed daughter. The Lord replied that He only came to help the lost sheep of Israel. She begged more intently for His intervention. Jesus explained, "It is not good to take the children's bread and throw it to the dogs." Ouch! Jesus must have missed that political correctness class.

The woman did not quarrel or argue whether she or her daughter were a dog, but used Jesus' metaphor to her daughter's advantage. Undeterred, she logically concluded that even dogs eat the crumbs that drop from the table. The deductive syllogism is:

- People eat bread
- People are messy and drop bread crumbs on the floor
- Dogs lick the bread crumbs people drop on the floor
- Jesus only gives bread to people
- Jesus called me a dog (if A)
- Give me crumbs (then B)

Jesus was impressed with her logic and said that her faith was great. Her daughter was healed immediately.

## Fringe Benefit
In the next chapter, a woman suffering from a hemorrhage for twelve years saw that if Jesus touched people, they were healed. The woman inductively reasoned, without revelation from God, that perhaps the reverse were true; if she touched the fringe of Jesus' robe, she might be healed (9:21). So, she touched the fringe of Jesus' robe and she was healed. Jesus called what she did faith, a faith that was logically created. Jesus said, "Daughter, take courage, your faith (inductively reasoned) has made you well." Critical thinking pleases the Savior.

## The Shepherd was not Sheepish
The Jewish religious leaders were trying to trap Jesus to accuse Him of some charge to condemn Him (Matthew 12:1-13). They asked the Lord of the Sabbath if it was lawful to heal on the Sabbath. The Lord used deductive logic and their own actions against them. Jesus subsumed "healing" in the broader category of "doing good" on the ladder of abstraction. Jesus asked who among the religious leaders would not, on the Sabbath, pull a sheep from a pit it fell into. Humans are more valuable than sheep (if A). So then, based on what you do, it is lawful to do good on the Sabbath (then B). The religious leaders had no response to Jesus' logic. The Jewish leaders could not pull the wool over Jesus' eyes. Shear brilliance (ooh, that was baaaad) on Jesus' part. He would not cotton to their yarn. Oh what a tangled web they weaved. Jesus' critical thinking again won the day.

## Mental Midgets Meet Messianic Match

Jesus confronted people with their own illogic. Matthew 12:22-29 recounts the story about Beelzebub. The Pharisees stepped into the batter's box and accused Jesus, the ace critical-thinking pitcher of the opposing team, of casting out demons by Beelzebub, the ruler of the demons (verse 24). Jesus immediately challenged them and their lack of critical thinking, hurling intellectual 120 m.p.h. fastballs right down the middle of the plate.

Jesus told the Pharisees that a kingdom divided against itself cannot stand. If Satan casts out Satan, he is divided against himself, and his kingdom will fail (verse 25). Strike one. Their reasoning was illogical, and Jesus used deductive logic to make that clear to them. Then the Lord conceived a conundrum for their consideration— if Satan is the one who casts out demons, then Jewish religious leaders who cast out demons are doing so by the power of Beelzebub. Swing, and a miss. Strike two. Jesus continued with more deduction by telling the Jewish religious leaders that since God casts out demons (if A), then He was from God, and they were opposing God (then B). Strike three. You're out!

Jesus then added that the Pharisees were guilty of the unforgivable sin when they inferred He cast out demons by the power of Satan. The Pharisees not only struck out, Jesus ejected them from the game. He was not playing with them anymore. The religious leaders' statement that Jesus was empowered by Satan was the straw that broke the Savior's back in that He was done with them. These religious leaders sealed their fate in Hell. If they had thought through the implications of their Beelzebub statement, this would not have happened. Illogic is spiritually dangerous—it leads to a lack of faith, and without faith, it is impossible to please God (Hebrews 11:6).

Jesus cautions us about not thinking properly. On the Day of Judgment, humans will be held accountable for every careless word spoken (Matthew 12:36). The best way to guard what you say is to first guard how you think.

Some people worry about committing the unforgivable sin, but that is impossible to do today. For someone to commit the unforgivable sin, that person must tell Jesus in His physical presence that His miracles are empowered by Satan. Since Jesus is not physically present performing miracles, no one can be guilty of committing the unforgivable sin, but we still should guard how we think and what we say.

## Puzzling Parables

After the Jewish leaders condemned themselves by their illogically-induced disbelief, Jesus altered His teaching tactics, beginning in Matthew 13. No longer would the Lord preach plainly, but instead He would proclaim perplexing parables (verses 10-17). It takes critical thinking skills to decipher them.

## Sow What?

For example, when Jesus explained the Parable of the Sower in Matthew 13:18-23, He gave clues about how to interpret the parables:

- Sower = someone proclaiming the gospel
- Seed = the gospel
- Birds = Satan/enemy
- Good fruit = new believer

So, a person shared the gospel. Satan snatched some seed and life problems snatched some seed, indicating these people were not believers, but make-believers. Only people represented by the good soil became true believers because they are the only ones who bore fruit.

Note that when we interpret the parables, Jesus never had the church in mind. Jesus does not define any element of the parable as referring to the church. Jesus expected His disciples to understand the parables, and they had no concept yet of the church. The church was still a mystery, an unknown (Ephesians 3:6). When we interpret the parables, since Jesus was not talking about the church, and the disciples did not know about the church, we have no right to interpret them as being about the church. The parables are about the much broader concept of the kingdom of heaven. Jesus was talking about believers and unbelievers in general.

## Tare Into this One

Jesus gives us clues to critically think through and understand the parables. Look at the next parable in verses 24-30. Jesus explained the parable in verses 36-43:

- Man sowing good seed = Jesus, the Son of Man
- Seed = believers

- Field = world
- Enemy = Satan
- Tares = false believers (opposite of good fruit)
- Harvest = the end of the age
- Reapers = angels

So, Jesus came to the Earth and made believers, but among them Satan sowed make-believers. At the end of the age, Christ will send His angels to sort them out, one from the other.

## Cutting the Mustard

Using the "Rosetta Stone" of Matthew 18-23 and 37-43, the Parable of the Mustard Seed is easily understood (verses 31-32). However, this parable also is often incorrectly interpreted because it is taken out of context. Many say this is a parable about how large and great the church will one day be, but that is an impossible interpretation. Remember, the church is a mystery when Jesus is speaking.

- Man sowing a mustard seed = Jesus, the Son of Man;
- Seed = the gospel;
- Garden plants/tree = believers;
- Birds = Satan/enemy.

This is not a positive statement; it is a negative one. Jesus is re-stating the Parable of the Wheat and the Tares, i.e., Satan will sow false believers among God's people.

The Lord expects us to understand the parables and gave us clues to do so. We need to and we can critically think our way through to the correct interpretation of these puzzles, as we can with all Scripture passages.

## Multiplication Examination

The time arrived for Jesus to test the critical thinking skills and faith of his disciples, as recorded in Matthew 14:13-21. This narrative is commonly known as the Feeding of the Five Thousand, although there were probably more than five thousand people present since women and children were not counted in the five thousand number (verse 21). Jesus had been teaching all day. About 3:00 p.m., the disciples told the Lord to send the people away so they could eat in the villages. Instead, Jesus told the disciples they should give the people something to eat.

This was a test. The disciples (just like the centurion, the "crumby" Canaanite woman, and the bleeding woman, who exhibited critical thinking skills and extraordinary faith) watched Jesus' miracles, including turning water into wine at the marriage feast in Cana in John 2. Would the disciples exhibit critical thinking leading to faith or would their logic, and therefore their faith, fail them? Could they reason inductively that if Jesus can control the wind and the sea, heal every person who asks (even from a distance), raise the dead, and make wine from water, He can multiply fish and bread?

The disciples did not use good inductive logic and failed the test, giving the answer that they only had five loaves and two fish. There is no indication that the possibility of Jesus multiplying the measly menu ever muddied their minds. In spite of the disciples' failure, Jesus multiplied the loaves and fish to feed all the people, with twelve baskets of leftovers, evidently one for each of the disciples. (I wonder if Jesus gave them each a basket to satisfy their hunger or to be a dramatic reminder of their lack of proper thinking and faith? I imagine it was for both reasons.) It was time for another exam. Will the disciples do better next time? Not so much.

## Praying Up a Storm

Jesus then sent the disciples by ship to the other side of the sea while He went up to the mountain to pray. Meanwhile, back on the Sea of Galilee, it was a dark and stormy night. The wind howled, the waves rose, the boat tossed. The seasoned sailors struggled with the wind and the waves. At about 3:00 a.m., in the midst of the chaos, Jesus walked on the sea toward the disciples. Mark 6:48 adds that Jesus intended to just walk by them. What a sense of humor. "Hi men. How's it going? Row, row, row your boat. Well, see you later." The disciples were aghast—"A ghost!" Jesus comforted them and told them to "buck up, take courage," in essence, think rightly.

Peter thought, "Wow, water-walking. Can I take a whack at it?" The Lord invited Simon Peter to join Him. Peter successfully walked on water until he stopped thinking correctly. Simon concentrated not on the fact that he was successfully walking on water, or that Jesus was and had been walking on water, or that Jesus can do great miracles. Instead, Pete (a.k.a. the Rock) thought about the wind. True to his name, he started to sink like a Simon. This was disciple critical thinking failure number two. The other disciples also failed the test because they never took any risk by staying in the boat. They lacked critical thinking, which resulted in a lack of faith. In the midst of the storm, the disciples "waved" off the idea of water-walking.

## Tradition Transgression

Have you ever met someone who can find the dark cloud inside every silver lining? The Pharisees and scribes were such people. My brother Bob once proposed that the first course they took in scribe school must have been Whining 101, and they must have all earned A's. In Matthew 15, these ungodly religious leaders complained that Jesus and His disciples transgressed the traditions of the elders, which were man-made, legalistic rules of conduct. The Jewish religious leaders were offended because Jesus' disciples put food in their mouths without first ceremonially washing their hands. Jesus counter-attacked with logic. Who do you think will win this argument?

Jesus condemned the Pharisees and scribes for transgressing the commandments of God. Hmmm, which is the sin, disobeying legalistic men or disobeying God? Even worse, the elders' traditions themselves were sin against God. Jesus unveiled the sinister scheme devised by these legalistic leaders to defraud their aged parents.

In the fifth of the Ten Commandments (Exodus 20:12), YHWH commanded, "Honor your father and mother." This included physically caring for and financially assisting your parents when they became elderly. In 1 Timothy 5:8, Paul said that anyone who does not provide for his parents has denied the faith and acts worse than an unbeliever. Even unbelievers take care of their aged parents; how much more so should believers? The Pharisees and scribes, however, dishonored their parents and sinned against God. These man-madelaw-loving legalists also loved loot. They taught that if your mom and dad knocked on your door asking for financial help, you should just turn and face your possessions and yell "Corban," meaning "Everything I have I dedicate and give to God."[2] After you yell "Corban," answer the door and say, "Sorry, but you are five minutes too late. I just gave everything I have to God, so I have nothing to give to you since it now belongs to Him. If only you would have come yesterday, everything belonged to me and I could have, and would have, helped. Be warmed and be fed. Have a nice life. Now stop dirtying my doorstep."

Then Jesus called them a bad name—hypocrites. In Matthew 15:7-9 Jesus said, "You honor me with your lips, but your heart is far from me. It is what comes out of your mouth ("Corban!") that defiles you, not what you put in your mouth (food from unwashed hands)." The Pharisees and scribes invalidated the Word of God in order to obey their traditions. Jesus was saying, "Here's what I think of you and your stinking traditions."

Jesus did not always play well with others. Critical thinking will not always allow you to play nice, either. It is too bad the Pharisees and scribes did not live in America. They could have filed a lawsuit through the ACLU because they were offended by what Jesus said. If you have not offended legalists and hypocrites (sorry for being redundant), you have not done your job. Jesus could not have cared less if He offended legalists. He added that legalists are just the blind leading the blind; they cannot think right and therefore have no faith. If you follow a blind legalist, both of you will end up in a hole.

## More Bread and Fish + Less People = Logic Meltdown

It was time for Jesus to give the disciples a re-test of their logic and faith. The Savior summoned the disciples and told them He felt compassion for the multitudes (four thousand men plus women and children) who had been with Him for three days and had not eaten (Matthew 15:32). The disciples whined that there were no McDonalds or greasy spoon restaurants that could feed this many people in such a desolate area.

What were they thinking? Had they lost their minds? The Lord just fed five thousand plus people with five loaves of bread and two fish. The disciples scoured the grounds and scrounged seven loaves of bread and a few fish. They needed Jesus to do a smaller miracle than He did before. Instead of deductively reasoning that Jesus had already fed five thousand plus people before with fewer loaves and fewer fish then we have now (if A), then Jesus can feed these fewer people with the food we foraged today (then B). Again, there is no indication that the possibility of Jesus multiplying the measly menu ever muddied their minds. In fact, based on what Jesus told the disciples at the feeding of the five thousand ("You feed them"), they could have performed this miracle themselves. However, they exhibited no logic; consequently, there was no faith, just whining. If we are whining, we are not thinking critically, and we are not pleasing God because we have no faith.

Jesus performed the same miracle as when He fed the five thousand.  As before, the people ate well, only this time there were only seven baskets of leftovers instead of twelve sacks of surplus.  The disciples will not have as much food to eat as they had last time.  They failed the test and the re-test because they did not reason rightly. They, therefore, exhibited no faith.

## Who Am I?

In Matthew 16:13-20, the Lord wanted the disciples to think deeply about Him.  He wanted them to use reason to determine who He was.  Jesus asked the disciples what they had heard other people saying about who He was.  They proposed various answers; then Jesus zeroed His question on them, "Who do you say that I am?"  It is logic time; it is faith time.  Based on what the disciples had seen and heard for more than a year, what is their conclusion?  Who is the One who can circumvent the laws of nature and physics?  Who is the One who is the most powerful speaker imaginable?  Who is the One who demonstrates limitless compassion for the needs of others?  "Based on the evidence, men, what is your logical conclusion?"  Jesus is throwing another fast ball.

Peter stepped up to the plate and knocked this one out of the park in verse 18.  "You are the Messiah, the Son of the Living God" ("Son of" means "equal to").  The Father enabled Peter to think rightly and demonstrate faith.  The Lord rewarded Peter for his thinking by making him the chief Apostle and by giving him the keys to the kingdom, the church (for the first time, Jesus told the disciples about the church, although they had no concept yet what it was to become). It is Peter who will preach on the Day of Pentecost, unlocking the door with the keys to let Jews into the church (Acts 2). It is Peter who will unlock the door with the keys to let Samaritans (half Jews and half Gentiles) into the church by enabling them to be baptized with the Holy Spirit (Acts 8). It is Peter who will unlock the door with those keys to let Gentiles into the church at the house of Cornelius (Acts 10). The Lord rewards logic-induced faith. Peter grabs the fringe of the robe momentarily, but he is unable to sustain the grasp.

## Why Am I Here?

The disciples now know the Lord's identity, but why is He on Earth? The Old Testament has much to say about the identity of the Messiah. The disciples evidently cherry-picked the Old Testament passages that referred to the Messiah in His second coming as a conquering King; they ignored the passages, like Isaiah 53, which prophesied that the Messiah in His first coming would have to die to pay the penalty for human sin.

Jesus attempted, on many occasions, to correct their thinking, beginning in Matthew 16: 21-23 (see also 17:22-23 and 20:17-19). He told the disciples He must go to Jerusalem, suffer at the hands of the religious leaders, die, and rise from the dead.

Peter decided to correct the Messiah's obvious obliviousness. In verse 22, Simon summoned the Son aside and scolded Him, "God forbid it, Lord! This shall never happen to you." Thankfully, the Savior was not swayed by "Rocky" logic. "Get behind me, Satan! You are a stumbling block to me; for you are not setting your mind on God's interests, but man's" (verse 23). Ouch, and double ouch. Peter had a thinking problem (he should have gone to AA—Adlebrain's Anonymous), allowing Satan to use his brain. Satan might as well have used it; Peter was not. Thinking well in one instance ("You are the Son of God") does not guarantee we will continue to think well in the next situation ("God forbid it, Lord!). Home run hitters also strike out. Keeping our minds focused and thinking logically calls for vigilance on our part. We cannot let down our guard. We have an enemy who is more than willing to do our thinking for us. Unfortunately, we are often too willing to comply with Satan. At those times, in essence, we let Satan think for us. We have lost our minds. This does not please our Lord.

## Why Can't We Do What You Do?

In Matthew 17:14-20, the disciples failed to heal a demon-possessed boy. Jesus cured the boy immediately. The disciples went to Jesus privately, asking why they could not cast out the demon. Jesus told them they could not exorcise the demon because they did not exercise their faith. They were not thinking logically about the abilities God had given them, resulting in petite belief and full-size failure. Faith-failure follows logic-failure.

Jesus was the quintessential critical thinker. He directed His life by thinking critically. The Lord always won arguments, and He always won His arguments with logic. The Apostles eventually learned critical thinking from the Master and consequently demonstrated stellar critical thinking skills.

## The Apostles were Critical Thinkers

The Apostles had to be critical thinkers. Although many Christians believe the Apostles were constantly bombarded with revelations from Heaven, or were led by the Holy Spirit to make decisions, the former rarely happened and the latter never happened. Remember, the majority of people believing something does not make it true. There was little revelation given to the Apostles, averaging about one revelation per year. They had to rely on what they knew about the Old Testament and their circumstances and then make logical decisions that led to faith. The disciples also used logic to make arguments.

## Feet Feat

In A. D. 33, Jews from all over the Roman Empire converged on Jerusalem to celebrate the Feast of Pentecost. Jesus had risen to Heaven ten days prior. According to Acts 2:9-11, they were "Parthians, Medes and Elamites; residents of Mesopotamia, Judea and Cappadocia, Pontus and Asia, Phrygia and Pamphylia, Egypt and the parts of Libya near Cyrene; visitors from Rome (both Jews and converts to Judaism); Cretans and Arabs." Hundreds of these Jews visiting Jerusalem believed in Christ and stayed in Jerusalem to learn from the Apostles' teaching. The non-native Jerusalem believers (also known as Hellenistic Jews) soon ran out of money. They needed financial assistance to survive. There were no MAC machines.

In Acts 4, new believers who lived in Jerusalem were selling their possessions to help provide for the Hellenists' needs. In Acts 5:1-11, Jerusalem natives Ananias and Saphira sold a piece of property. They secretly stashed some of the cash and then lied to the Apostles that the amount they were giving was the amount of the sale. Peter confronted Ananias about this, using deductive logic. In essence, Peter argued that before Ananias sold the land, it belonged to him and his wife. After the land was sold, the money was under Ananias' and Saphira's control (if A). They did not have to give all of the money to the cause (then B). They did, however, have to tell the truth about the sale of the land. Peter said they ultimately lied to God, and both Ananias and Saphira died. Where would I be, where would you be if, when we lied, God struck us dead? I will tell you where I would be—writing books with no one alive to read them (I better watch for lightning bolts). (Notice in verse 9 that feet carried out Saphira and buried her—the non-figurative interpretation paints an interesting picture.)

## We Already Did Our Entry-Level Job at McDonalds

Satan tried a back door attack on the church in Acts 6. The number of disciples was rising rapidly, and the native Israeli Jewish believers were overlooking the Hellenistic Jewish widows in the daily serving of food (I guess the fellowship and camaraderie of chapter two waned by chapter 6). The Hellenists complained to the Apostles about this, evidently wanting the Apostles to be the widows' waiters. True, the Apostles had served food before at the feeding of the five thousand plus and the feeding of the four thousand plus, but it was an unwise use of their time to be waiters now, just as it was unwise for Moses to judge all the cases brought before him by the Hebrews. Satan attempted to distract the Apostles from their main role and priorities of Bible study and evangelism.

Using deductive logic, the Apostles told the congregation that if their job was to dedicate themselves to the Word of God (if A), then it was not wise for them to wait tables (then B). They told the congregation to select seven godly men to do this task. The logic pleased the congregation, who chose seven Hellenistic men to do the job. As a result, people kept getting saved, including Jewish priests.

Be careful about what you think your Church leaders should be doing. Although many pastoral and elder job descriptions contain more than thirty responsibilities, their main priority is the spiritual care of the congregation. If your pastor is doing anything more than studying Scriptures, praying, giving spiritual counsel, evangelism, and leading worship, he is not concentrating on his main priorities and responsibilities. Be the critical thinker in your Church and speak up about it; get the Church's priorities changed to God's priorities.

## Heaven is a Stone's Throw Away

Stephen was one of the godly seven waiters chosen to feed the widows in chapter 6. Some Hellenistic Jewish unbelievers started a logical argument with him (Acts 6:8-10) but were unable to win the argument because of Stephen's wisdom and his grace (he did not quarrel with them). These Hellenistic Jews enticed people to lie about Stephen. The Jewish religious leaders consequently arrested Stephen and put him on trial before the Jewish Council.

Stephen delivered a powerful, logical argument, recounting the history of God's dealing with Israel and how Israel had consistently opposed God. Stephen concluded, saying in verses 51-53, "You stiff-necked people, with uncircumcised hearts and ears! You are just like your fathers: You always resist the Holy Spirit! Was there ever a prophet your fathers did not persecute? They even killed those who predicted the coming of the Righteous One. And now you have betrayed and murdered Him—you who have received the law that was put into effect through angels but have not obeyed it."

Ouch. Jesus would be proud of that speech. It did not have one iota of political correctness in it. In fact, Jesus was proud. Stephen saw Heaven open and Jesus standing at the right hand of God, welcoming him home.

The Jewish leaders had the same reaction to Stephen as they had to Jesus. Instead of repenting, the Jewish leaders stoned Stephen to death. Logic may not win friends for you, or rise to the level of proof with the people who hear you, but it does please the Son of Man.

## Jews and Gentiles in a Giant Jam

Peter did the unthinkable for a Jew—he preached to Gentiles at the house of Cornelius and they decided to follow Christ. This caused no small furor among the Jews in Judea and Jerusalem. They could not believe Peter would do such an evil thing. Jews did not talk to Gentiles unless they had to. No Jew ever *had* to evangelize a Gentile (The Jonah Syndrome?).

Peter explained to his Jewish Christian brethren what had happened at Cornelius' house using a deductive, logical, and orderly argument (Acts 11:4). He described how God told him to go and preach to the household of Cornelius. Simon says, as he was preaching, the Gentiles were baptized with the Holy Spirit. "If God therefore gave to them the same gift as He gave to us also after believing in the Lord Jesus Christ (if A), who was I that I could stand in God's way (then B)?" The argument was effective because the rage receded as the offended acknowledged God was also saving sinful Gentiles. Well-reasoned logic on one person's part may lead to faith in other people.

## Must Gentile Christians be Converted into Jews?

Some Jewish believers told Gentile believers they had to be circumcised or they could not be saved. God gave no revelation about how to handle this potentially explosive and destructive issue except that circumcision is not required for salvation; the disciples and elders debated the matter at length (Acts 15:6-7). Peter argued that Gentiles were saved by grace through faith the same way Jews were saved. Paul and Barnabas then related how God worked through them among the Gentiles. James, the Lord's brother, argued that the Prophets told of a time when God would call Gentiles to salvation. James' conclusion was that they should not trouble the Gentiles with circumcision. The Gentiles were happy to hear that. Reason, not revelation, ruled the day.

In the next chapter, Paul meets Timothy, who is an uncircumcised half-Jew. Using inductive logic, Paul determined that Timothy not being circumcised could result in Jews being offended (have you ever wondered how they would know), and thereby be an impediment to the preaching of the gospel. Paul reasoned that Timothy's not being circumcised was not a valid reason to block Jews from becoming true believers in Jesus. If the Jews became offended, they would not believe in Christ (if A), so Paul circumcised Timothy (then B). Paul received no revelation to circumcise Timothy. Paul used logical thought and critical thinking skills so as not to hinder the gospel.

## Reasoned Preachin'

Acts 17:1-3 records Paul's visit to the synagogue in Thessalonica, where for three Sabbaths, he "reasoned with them from the Scriptures, explaining and giving evidence that the Messiah had to suffer and rise from the dead." Paul made rational, logical arguments as he presented the gospel. For some, the rational arguments led to faith and salvation (verse 4). Paul then traveled to Berea. He followed the same logical approach in Berea he used with the Thessalonicans. The Bereans examined the Scriptures to see if what Paul was saying was true. Again, reasoned argument led to faith and salvation (verse 12).

Paul journeyed to Athens and preached a logical discourse; some sneered, some believed. What Paul said rose to the level of proof for some but not for everyone. Our job is not to prove that the Bible is true, but to present a logical argument and leave the results up to God. As the Apostle Paul said, some people plant the seed, others water it providing evidence, but it is God who makes the seed grow, resulting in proof and salvation (1 Corinthians 3:6).

Paul made logical arguments, supported with evidence, whenever he preached. Paul reasoned with the Jews in the synagogue in Ephesus. In Acts 19, he returned to Ephesus, reasoning with and persuading people in the synagogue for three months. Then he daily reasoned in the school of Tyrannus for two years. Paul gave a logical defense of Christianity before Felix, Festus, and King Agrippa. Paul spent the remaining time discussed in the Book of Acts in Rome under house arrest where he reasoned with people about the gospel. Throughout his ministry, Paul preached logical sermons to evangelize the lost and logical discourses to mature the saints. If, as stated previously, logic and critical thinking produce faith, and if preaching is to help people come to faith in Christ or to grow in their faith in Christ (if A), then sermons and discourses must be based on the principles of logic and critical thinking (then B).

## Salvation Logic

The path to saving faith is down the road of critical thinking and is logically induced. Our job is to give pre-Christians facts by which to make a decision to follow Christ. We tell pre-Christians God is holy (If "A"), and they sinned against Him (then "B"). God is just and judges sin (If "A"), so they are bound for Hell because the wages of sin is death (then "B"). God is love and became a man, Jesus Christ, to die on the cross in our place for our sins (If "A"). They must believe this and confess that Jesus is God (Romans 10:9-13), committing their eternal destiny to Jesus Christ and His grace and mercy (then "B").

The evidence is clear from the entire Bible—logic leads to faith. Do you lack faith? Your problem may be your thinking. We saw how the Apostles were logical, critical thinkers who were men of faith. How did they make decisions about everyday life? We will investigate this in the next chapter.

## For Review and Discussion

- Give three example of God being a critical thinker.

- Explain why Christ had to die on a cross.

- Explain why Abraham was critical thinker.

- Explain how Joshua and Caleb were critical thinkers.

- Explain why the story of David defeating the dwarf was not a matter of "Name it and claim it."

- Describe Esther's faith.

- Contrast the Centurion's faith with the disciples' faith.

- Was the church built on Peter? Why, or why not?

- In what ways were Jesus and Stephen not politically correct?
- What logic convinced you to trust Christ for salvation?

## ENDNOTES

1. Keathley, Hampton.    "Our Daily Bread: Five Smooth Stones." <u>Bible</u>.2005. <http://www.bible.org/illus.asp?topic_id=1463>.

2. Hendricksen, William. <u>New Testament Commentary: Matthew</u>. Grand Rapids, MI: Baker Book House, 1973, p. 613.

Each indecision brings its own delays

And days are lost lamenting over lost days...

What you can do or think you can do, begin it.

For boldness has magic, power, and genius in it.

Johann Wolfgang von Goethe

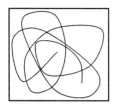

CHAPTER FIVE

# The Process of Making Biblical Decisions

A common belief among Christians is that God will tell you what to do when you have to make an important decision, usually supported by Proverbs 3:5-6 in the KJV, "Trust in the LORD with all Thine heart; and lean not unto Thine own understanding. In all thy ways acknowledge him, and he shall direct thy paths." Christians, who supposedly had their path directed by God, will refer to this direction with the phrase, "The Lord led me."

Quizzically, no one in the New Testament used such terminology. How did believers in the New Testament make decisions? What can we learn from them?

## Paul the Planner
Without revelation from God, Paul decided to go through Macedonia and Achaia, next to Jerusalem, and then to Rome (Acts 19:21). Paul often used logical reasoning to make decisions. He never said he felt "led of the Spirit" to do something. The Holy Spirit did give Paul revelation at times, but not often.

## When in Rome

Paul told the Roman Church he had made plans to visit them on several occasions, but was hindered from doing so; he does not say by whom or what (Romans 1:13). Evidently, since the Lord was not "leading"[1] him, Paul made decisions that did not always work out.

Some modern-day Christians look to prophecy to get answers about a decision they need to make. "When we encounter situations which do not appear to have a clear answer in Scripture, we may need access to prophetic ministry. This ministry will echo Scripture faithfully, will drive us to the feet of Jesus, whilst not usurping our will or forcing us into unsound judgments or actions."[2] However, Paul, an apostle, did not look for prophecy from God to figure out what to do.

Other Christians look for the "leading or guiding of the Holy Spirit," a supposed inward impression or outward sign that God gives, indicating a correct choice in a decision. I was reared under this oppression. For example, I was told to use the fleece method to buy a car. You go to the car lot, choose the car you want, and "put out a fleece" like Gideon did. You pray, "Lord, if You want me to purchase this car, allow no one to buy it for three days." If the car is still there when you return, it is God's will for you to buy this vehicle. It never seemed to occur to the purveyors of this procedure that the car may still be on the lot because everyone else knew it was a lemon. Believe it or not, using this method resulted in me making some poor car purchases. I became soured about buying cars. One of the automobiles spontaneously caught fire and was totaled with one car payment remaining. I like extra crispy chicken, but not cars. I was fleeced. Besides, Gideon laid out his fleece after God told him what to do by direct revelation—the fleece was a sign of faithlessness. In April 1986, Larry Burkett (on his radio program) spoke of a young couple that wanted to buy a home, but felt it was too expensive for them. They told God, "If you want us to buy it, (1) have the contractor accept only 1/2 of what he's asking for the down payment, and (2) have the bank approve our loan." Both events happened and they bought the home. They soon began to go into debt. The problem: what to do now, since God "directed" them to do this![4] Did God direct them?

Paul further elaborated on his plans in Romans 15. Paul's aspiration was to preach in areas where people had not heard the gospel, to fulfill Isaiah 52:15. Since preaching to unreached people was his highest priority in life, this goal kept Paul away from Rome (verses 20-22), which already had been reached with the gospel. He told the Romans that he planned to stop by to see them eventually, but first he had to deliver an offering to the Jerusalem Church. Taking the offering to Jerusalem was a higher priority to Paul than visiting Rome. Paul prioritized his goals and followed those priorities. Setting priorities requires logic and critical thinking.

Paul had goals that motivated his decision to go to Rome. Paul could have visited many cities, so he set priorities because there was not enough time to visit every one. The reasons he listed for going to visit Rome were to impart a spiritual gift that would help them grow spiritually (1:11), to encourage their faith and for them to encourage his faith (1:12), to enjoy their company, and to secure financial aid for a trip to Spain (15:24). He never gave "I felt led," or "God told me" as a reason for visiting. Paul evidently wanted to go to Spain to preach to the undetached, which was the overarching reason to go to Rome, which was conveniently located on the way to Spain. The Apostle Paul's decisions were logical, based upon priorities and goals, not revelation from God. He detailed the reasons for his decisions; revelation from God or the leading of the Holy Spirit were not among them. God wants us to make decisions the same way Paul made them.

## Maybe He Will, Maybe He Won't

In 1 Corinthians 16:3-9, Paul outlined travel plans that included the Church at Corinth. He told the Corinthians to select one of their own members to deliver their financial gift to the Church at Jerusalem. Paul added that "if it is fitting," he would go to Jerusalem also. He did not say that if he received revelation, he would go, or if he feels led of the Spirit he would go. He said if it is fitting, he would go. "Fitting" means if it seems like the right thing to do, based on a logical decision. Paul does not delineate the criteria he will use to decide if it is fitting for him to accompany the financial gift and the person carrying the gift to Jerusalem, but he planned to use logic skills to determine his course of action. He told the Corinthians that perhaps he will stay with them, or even spend the winter. That does not sound like being led of the Spirit or revelation. Paul was making plans absent these types of direction from God. He stated that he did not want to just see the Corinthians in passing, but then rendered the caveat, "if the Lord permits" (see James 4:13-15). God may change Paul's plans or erect obstacles to them, but that does not stop Paul from planning.

Paul explained why he would not come to Corinth immediately; he planned to stay in Ephesus until Pentecost, not because the Lord or the Holy Spirit told him to do so, but because there was a vast opportunity for ministry. Again, preaching to those who had not heard the gospel was Paul's top priority, and that priority drove his decision-making.

In 2 Corinthians 1:15-2:4, Paul says his plans to visit Corinth did not materialize. Paul does not say he failed to make the trip because he was led of the Spirit or received revelation not to go. He says in 2:1, "But I determined this (not to come to Corinth) for my own sake, that I would not come to you in sorrow again." Not coming to Corinth was Paul's reasoned decision, not one divinely revealed. Paul was avoiding Corinth because of the emotional anguish the Corinthians caused him, not because God told him not to go. In 13:1, Paul stated future plans to visit Corinth. The Corinthian Church had issues to deal with before Paul would visit again.

## Guess Who's Coming to Dinner?

Paul recounted a confrontation he had with Peter in Galatians 2:11-14. Peter went to Antioch and ate with the Gentiles, but when Jewish representatives arrived from James in Jerusalem, Peter became aloof from the Gentiles. Peter led other Jews to participate in his hypocrisy. Without revelation or leading of the Holy Spirit, Paul said, "When I saw that they were not straightforward about the truth of the gospel, I said to Cephas in the presence of all, 'If you, being a Jew, live like the Gentiles and not like the Jews, how is it that you compel the Gentiles to live like Jews?'" Paul confronted Peter about his hypocrisy in front of everyone.  Paul used deductive logic.  He explained the premises that led to his conclusion in verses 15-21. (1) Those Jews who believed in Christ died to the Old Testament law and should not follow it; (2) those believers who now follow the Old Testament law nullify grace; (3) those believers who nullify grace are saying that Christ died needlessly; (4) to say that you are a believer in the Lord Jesus Christ and say by your actions that Christ died needlessly (if A) leads to the conclusion that such believers are hypocrites (then B).  Paul figured this out logically without revelation or the leading of the Holy Spirit.  Based on logic, Paul confronted Peter to highlight his hypocrisy.

## Philippi By and By

Philippians 2:23-28 records Paul making decisions to visit the Philippian believers. He planned to send Epaphroditus back to the Philippian Church, but not immediately.  Paul was waiting to visit Philippi, not because he was waiting for revelation from God or the leading of the Holy Spirit, but to see what would happen to him as he sat in prison. As soon as Paul understood his fate, he said he would send Epaphroditus to see the Philippians.

Paul gave deductive logical reasons for his plans.  The Philippians sent Epaphroditus to Paul to minister to him, but while Epaphroditus was ministering to Paul, Epaphroditus became ill and almost died.  Instead, Paul had to minister to Epaphroditus.  The Philippians heard of Epaphroditus' illness, which upset him; Epaphroditus did not want his home Church to worry about him.  Epaphroditus wanted to go home to Philippi, and Paul wanted the Philippians to see that Epaphroditus was well (if A).  This would lessen the Philippians' anxiety about Epaphroditus as well as lessen Paul's concern for the Philippians (then B). This is sound reasoning based on deductive logic.

## The Best Laid Plans

Paul tried on several occasions to visit the Church at Thessalonica, but Satan hindered him. The Lord did not tell Paul to visit the church (1 Thessalonians 2:18). Just like us, Paul made a plan that did not pan out. Instead, Paul "thought it best" to stay in Athens alone and to send Timothy to Thessalonica to find out about the condition of the Thessalonians' faith (1 Thessalonians 3:1, 2, and 5). Note that Paul logically thought this was the best thing to do. He did not receive revelation from God or a leading of the Holy Spirit. He thought, planned, and then executed the plan. Paul does not explain how Satan does so, but the Devil can thwart our plans. Paul's planning was not the problem; the problem was the power of Satan.

## Are You Telling Me What to Do?

Paul made plans for others as well as himself. He sent Tychicus to the Ephesian Church for the logical reason of making "everything known to you ... about us" (Ephesians 6:21-22). Similarly, Paul told the Church at Colossae that he was sending Tychicus to them so they would know about Paul's circumstances and for Tychicus to encourage them. In 2 Timothy 4:9-21, Paul wanted Timothy to make every effort to visit him soon. Paul needed his cloak and told Timothy, therefore, to come before winter. Paul did not seek revelation or the leading of the Holy Spirit. He did not instruct Timothy to search for revelation or the leading of the Holy Spirit to determine what God wanted him to do. "Come as soon as you can and get here before winter."

Paul devised and implemented a plan for Titus to stay in Crete to "set in order what remains, and appoint elders in every city" (Titus 1:5). Paul later urged Titus to come see him at Nicopolis, where he planned to spend the winter (Titus 4:12). Paul did not seek revelation or the leading of the Holy Spirit. He did not instruct Titus to search these two avenues to determine what God wanted him to do. The text is very clear regarding the origin of the decision: Paul said, "I have decided."

Paul instructed Philemon to prepare lodging for him because he hoped, because of prayers offered to God, soon to be released from prison (Philemon 22). Paul did not receive revelation or the leading of the Holy Spirit about being released from prison or about staying with Philemon. Paul did not instruct Philemon to search these two avenues to determine what God wanted him to do. Paul told him to pray and to prepare. Paul consistently used logic to plan for himself and to plan for others.

## Divide and Conquer
In Acts 22, some Jews wrongly thought Paul took a Gentile into the Temple in Jerusalem. A riot erupted. Roman soldiers subdued Paul and took him before the Jewish Council. Using inductive logic, Paul supposed he could escape this mess by getting the Council members to fight among themselves. The Council was comprised of Pharisees and Sadducees. The Pharisees believed in the resurrection of the dead; the Sadducees did not believe in

resurrection. Paul cried out in the Council, "Brethren, I am a Pharisee, a son of Pharisees; I am on trial for the hope of the resurrection of the dead." God gave no revelation to Paul to say this. It was what Paul "perceived" (23:6), or logically reasoned. The Council members began to quarrel and the assembly was divided. Some of the Pharisees began to defend Paul's innocence. Tempers in the room became overheated. Fearing for Paul's life, the Roman commander whisked Paul to safety, detaining him in the soldiers' barracks. Paul's critical thinking saved the day.

## What We Learn from Paul
Unlike what we see today in Christian circles, Paul did not look for a "leading of the Holy Spirit" or prophecy to make decisions. He used logic, critical thinking, and goals to craft his decisions. We are wise if we follow his example.

## John the Planner
The Apostle John also made plans without revelation or the leading of the Holy Spirit. In 3 John 14, John said he hoped to see the letter's recipient shortly. His goal was to speak face-to-face with this person. John made a logical decision.

## Are Marriages Made in Heaven?
In 1 Corinthians 7:25-40, Paul, guided by the Holy Spirit, gave directions about how to find a marriage partner. Paul and the Holy Spirit do not command us to seek revelation or the leading of the Holy Spirit. Paul said that since Christians will have trouble in this life if they marry (particularly during times of persecution), and since it is difficult to devote more time to serving the Lord, it may be

better not to marry. However, even though there will be persecution and less time to serve God if one is married, Christians are free to marry if they wish. Each person is to weigh the consequences and responsibilities of marriage before getting married. There are no commands to search for "God's choice" in the marriage. We are not told to seek God's will about whether we should marry or even whom we should marry. Paul and the Holy Spirit only instructed us to think through the ramifications of the decision we make. However, when I was a boy, my Church taught that God had chosen someone for me to marry and I must find her to be in his "perfect will."

Whom should you marry? Alan, age 10, responded, "You got to find somebody who likes the same stuff. Like, if you like sports, she should like it that you like sports, and she should keep the chips and dip coming."[3]

Whom may a Christian marry? How do you find that person? Kristen, age 10, said, "No person really decides before they grow up who they are going to marry. God decides it all way before, and you get to find out later who you're stuck with."[5] Paul has two guidelines: the person must be a believer and the person must be someone who pleases you (verse 39). You are neither to seek revelation from God on this matter nor try to determine the leading of the Holy Spirit for your life mate. Paul says you may marry anyone you wish who meets his two criteria. It is your decision, based on what believer you like (a believer who likes you would be helpful as well). God puts the decision, after you meet these two criteria, squarely on your shoulders. God sets the parameters of your decision (see chapter 11) by the people He allows you to meet, but as long as the person is a believer and you want to marry that person and that person wants to marry you, God is pleased with your decision. God is not hard to please—just obey His Word.

What would be the implications of God choosing someone for a person to marry, but then that person marries someone else. For argument's sake (although the Bible never says anything even remotely that God does this), suppose God wants Bob and Sue to marry, but Sue decides to disobey the will of God and marry Pete (Pete would not, therefore, be God's "second best," but disobedience to God). Now Sue and Pete are out of God's will, and through no fault of his own, so is Bob if he were to marry someone else or not marry at all, since he was supposed to marry Sue. Suppose God wanted Pete and Amanda to get married, but now that Pete married Sue, lonely Amanda meets lonely Bob and they marry. Although both couples are out of God's will, it is only four people, total, who are out of God's will. However, suppose Amanda and Bob never meet each other and marry other people whom God wanted to marry other people, and God wanted the two people they marry to marry someone else, and so on for centuries.

Two people's disobedience to the will of God (Sue and Pete) can lead to a snowball affect of people marrying someone who is not God's will for them. To avoid all of that, and for other reasons as well, among them that God lets us exercise free will (see chapter 11), God says we are free to be single or we are free to marry any believer who pleases us, and even to re-marry if we are widows (1 Corinthians 7:39), if we are sexually sinned against by our spouses (Matthew 19:9), or if we are abandoned by an unbelieving spouse (1 Corinthians 7:15). We have to make a logical decision regarding marrying the person we want to spend the rest of our lives. So, do not blame the Lord for your marriage choice. The person you married was your choice, not God's. I hope you choose as well as I have.

## Conclusions

In These Last Days Words are important. The most important words ever spoken come from our God, recorded for us in the Bible. Have you ever wanted to hear God speak? Have you ever said in a moment of desperation, "O God, if you would only speak! If I could only hear Your voice. If you would only talk to me and not be so silent!"

Hebrews 1:1-2 shouts loudly that God has not been silent. God is not withdrawn and uncommunicative. These verses teach us that God spoke to us before the coming of the Son of God to this planet and *through* the Son of God's coming into the world. These verses also teach us that God has finished speaking for now.

## God Spoke Through the Old Testament Prophets

Hebrews 1:1 says, "In the past God spoke to our fore-fathers through the prophets at many times and in various ways." God spoke. However, God did not speak directly to the masses of humanity; He spoke through the prophets. God did not whisper His Word into the heart of every believer. His usual way was to call a prophet and then empower that person to speak and to write to the people what God wanted said.    Prophets were the only instruments God used to communicate to the world.

God spoke in many ways and at many times to give us the Old Testament.  He delivered His Word through more than thirty authors over a period of 1,100 years.  This is known as progressive revelation, meaning that God only revealed pieces of His Word at any given time.  God spoke directly to Moses (Exodus 3).  When Moses was on Mount Sinai, God gave him the Law, accompanied by thunder and lightning (Exodus 20).  God spoke to Jacob (and many others) in a dream (Genesis 31:11).  God spoke to the Israelites through a fable in Judges 9.  Daniel saw a vision (Daniel 9).  The Angel of the Lord gave revelation to some (Judges 6).

God's revelation in the Old Testament was incomplete. 1 Peter 1:10-12 says, "Concerning this salvation, the prophets, who spoke of the grace that was to come to you, searched intently and with the greatest care, trying to find out the time and circumstances to which the Spirit of Christ in them was pointing when He predicted the sufferings of Christ and the glories that would follow. It was revealed to them that they were not serving themselves but you." The Old Testament was infallible, without error.  2 Peter 1:21 says, "Above all, you must understand that no prophecy of Scripture came about by the prophet's own interpretation. For prophecy never had its origin in the will of man, but men spoke from God as they were carried along by the Holy Spirit."

The Old Testament Scriptures are valuable and powerful. 2 Timothy 3:15-17 says, "from infancy you have known the Holy Scriptures, which are able to make you wise for salvation through faith in Christ Jesus. All Scripture is God-breathed and is useful for teaching, rebuking, correcting and training in righteousness, so that the man of God may be thoroughly equipped for every good work."

The prophets' writings were profitable and good, but they were also fragmentary and incomplete. Something more was needed. God has a superior way to communicate with us.

## God Became One of Us to Speak to Us

Hebrews 1:22 says, "but in these last days He has spoken to us by His Son." God did something unique to communicate with us—He sent His Son. This is different. Jesus is not just another prophet. He is the Son of God. God narrowed His revelation down to One Source—Jesus.

The New Testament centers on Christ. The Gospels tell about Jesus' life, death, and resurrection. The Epistles tell us what difference Christ's life can make in our lives. The Book of Revelation tells us what Jesus will do in our future. Jesus not only brought revelation from God; He was the Revelation of God. John 1:18 says, "No one has ever seen God, but God the One and Only, who is at the Father's side, has made the Father known." Jesus revealed and explained God. God is no longer hidden. Contrast the prophets' message with Jesus' message. The prophets said, "Thus says the Lord" more than four hundred times. Jesus said, "Truly, truly, I say to you." The Word of God in His Son is so complete that there will be no more revelation, which is what "in these last days" means. The written revelation of God in Christ will not be followed in the Church Age by any other revelation. Jesus is the Word of God. God commands us in Hebrews 3:1 to "fix our thoughts on Jesus."

God has given us *everything* that pertains to life and godliness (2 Peter 1:3). Why would we need anything else from God? The answer is simple: we do not! We have all we need to live a life of faith. Christians need to stop wondering when God is going to tell them what to do and look at what He has told them to do through His Word. There is no more revelation. God finalized it in His Son. Use your mind and think.

The Gospels and the Epistles recount many occasions where Jesus and the Apostles used critical thinking and logic. Logical reasoning that led to acts of faith and courage was the foundation of decision-making in the New Testament.

We arrive at most of the decisions we make in life inductively. We make observations about the situation, then combine that information with other truths we know about the Bible and our life experiences to make a decision. Inductive arguments do not come with mathematical certainty. We make the best decision we can based upon the information we have available at the time. In explaining the decision we made, we will not say that the Lord led me, but along with the Apostle Paul we will say, "'It seemed best to me,' based on my critical thinking skills."

A thinking skill God wants you to hone is the ability to study and interpret His Word. You must develop this skill so you will know the truth and be able to tell if you arc being taught errors, like those associated with "the leading of the Holy Spirit." You cannot afford to have your spiritual growth stunted by not knowing how to determine if you are being told the truth about the Bible. We will look at how to study and interpret God's Word in chapter six.

## For Review and Discussion

- Describe how Paul made decisions.

- What is your conclusion about "the Lord led me?"

- How do you think you should make decisions? How does this compare to the way you currently make decisions?

- Do you believe God chose someone for you to marry? Explain your answer.

# ENDNOTES

1.  See Gary Friesen's <u>Decision Making and the Will of God: A Biblical Alternative to the Traditional View</u>. Portland, OR: Multnomah Press, 1982.

2.  Cooke, Graham. <u>Developing Your Prophetic Gifting</u>. Ventura, CA: Sovereign World, 1994, p. 17.

3.  Snodgrass, Klyne. <u>Between Two Truths: Living with Biblical Tensions</u>. Grand Rapids, MI: Zondervan Publishing House, 1990, p. 179.

4.  <u>"How Do You Decide Whom to Marry?" Car Talk. 2005. <http://www.cartalk.com/content/read-on/2000/03.18.html>.Ibid.</u>

5.  Ibid.

The man who does not read

Has no advantage

Over the man who cannot.

Mark Twain

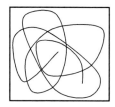

CHAPTER SIX

# The Process of Biblical Interpretation

## Do Your Best

In 2 Timothy 2:15 God commands, "Do your best to present yourself to God as one approved, a worker who does not need to be ashamed and who correctly handles the Word of Truth." The Lord *commands* us to work hard at doing our best possible Bible interpretation. Doing our best study is not an option; it is every Christians' obligation.

Interpretation means we discover the meaning the author intended for the text. Interpretation is guided by hermeneutics (the science of correct interpretation), using principles and rules to extrapolate the author's meaning. Dr. David L. Cooper's Golden Rule of Interpretation stated it well, "When the plain sense of Scripture makes common sense, seek no other sense; therefore, take every word at its primary, ordinary, usual meaning unless the facts of the immediate context, studied in light of related passages and axiomatic and fundamental truths, indicate clearly otherwise."[1] Or, as my college professor Dr. Thomas Figart used to say, "When the plain sense of Scripture makes common sense, seek no other sense, or it is nonsense."

Christians disagree about how certain passages should be interpreted. However, the biblical writers did not want to confound, confuse, or conflict us. Just like everything you say and write has a specific meaning, every passage of Scripture has but one correct interpretation. Our job is to discover it.

Correct biblical interpretation may mean accepting the simplest answer. In the 1960's, NASA decided it needed a ballpoint pen to write in the zero gravity of space. Finally, the Astronaut Pen was developed at a cost of $1 million. The pen worked. The USSR, faced with the same problem of writing in zero gravity, used a pencil.[2] Often, the simplest answer is the best answer.

Correct biblical interpretation may be the simplest answer, but it is hard work nonetheless—God commands you to be a worker. Correct interpretation of Scripture is an act of dedicating yourself to God and is therefore an act of worship. "How this thought ought to drive out even loose carelessness, to say nothing about arrogant opinions, following human authorities, popular errors, and practices!"[3] We have no right to take interpretation lightly, and we must do it rightly.

The goal of interpretation is to do it so well that God approves of your work. God commands us to worship Him by finding the right interpretation of every passage, that is, the meaning He intended. Any other interpretation than the one God intended is mishandling the Word of God and is in opposition to the worship of God. Your goal in interpretation is not, "What this verse means to me is...," but, "What this verse means to God is..." Hollis Green, Chancellor of Oxford Graduate School said, "If you misinterpret Shakespeare, you damage him; if you misinterpret Scripture, you damage the kingdom of God."[4] To teach the wrong interpretation of a passage is spiritual abuse and fraud. It is being a careless worker; God is watching.

We should be ashamed to get our interpretation wrong. We are to be workers who do not need to be ashamed. The word "ashamed" means embarrassment that arises from guilt due to sin. "Ashamed" means being disgraced before God. Do you feel disgraced, embarrassment that arises from guilt due to sin, for not doing your best to diligently, personally study the Word of God? If you are guilty of not doing your best and you do not feel shame, what is wrong with your view of the Christian life? God says your goal is to be a worker who is not ashamed because you rightly interpreted the Word of truth. I know many times I have sloughed off from studying God's Word and have felt no shame for it. I need a continual fresh view of my need to study the Bible and how the lack of study offends a holy God.

Studying the Bible is not rocket science; it is more important than that. Studying the Bible is a science, the science of hermeneutics. We need a scientific process to discover and draw out the information from the Text to make correct interpretations of Scripture.

Correct biblical interpretation is something you work at, think about, and pursue, not something you dabble in, play with, or trivialize. Correct biblical interpretation is hard work. Correct biblical interpretation includes using critical thinking skills if you are going to do your best as a worker to rightly handle the Word of Truth. Studying and interpreting the Bible correctly requires the use of inductive logic.

I find it much easier to listen to a sermon or a Sunday School lesson, or to read a devotional commentary, than to analyze a text of Scripture on my own. Christians do not study the Scriptures on their own for various reasons. Some do not study because they are lazy. Others do not take the time to study (these people usually say they do not have time to study, but I find that I find time to do what I want to do). This chapter cannot help you if you fall into these two categories. You have decided not "to do your best." You have decided to disobey God and not worship Him.

Some Christians do not study because they think they do not know enough Bible or theology to interpret the Scriptures correctly. They feel much like the students who had a one-question essay test: Define the universe; give three examples. Follow God's commandment—do your best. Get a good study Bible, a Bible Dictionary, Bible software, and a word study book like "Little Kittle" by Bromiley. Invest in some good critical commentaries (critical commentaries deal with the Hebrew and Greek texts and are written above the devotional and popular levels), but only use them after you have done your own study so you can develop your own research abilities. Besides, you remember most what you discover on your own.  After making these purchases, follow the steps in the remainder of this chapter.

## Communication Conundrum

Writing is the most inefficient form of communication because we interpret words best when we can see others' facial expressions and hear their tone of voice, which account for about 90% of the communication process. How often have people misconstrued the message of an e-mail you sent, and how often have you misinterpreted something written to you?  In many of these cases, misunderstandings would not have occurred if you had talked to the person face-to-face.  Interpretation is much more difficult if we cannot see and hear the person. Writing is inefficient; the Bible is written.

What does it mean to communicate with someone? Communication is the response of someone to the symbolic behavior of someone else.  Words are symbols that represent thought.  Communication only occurs when the message is received in the way the sender intended it to be received, when what is in the mind of the sender is the same message received and understood in the mind of the receiver.

Claude E. Shannon and Warren Weaver designed a model, a symbol of the communication process (see Figure 6-1). An information source, God in our case with Bible study, encoded or chose the words He wanted us to know and transmitted that message through the pages of His Holy Word. We receive this information by reading and studying the Word of God, decoding what is written, with the goal of discovering authorial intent, that is, what God actually meant. What an awesome responsibility and astounding privilege, but the process is fraught with difficulty.

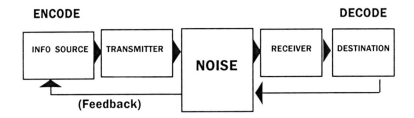

**Shannon and Weaver Communication Model**
**Figure 6-1**

Our feedback is limited. We can tell God we do not understand what He said, but we cannot ask Him questions about what He meant as we can in conversations with humans. Communication from God is, practically speaking, one way and completed.

Unfortunately, before the information God encoded and transmitted gets to us, it passes through the noise of different languages, different cultures, contextual meaning, an absence of facial expressions and tone of voice on God's part, our biases, and our faulty logic. When we hear sermons or read commentaries, emotions, authority figures, and illogical reasoning masquerading as logic can sway us. Our lack of critical thinking when we study and interpret the Scriptures can keep us from our doing our best, which can hinder the Holy Spirit from renewing our minds like we need Him to do.

## Interpretation Aids

In one sense, the Bible is different from all other books. It alone is the special revelation of God to humans. Only the Holy Scriptures are inspired and inerrant in its original writings, the autographs. God never had to do a second edition or a Version 2.0 because He had to correct errors. (Unlike copies of the Bible. One revision of the King James Bible was dubbed "The Murderer's Bible" because the revisers forgot the word "not" in "Thou shalt not kill.")

This is not true with other writings. On March 29, 2005, Eric Slater wrote "Hazing Death Highlights Chico's Greek Life" for the Los Angeles Times. After a local Chico newspaper contradicted Slater's article, the Times wrote a retraction:

> An article in Tuesday's California section about hazing at Cal State Chico mistakenly said that a pledge to a fraternity at nearby Butte Community College died of alcohol poisoning. He did not die but was hospitalized. The article also said Chico has a population of 35,000; according to the city, the population is 71,317. In addition, University President Paul Zingg was quoted saying the school would shut down its Greek system if problems with hazing did not abate. Zingg made his comments to a group of 850 students and others, and his remarks were quoted in the local media. He did not speak with The Times. Also, although the article characterized the school as being well known for its basketball program, its winning baseball program may be best known outside campus.[5]

God has never needed to write a retraction. The Bible is God's Word that the Holy Spirit, supernaturally superintended to say precisely what God wanted said. The Bible is not what the writers of Scripture wanted to say. "The biblical writers seek consciously to recede into the background. They point away from themselves to God as the author of their message. They spare no effort in putting God before the reader."[6]  Since God is its author and the Bible is the only Book He wrote, only the Word of God gives us true information about God, salvation, and the future destiny of the universe.  It alone is absolute truth.  There are depths to Scripture that can only be fathomed with the aid of the Holy Spirit since He is its author (1 Corinthians 2:14). So, in one sense, the Bible is different from all other books.

In another sense, the Bible is no different than any other book.  It was written in human languages (Hebrew, Aramaic, and Koine Greek) just like any other book.  The writers of Scripture had a message to communicate in a historical setting for a particular purpose, and they communicated that message following the rules of syntax and grammar, just like any other book.  "An author of a book of the Bible composed his work according to normal writing procedures.  He had a main purpose in writing, and subordinate ones as well."[7]

We need help to bridge the gap between the writers of Scripture and the readers of today.  Printed books, computer software, and the Internet provide historically unparalleled access to information about the Bible and its contextual settings.  There are many aids to make sure we "do our best."  Some of that information is good, and some, well, is not good.  How can we discover which resources are valuable and which ones we should avoid? Information Literacy Research[8] can help us in our quest. The American Library Association said, "To be information literate, a person must be able to recognize when information is needed and have the ability to locate, evaluate, and use effectively the needed information."[9] Either we know something about the Bible or we must know where to find information about the Bible.  For most of us, it is the latter more than the former.  Information Literacy is knowing how to find information, evaluate it, and use it effectively in interpreting Scripture.

## Evaluating Internet Resources

Internet research usually starts with a search engine like Google or Yahoo.  The search engine will list everything from an eight-year-old's Web page to scholarly documents. Not every site listed will be valuable to your research.

The first thing I evaluate is the Web address, or the URL. Those I consider of the highest caliber end in .edu, meaning a college or university sponsors them.  The information on these sites is not infallible, but a scholar in the field probably wrote what is written there.

Anyone can host a Web site; that does not make that person an expert.  I rank Web sites validity in this order:

- .edu for educational or research material
- .gov for government resources
- .com for commercial products or commercially-sponsored sites
- .org for a non-profit resource

A name in the URL may mean a personal home page with no official sanction. URL's ending in .com or .org may be less reliable than a .edu Web site because the person writing may not be a scholar or be peer reviewed for accuracy. Be cautious of Web sites containing someone's name. It is probably a personal home page and is not peer reviewed.

The second thing to evaluate is the author of the Web site. Is the author identifiable? Does the author document his or her expertise on the subject as indicated on a credentials' page? If there is no such page, go back to your search engine, type in the author's name, and discover what you can about this person. You may need to trace back in the URL (Internet address) to view a page in a higher directory that has background information. NetworkSolutions' Web site provides a comprehensive search across multiple WHOIS databases. It includes all domains and extensions regardless of where they are registered.[10] They help to identify the person.

Thirdly, when evaluating Internet resources, determine the intended audience of the page—for whom was this written? Was it written for your needs? Next, is the source of the information documented? Do not accept the information presented without some skepticism. Web sites are rarely referred or reviewed, as are scholarly journals and books. There are no means to evaluate the scholarship of most non-.edu Web sites. The source of the information should be clearly stated, whether original or borrowed from elsewhere, or I recommend ignoring it. If the source is stated, check to see the source meant what he or she was credited with saying. Was the source taken out of context?

## Bias by Us

The last thing to evaluate is the author's bias. Many .org's and .com's are sponsored by cults and try to hide that information from you. Others take theological positions that may be contrary to what you believe or what the Bible teaches, or both.

What is bias? Bias means to skew toward a particular position in an argument due to preconceived views. Because you have a bias does not mean you are wrong. Your bias may exist because what you believe is true. Bias is not necessarily bad, but we often view it negatively.

People tend to limit bias to newspaper reporting and political commentary. Political bias, which is often formulated by applying biblical principles to political issues, runs the continuum from liberal to conservative. On the right side of the continuum are fiscal, federalist, and social conservatives. Fiscal conservatives tend to favor less taxes, less government, and are therefore believers in supply-side economics. Federalist conservatives favor less government intrusion in Americans' daily lives and hold an "originalist's"[11] view of the Constitution, meaning the legislature makes laws, not the courts, and the courts must interpret the Constitution according the Framers' intent. Federalist conservatives tend to believe there are God-given rights as outlined in the Bill of Rights. Since God gives these rights, any government that infringes on those rights usurps the prerogatives of God and is therefore a tyrannical government, which according to the Declaration of Independence, the people have a right to overthrow. Social conservatives promote adherence to high moral values (although no one is capable of always acting according to those values—it does not make us hypocrites, just human and inconsistent), such as being truthful, the sanctity of marriage, and the sanctity of life, resulting in being anti-abortion/pro-life, and pro-death penalty.

On the left side of the political continuum are fiscal, anti-federalist, and social liberals. Fiscal liberals tend to favor higher taxes and massive government spending. They are usually Keynesian in their economic views and have a predilection for the teachings of socialism and Karl Marx. Anti-federalist liberals view the government as the solution to society's problems and use the courts to find rights not previously delineated in the Constitution, bypassing the legislature (Roe v. Wade, for example).

Anti-federalist liberals have a propensity for what they call the separation of church and state (a phrase coined by judicial activists and not found in the Bill of Rights). Their purpose seems to be to remove God from the culture. If they can accomplish this goal, then it is not our Creator who endows our rights, but it is government who gives us our rights. If government endows our rights, then government can revoke those rights, such as limiting free speech, firearm ownership, and the right to freely worship God.

Social liberals slant toward a reduced value for human life (often based in not believing humans are created in the image of God).  Social liberals, therefore, support abortion on demand, homosexual marriage (sex without procreation), forms of euthanasia (the murder of Terri Schiavo by the courts, for example), and are anti-death penalty (taking a human life is not important enough to take another human life in its place).  For example, Princeton University professor Peter Singer spoke at the Governor's Commission on Disability, in Concord, New Hampshire in 2001.  The Associated Press reported:

> 'I do think that it is sometimes appropriate to kill a human infant,' he said, adding that he does not believe a newborn has a right to life until it reaches some minimum level of consciousness.
>
> 'For me, the relevant question is, what makes it so seriously wrong to take a life?' he asked.
>
> 'Those of you who are not vegetarians are responsible for taking a life every time you eat. Species is no more relevant than race in making these judgments.'[12]

People fall all along the continuum in their beliefs.  They may be fiscally conservative yet socially liberal, or fiscally liberal and socially conservative.  Countless possibilities exist.

## Pious Bias

Bias is not limited to newspaper reporting and political commentary.  We all have biases, and we all have biases we bring to our interpretation of Scripture, on a continuum from liberal to conservative.

In the broad category of theology, conservatives have two main biases—covenant theology and dispensational theology. Covenant theologians see the salvation of the elect (soteriology) as God's overarching reason for doing what He does.[13] In my view, many covenant theologians tend to elevate God's sovereignty above the rest of His attributes. Covenant theologians rely heavily upon the teachings of Luther and Calvin. The Westminster Confession of Faith of 1647 delineates covenant theology:

> Covenant theology is a system of interpreting Scripture on the basis of two covenants: the covenant of works and the covenant of grace. . . . God initially made a covenant of works with Adam, promising eternal life for obedience and death for disobedience. Adam failed, and death entered the human race. God, however, moved to resolve man's dilemma by entering into a covenant of grace through which the problem of sin and death would be overcome. Christ is the ultimate mediator of God's covenant of grace.[14]

Dispensational theologians (my bias) believe God's overarching reason for doing what He does is to bring glory to Himself. Even the purpose of salvation for humans is to bring glory to God (see Ephesians 1:3-14). Dispensationalists sharply distinguish between Israel and the church and prescribe to a literary, or literal interpretation of Scripture. This type of interpretation says you interpret the Bible the way you normally interpret any piece of literature. If a passage is figurative, you interpret it figuratively; if it is literal, interpret it literally.

One of the key differences between covenant theology and dispensational theology is that dispensationalists interpret prophecy literally, not figuratively. Most see a future rapture of the church, the Tribulation, the second coming of Christ, the Millennial reign of Christ, the Great White Throne Judgment of unbelievers to an eternity in Hell, the destruction and recreation of the universe, and eternity with God for the elect.

Although covenant theologians and dispensational theologians disagree on these topics, as conservatives, they agree on other doctrines. Conservatives Christians are prone to believe in creation by a divine act of God's will. (Conservatives do disagree about the age of the Earth. Some believe God created the universe in six 24-hour days; others believe God took billions of years to create the universe and the Earth—in context, the word day in Genesis 2:4 not only refers to each creation day, but for all seven days, indicating the word means a long period of time.) Conservatives believe God created all life forms without using any macro evolutionary (Darwinian evolution) processes. Most do believe in microevolution (adaptation and change within a species, for example, different breeds of dogs have a common ancestor—a dog). Christian conservatives promote the sanctity of marriage, are anti-abortion, and pro-death penalty.

Liberals believe that God may have been involved in the writing of the Bible, but debate which passages, if any, He authored. The Scriptures, being authored by men, are therefore fallible. Some liberals may believe God created the Universe, but most believe in the macro evolutionary process to bring about life on Earth. Most liberals promote homosexual marriage, homosexual ordination of clergy, are pro-abortion, and anti-death penalty. Christians fall all along the continuum in their beliefs.

As you do observation, interpretation, and application when you study the Bible, your bias colors your study. You exhibit bias in the way you present the information you have discovered, just like I do as I am writing.

## Main Types of Bias

"Selection bias" means we choose only the evidence that supports our beliefs and reject evidence contrary to our beliefs. I find this so easy to do. For example, if my bias is pro-death penalty, I may ignore statistics in my argument related to those who are wrongly sentenced to death. If my bias is anti-death penalty, I will concentrate on those who are wrongly sentenced to death, but ignore those wrong convictions that are later overturned on appeal. A pro-abortionist discounting scientific evidence supporting the humanity of the fetus is selection bias.

Simon Says:
Many Christians' interpretation of Matthew 16:15-20 provides a good example of selection bias:

"But what about you?" He asked. "Who do you say I am?" Simon Peter answered, "You are the Christ, the Son of the living God." Jesus replied, "Blessed are you, Simon son of Jonah, for this was not revealed to you by man, but by my Father in heaven. And I tell you that you are Peter, and on this rock I will build my church, and the gates of Hades will not overcome it. I will give you the keys of the kingdom of heaven; whatever you bind on earth will be bound in heaven, and whatever you loose on earth will be loosed in heaven." Then He warned his disciples not to tell anyone that He was the Christ.

Adam Clarke (1762 to 1832) wrote concerning the rock upon which the church will be built:

> Peter, *petros*, signifies a stone, or fragment of a rock; and our Lord, whose constant custom it was to rise to heavenly things through the medium of earthly, takes occasion from the name, the metaphorical meaning of which was strength and stability, to point out the solidity of the confession, and the stability of that cause which should be founded on THE CHRIST, the SON of the LIVING GOD.
>
> Upon this very rock, *epi taute te petra*—this true confession of thine—that I am THE MESSIAH, that am come to reveal and communicate THE LIVING GOD, that the dead, lost world may be saved—upon this very rock, myself, thus confessed (alluding probably to Psalm 118:22, The STONE which the builders rejected is become the HEADSTONE of the CORNER: and to Isaiah 28:16, Behold I lay a STONE in Zion for a FOUNDATION)—will I build my Church, *mon ten ekklesian*, my assembly, or congregation, i.e. of persons who are made partakers of this precious faith.  That Peter is not designed in our Lord's words must be evident to all who are not blinded by prejudice.  Peter was only one of the

builders in this sacred edifice, Ephesians 2:20 who himself tells us, (with the rest of the believers), was built on this living foundation stone: 1 Peter 2:4, 5, therefore Jesus Christ did not say, on thee, Peter, will I build my Church, but changes immediately the expression, and says, upon that very rock, *epi taute te petra*, to show that he neither addressed Peter, nor any other of the apostles.  So, the supremacy of Peter, and the infallibility of the Church of Rome, must be sought in some other scripture, for they certainly are not to be found in this (author's emphasis).[15]

Clarke interprets Jesus using a play on words—little rock and big rock from Peter's name.  According to Clarke, to hold a contrary view can only be prejudice.  G. Campbell Morgan (1863 to 1945) agreed:

Now thou art *Petros*, rock.

Then what? "Upon this rock"—not *Petros*, a piece of rock, a fragment of the rock nature, but *Petra*, the essential rock—"Upon this rock I will build My Church." Thou art of the rock nature, and thou shalt be built upon the rock foundation.

"Upon this rock."  Remember, He was talking to Hebrews. If we trace the figurative use of the word rock through the Hebrew Scriptures, we find that it is never used symbolically of man, but always of God.  So here at Caesarea Philippi, it is not upon Peter that the Church is built.  Jesus did not trifle with figures of speech.  He took up their old Hebrew illustration—rock, always the symbol of Deity—and said, Upon God Himself I will build My Church. My Kingdom shall consist of those who are built into God, "partakers of the Divine nature: "Mark the intention carefully by taking Peter's final words first—"The living God." Then the word immediately preceding—"the Son of the living God;" and then the first word—"Thou art Messiah." Jesus said; On that, I will build My Church, on Jehovah God, manifest in time in His Son, administering the affairs of the world through that Son as Messiah. Peter had found the foundation, had touched Jehovah, and by touching Him had become petros.[16]

John F. Walvoord and Roy B. Zuck of Dallas theological Seminary agreed as well:

Peter (*Petros*, masc.) was strong like a rock, but Jesus added that on this rock (*petra*, fem.) He would build His church. Because of this change in Greek words, many conservative scholars believe that Jesus is now building His church on Himself. Others hold that the church is built on Peter and the other apostles as the building's foundation stones (Ephesians 2:20; Revelation 21:14). Still other scholars say that the church is built on Peter's testimony. It seems best to understand that Jesus was praising Peter for his accurate statement about Him, and was introducing His work of building the church on *Himself* (1 Corinthians 3:11).[17]

Although the preceding arguments may sound like viable interpretations of the Text, they are all guilty of selection bias. One of the main problems with Peter being a little rock and Jesus being the big rock upon which the church will be built is Jesus spoke in Aramaic, and there is no distinction in Aramaic in the word for big rock and little rock—they are the same word.   William Hendricksen explained:

> My inability to accept the theory [big rock, little rock] in its entirety is based on the following: a. On the basis of what is known about Aramaic it must be regarded as very probable that the same word was used in both cases.  The question will be asked, "Then why not the same word in Greek?" Answer: for the simple reason that petra, the common word for stone or rock, being feminine, had to be changed to a masculine—hence to petros—to indicate the name of a male person, Peter.  As to *petros* and *petra* differing in meaning, this is not always true.  A very frequent meaning of *petra* is *rock* or *stone*.  It does not always mean . . . "rocky ledge" or "rocky cliff".

> . . .The meaning is, *You are Peter, that is, Rock, and upon this rock, that is, on you, Peter, I will build my church.*  Our Lord, speaking Aramaic, probably said, 'And I say to you, you are *Kepha* and on this *kepha* I will build my church.' Jesus, then, is promising Peter that he is going to build his church *on him*![18]

The big rock, little rock interpretation is impossible and selection bias.  Albert Barnes (1798-1870) established the reason for the selection bias:

And upon this rock . . . —This passage has given rise to many different interpretations. Some have supposed that the word "rock" refers to Peter's confession, and that Jesus meant to say, upon this rock, this truth that thou hast confessed, that I am the Messiah and upon confessions of this from all believers, I will build my church. Confessions like this shall be the test of piety, and in such confessions shall my church stand amid the flames of persecution, the fury of the gates of hell. Others have thought that Jesus referred to himself. Christ is called a rock, Isaiah 28:16; 1 Peter 2:8. And it has been thought that he turned from Peter to himself, and said, "Upon this rock, this truth that I am the Messiah—upon myself as the Messiah, I will build my church." Both these interpretations, though plausible, seem forced upon the passage to avoid the main difficulty in it. Another interpretation is, that the word "rock" refers to Peter himself.

This is the obvious meaning of the passage; and had it not been that the Church of Rome has abused it, and applied it to what was never intended, no other interpretation would have been sought for.[19]

Truth is truth, and as J. S. Mill said, we must follow it wherever it leads. It does not matter who misuses a passage of Scripture; our job is to study the historical and literary contexts, do word studies, and reach conclusions regardless of where they lead us. Discovering what Jesus meant is our goal. I can say Christ built the church upon Peter and all the apostles and not make Peter the first pope. In Acts 2, Peter was present when Jews first entered the church, Samaritans could not enter the church until Peter arrived in Acts 8, and Peter brought the Gentiles into the church in Acts 10. Peter had to be there for these three events to occur because Jesus gave him the keys to the kingdom. Peter unlocked the doors to build all believers on the foundation of the apostles and prophets (Ephesians 2:20). Not to give the evidence that supports Peter is the rock is selection bias and a bias against giving Roman Catholicism ammunition for its doctrinal error.

Another form of bias is "bias by omission," selecting certain information to include and certain information to exclude. For example, if there were a forum of scientists who are Christians discussing the age of the Earth, I can report in a Christian magazine, "Scientists say that belief in an old Earth means belief in Darwinism." I then can give details about what the five scientists at the forum said to support that claim and end my column. It sounds like this was the only view presented.

However, let's say that in reality there were not just five Christian scientists at the forum, but eight Christian scientists. The other three scientists debunked the notion that believing in an old Earth also meant belief in Darwinism. The three other scientists not mentioned in the magazine column found the idea of Darwinism repugnant and presented evidence for progressive creation by God over eons of time. If this were the case, I, the writer of the newspaper column, would obviously have a bias for a young Earth position. I would be guilty of bias by omission. I told the truth, but I did not tell the whole truth.

That can be good and that can be bad, depending on my motive.

God regularly used bias by omission, and it has given liberals grenades to lob at the divine origin of Scripture. For example, Matthew 8:28-29 says there were two demoniacs, while the same event in Mark 5:1-2 says there was one demoniac. Liberals say this is a contradiction, supporting errancy. It looks like an error, but is it? Since I have a bias of inerrancy, I say there is no mistake. Matthew and Mark had different purposes they were trying to convey. Only one demoniac repented, and Mark concentrates on that. Matthew tells us what occurred with both of the demoniacs. If there were two demoniacs, by definition there had to be one demoniac. There is no contradiction, just bias by omission. This type of bias by omission's motive is not to influence others' beliefs by hiding some of the evidence as the Christian reporter did with the age of the Earth forum. It is like the headline in one newspaper saying "Baseball Returns to the Nation's Capitol with the Washington Nationals Home Opener Baseball Game," while another newspaper headline says, "President Bush Throws Out the First Pitch at the Washington Nationals Home Opener Baseball Game." There does not have to be an error; both statements are true. It is simply bias by omission. Each writer wanted to convey a different message, not hide evidence to influence belief.

So, to determine bias, evaluate the way in which the author is assessing the facts and issues. What can you decipher about the way some aspects are accentuated and other details are diminished?

## Appraising a Book

How can you tell the value and validity of a book? Start by evaluating the publisher. Is this a reputable company? Although the fact that the publisher is reputable does not necessarily guarantee quality, it improves the odds. On the other hand, just because you aren't familiar with the company does not mean the book is not reliable. You will just have to work harder to discover the book's validity.

Next, evaluate the gravitas, the substance and "weightiness" of the book. Evaluating the authority and reliability of the information you discover is a vital step in doing research. Is this a scholarly or a popular book or journal? This distinction is significant because it indicates different levels of difficulty in dispensing ideas. Scholars generally write scholarly works for other scholars or experts in the field of study. Scholarly works *always* cite their sources in the form of footnotes or endnotes. The profundity of scholarly works assumes some scholarly training by the reader. The main purpose of a Christian scholarly journal or book is to report on original research in order to make such information available to the rest of the scholarly community, and these works can add gravitas to support your argument.

Popular works, on the other hand, are intended for the interest and intelligence of the laity at large. Popular publications do not cite sources as prolifically as scholarly authors do, and many of these works rarely cite sources. Information is often second or third hand and may contain more opinions than well-reasoned arguments. These works are usually written at an eighth-grade reading level and often only give a cursory treatment of a topic.

## Scan the Book

Read the preface to determine why the author wrote the book and for whom it was written. Is this source too childish, too complex, or just right for your needs (it sounds like the Goldilocks method)?

The book should list the references it cites so you can check the author's sources. Just because the author of the book you are reading quoted another author does not mean the quoted author said what your author said he said. Your author may have taken the other author out of context. If you want to quote an author, always use the original author's text and see if the writer actually meant what the book you are reading attributed to him or her.

Does the information seem well researched, or does supporting evidence not buoy it? In other words, does the author display an understanding of critical thinking skills? Do the ideas and arguments advanced agree with other works you have read on the same topic? The more unique an author's views, the more you must use critical thinking skills to scrutinize the writer's ideas. Just because an idea is new makes it neither right nor wrong. Do not accept or reject any idea until you have investigated it as thoroughly as you can. Determine the author's bias.

## Doing the Study

Knowing how to do information research can greatly aid your Bible study. The more information you can access, the better your chances of doing your best Bible study, and thereby please and worship God. Following are some strategies to improve the results of your study.

## Bloom Where You are Planted

Following the 1948 Convention of the American Psychological Association, a collection of colleges selected delegates to devise a classification of "the goals of the educational process."[20] In 1956 they published their research, having developed a taxonomy of levels of intellectual behavior important for learning to occur. Although the book is known as Bloom's Taxonomy, he was just the first editors' name listed on the title page.

The taxonomy, or hierarchy, consists of six levels (see Figure 6-2). Bloom's committee postulated that learning occurs best at the upper level of the hierarchy, but everyone must begin at the bottom level and work up the ladder. Bible study is advanced when you begin at the lower level as well

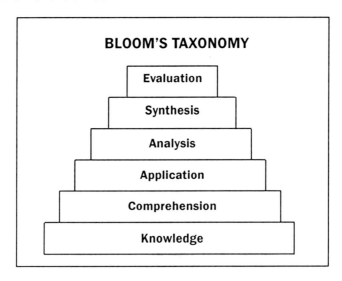

**Figure 6-2**

In Bible study, the first four lower levels of Bloom's Taxonomy will be answering the question, "What does the text say?," also known as observation. Observation means to give comprehensive and careful concentration to what you see.

The bottom, foundational level is "Knowledge"—just the simple recall of information. Memorizing and reciting John 3:16 would be learning at the Knowledge level. The Knowledge level also entails doing an observation of the text. First you want to read the passage, the more times the better. The more you read the pericope, or section you have chosen, the more you will observe. G. Campbell Morgan used to read a passage thirty to forty times before he started to study it.[21]

Next, you will want to ask questions about who the characters are in the account, where does the passage take place, when did it occur, what happens, and how does the story end. For example, examine the crucifixion account in Matthew 27. Who are the governor's soldiers, who was Simon of Cyrene, who were the two thieves, where is Golgotha, why is verse 45 important—"From the sixth hour until the ninth hour darkness came over all the land?" You do not yet answer the questions; you just write them down. The best critical thinking occurs only after we have asked the best possible questions.

Be sure to write down your questions and eventually your answers. We get careless and miss important information if we do not write down our observations. Louis Agassiz, 19th century professor of zoology at Harvard University said, "A pencil is the best of eyes."[22]   Rick Warren attributed Dawson Trotman, founder of the Navigator's with saying, "Thoughts disentangle themselves when they pass through the lips and the fingertips."[23] Write down the information you observe and more will come to the fore.

Oletta Wald[24] listed specific observation information to discover:

- Key words
- Advice, admonitions, warnings, and promises
- Reasons for and results of doing things
- Contrasts, comparisons, and illustrations
- Repetition and progression of ideas
- Questions
- Prepositions and conjunctions
- Grammatical construction—verbs, nouns, pronouns, adverbs, adjectives
- Atmosphere, mood, and tone
- Literary form or genre

Knowledge is the first step to doing Bible study. The second level is "Comprehension," which assumes you know the information from the first level; now you put the information in your own words. Paraphrasing John 3:16 would be learning at the Comprehension level. Comprehension is summarizing what you saw when you observed the text.

The third level is "Application," taking learned material and using it in a new situation. Teaching someone else what John 3:16 says would be learning at the Application level. It is also telling someone else what you observed.

Personal Bible study should not be done in isolation. Pick a partner.

The fourth level is "Analysis." Analysis is taking the verse apart word-by-word and phrase-by-phrase to determine its meaning. Analysis determines the historical context of the verse—who wrote it, why was it written, and to whom was it written. Doing a word study and background study of John 3:16 would be learning at the Analysis level. Although this is still observation, you are doing your final preparation before interpretation.

The fifth level of Bloom's Taxonomy is "Synthesis." Synthesis is creatively putting the pieces of your research together to make a reasoned conclusion about the passage. You do your interpretation at the Synthesis level. Giving interpretive conclusions about John 3:16 would be learning at the Synthesis level.

The top level is "Evaluation," which is applying the biblical text to daily life. Evaluation is making judgments about the value of ideas. Discussing the question, "Do you think, based on John 3:16, that people from other religions can get into Heaven? Why, or why not?" is an example of learning at the Evaluation level. The Evaluation level applies the text to specific life situations. It asks, "What am I supposed to believe or do?"

Following these steps of observation, interpretation, and application will greatly enhance your Bible study. To show you how to use these principles of interpretation, I will first apply these principles to a text of Scripture, then, in the next chapter, to a topic of Scripture.

Let's study Mark 1:21-28:

> They went to Capernaum, and when the Sabbath came, Jesus went into the synagogue and began to teach. The people were amazed at his teaching, because he taught them as one who had authority, not as the teachers of the law. Just then a man in their synagogue who was possessed by an evil spirit cried out, "What do you want with us, Jesus of Nazareth? Have you come to destroy us? I know who you are—the Holy One of God!"

> "Be quiet!" said Jesus sternly. "Come out of him!" The evil spirit shook the man violently and came out of him with a shriek.

> The people were all so amazed that they asked each other, "What is this? A new teaching—and with authority! He even gives orders to evil spirits and they obey Him." News about him spread quickly over the whole region of Galilee.

List your observation questions from the Knowledge level, like:

Verse 21
- Who are "they?"
- Where is Capernaum?
- What historical facts can be found about this city?
- What can be found about the culture of the city?
- Where else is Capernaum mentioned in the Bible?
- Why did Jesus go to Capernaum?
- Where was He before He went to Capernaum?

- What is the Sabbath?
- What is the original Greek word and definition?
- Is it the same as Sunday?
- What other significant events occurred on the Sabbath in the Bible?
- Why was the Sabbath mentioned in the text?
- What was a synagogue?
- What is the original Greek word and definition?
- What other significant events occurred at synagogues in the Bible?
- How could Jesus just start teaching in a synagogue?

Verse 22
- What does teaching with authority mean?
- What authority was lacking from the scribes' teaching?

Verse 23
- What is an evil spirit?
- How are they different from good spirits?
- Where else are evil spirits mentioned in the Bible?
- Are they the same as demons?
- What does evil mean?
- How can an evil spirit possess someone?
- What did the person have to do to get possessed?
- Can it happen to me?
- Why was someone with an evil spirit in a synagogue?
- Why did the evil spirit cry out?

Verse 24
- Why did the evil spirit call the Lord "Jesus of Nazareth?"
- How can Jesus destroy evil spirits?
- How does the evil spirit know who Jesus is?
- Why did the evil spirit call the Lord "the Holy One of God?"
- What does holy mean?

Verse 25
- Why did Jesus sternly tell the evil spirit to be quiet?
- Did Jesus really say, "Shut up!"?
- Is telling the evil spirit to come out of the man the same as destroying    the evil spirit?

Verse 26
- Why did the evil spirit shake the man violently?
- Why did the evil spirit shriek when he came out?
- What does shriek mean?

Verses 27-28
- Why is what Jesus did so amazing to these people?
- What and where is Galilee?
- Why did the text tell us news about Jesus spread throughout Galilee?

Next, summarize the passage for the Comprehension level.  "They (Jesus and others evidently) went to Capernaum (which was probably in Galilee—verse 28). On the Sabbath, Jesus entered the synagogue and began teaching.  The people could not believe the authority with which Jesus spoke to them. A man possessed by an evil spirit confronts Jesus, yells at Him, calling the Lord, "Jesus of Nazareth" and "the Holy One of God." The evil spirit wants to know if Jesus plans to destroy him. Jesus yells back at the evil spirit to be quiet and come out of the man. The evil spirit complies with a shriek after violently shaking the man. The people are amazed an evil spirit listens to Jesus, and news about Jesus spreads like wildfire throughout Galilee."

I may not know what most of what I just said means, so my ignorance should impel me to the next level. Move into the Application level by explaining what you learned so far to someone else. Whet their appetite to study the passage as well. Having a partner who is also studying the same text may encourage you to keep at your endeavor and to do your best, and that person may observe things you missed and you may observe things your partner missed. Having a partner can improve your outcome.

Now it is time for the Analysis level. Use your study tools—a study Bible, a word study book, Bible software, and a Bible dictionary. You now want to answer as many questions as you can from the Knowledge level. I will answer a few of them.

Verse 21
- Who are "they?" "They" refers to Jesus and at least four of His disciples—verses 16-20.

- Where is Capernaum? What historical facts can be found about this city? What can be found about the culture of the city? Where else is Capernaum mentioned in the Bible?

Capernaum was a town located on the northwest shore of the Sea of Galilee and was approximately eighteen miles northeast of Jesus' hometown of Nazareth. Capernaum is mentioned sixteen times in the New Testament. The town was on a major trade route between Egypt and Damascus. A Roman garrison was stationed there.

From other passages of Scripture we learn that Capernaum was the home of the four disciples mentioned in verses 16-20, the closest friends of Jesus. Jesus moved to and lived in Capernaum during most of His earthly ministry. It became His home base of operations. In Capernaum, the centurion asked Jesus to heal his son. The people of the town rejected Jesus and He said it will be more tolerable for the people of Sodom in the judgment than for those from Capernaum. This was the city where four men carried a paralytic man on a stretcher so Jesus could heal him. The crowd was so large outside the house where Jesus was speaking, the four men had to "unroof the roof" (Greek text) to get the man to Jesus. Jesus sent the disciples to Capernaum after the feeding of the 5,000 plus. The disciples were straining at sea on their way to Capernaum when they saw the Lord walking on the water. Jesus gave His "I am the Bread of life" sermon in Capernaum.

- Why did Jesus go to Capernaum? Where was He before He went to Capernaum?

Jesus not only goes to Capernaum, He moves there. A parallel passage is found in Luke 4. In verse 4:16 we find that one of the first ministry places Jesus visited was His hometown of Nazareth. He went to the synagogue on the Sabbath and stood up to read. He was handed the Isaiah scroll that "just happened" to be at chapter 61. Jesus read: 'The Spirit of the Lord is on me, because He has anointed me to preach good news to the poor. He has sent me to proclaim freedom for the prisoners and recovery of sight for the blind, to release the oppressed, to proclaim the year of the Lord's favor.' Then He rolled up the scroll, gave it back to the attendant, and sat down. The eyes of everyone in the synagogue were fastened on Him, and He says to them, 'Today this Scripture is fulfilled in your hearing.'

Jesus then told the people of Nazareth a prophet has no honor in his own country, and like prophets of old, He would do no miracles for them. The townspeople went ballistic. They ran Jesus out of town and tried to throw Him off a cliff, but He walked through the crowd like the Israelites walking through the Red Sea and eluded their grasp.

Then Jesus went to Capernaum, the hometown of Peter, Andrew, James, and John, His new disciples. Because of His rejection in His hometown of Nazareth, Jesus made Capernaum His new place of residence.

- What is the Sabbath? Is it the same as Sunday? What is the original Greek word and definition? What other significant events occurred on the Sabbath in the Bible? Why was the Sabbath mentioned in the text?

God initiated the Sabbath as a day of rest and worship. The Jews observed it from sundown Friday to sundown Saturday. So, Sunday is not the Sabbath. The Sabbath was a day to worship God and a day to be concerned for the welfare of others (Deuteronomy 5:14). The scribes and Pharisees made many rules governing the Sabbath, and it was impossible for the people to keep the rules. The scribes and Pharisees would later get angry with Jesus for doing good for others on the Sabbath, and determined to kill Him. The Greek word for Sabbath is *sabbaton*, and means rest from labor. One of the Ten Commandments says to keep the Sabbath holy. It is the only commandment not restated in the New Testament for Christians to follow.

- What was a synagogue? What is the original Greek word and definition? What other significant events occurred at synagogues in the Bible? How could Jesus just start teaching in a synagogue?

The original Greek word for synagogue is *sunagoge*, and it means a place to gather together. The presence of a synagogue in a city meant that at least ten Jewish males lived there. The synagogue served as a school for children and a judicial center Sunday through Friday at dusk, and a place of worship and a place to teach the Law on the Sabbath. Worship attendees took turns reading the Old Testament scrolls, which were read on a three-year rotation. Visitors from other towns were invited to teach in the synagogue.

Verse 22
- What does teaching with authority mean? What authority was lacking from the scribes teaching?

The scribes did not teach directly from the Scriptures. They taught from commentaries written about the Scriptures. They would teach what Rabbi Z said. Rabbi Z wrote about what Rabbi Y said. Rabbi Y wrote about what Rabbi X said. Rabbi X wrote about what Rabbi W said. Rabbi W wrote about what Rabbi V said. Rabbi V wrote about what Rabbi U said, and so on. By the time the scribes taught the people, what they said was dead and lifeless because what they taught was so far removed from the authority of Scriptures. However, Jesus taught directly from the Scriptures as His own authority. He gave the correct interpretation of the passages He taught.

The closest analogy to explain how the scribes taught can be seen in the modern interpretation of the U.S. Constitution. Alan Sears, executive director of the Attorney General's Commission on Pornography under President Ronald Reagan said, "Activist judges seldom rely on the words of the Constitution, but on opinions of other judges that can be stretched and re-interpreted to fit the causes activists choose to promote or protect. Over time, the original intent of the Constitution gets lost in the sediment from layers of judicial interpretations."[25] One such ruling was the expansion of the U.S. Supreme Court's 2003 decision to outlaw sodomy laws *(Lawrence v. Texas)* based on another opinion from Roe v. Wade that found a right to privacy in the Constitution. *Lawrence v. Texas* was then the basis for U.S. District Court Judge Gary Lancaster's ruling that struck down a ten-count obscenity charge for pornography depicting rape and murder of women. Judge Lancaster said the *Lawrence* ruling could, "be reasonably interpreted as holding that public morality is not a legitimate state interest sufficient to justify infringing on adult, private, consensual sexual conduct even if that conduct is deemed offensive to the general public's sense of morality."[26] The Constitution then loses its intent, just like the Bible lost God's intention by the way the scribes interpreted rabbis, ignoring the Scriptures.

Verse 23
- What is an evil spirit? Are they the same as demons? Why was someone with an evil spirit in a synagogue?

An evil spirit is a demon (Luke 4:33). They are fallen angels who can do nothing but sin against God and who try to destroy humans' relationship with God. They are incapable of redemption, and along with their master Satan, have made permanent reservations in Hotel Hell (Matthew 25:41).

Verse 24
- Why did the evil spirit call the Lord "Jesus of Nazareth?" How can Jesus destroy evil spirits? How does the evil spirit know who Jesus is? Why did the evil spirit call the Lord "the Holy One of God?" What does holy mean?

Jesus had just come to Capernaum from Nazareth where He was rejected by His town folk. Since Jesus is God, He has authority over demons and they must obey Him. On many occasions, Jesus cast out demons, even once letting them go into a herd of swine (this was the first recorded recipe for deviled ham). Evil spirits are intelligent creatures and always recognized Jesus. Holy is the opposite of evil, and means total pureness and a total rejection of evil.

## Interpretation

Let's do an interpretation of Mark 1:21-28, the Synthesis level of Bloom's Taxonomy. Jesus took His disciples to their hometown of Capernaum. As was Jesus' custom, He went to the synagogue sometime between dusk on Friday and dusk on Saturday. Being a visitor to the town, He was invited to speak and amazed His audience because He did not teach from the rabbinical writings, but gave the correct interpretation of the passage, using the Scripture as His authority. The power of the Word of God overwhelmed the people. They had never heard anything like this before since their scribes did not use the Scriptures as their authority to teach.

While Jesus was teaching, a man possessed by an evil spirit cries out, "What do you want with us, Jesus of Nazareth? Have you come to destroy us? I know who you are—the Holy One of God!" The demon was probably making fun of Jesus, trying to rub salt in His wound because He was no longer Jesus of Nazareth. Jesus' town folk ran Him permanently out of His hometown of Nazareth. At that moment, Jesus was not part of any town, although He is in the process of moving to Capernaum. The demon knew his time of possessing the man was soon over. In the presence of a holy God, the evil demon had to profess that holiness. Jesus rebuked the demon and exorcised him. This just added to the people's amazement, and they had to tell everyone about it.

Once you reach this point in your study, research critical commentaries to glean further information. If your interpretation disagrees with any of their interpretations, read the argument the author makes to see if it makes sense to you. You may want to alter your interpretation, or you may not. Do your best.

## Application

Let's do the application to our daily lives of Mark 1:21-28, the Evaluation level of Bloom's Taxonomy.

1. Correct interpretation of Scripture will lead to people listening intently, thereby enabling the Holy Spirit to transform people's minds.

2. Correct interpretation of Scripture stirs demons into action. Demons do not care if we get an interpretation of Scripture wrong; they do get upset when we get it right, and they then try to thwart God's message. Expect demons to disrupt your Bible study.

3. Expect demons to be at your next worship service.

4. Pray for those who teach you the Word of God. They face much spiritual opposition.

5. God is stronger than any demon. God's will be done on Earth as it is in Heaven. We need not cower in the corner dreading demons.

6. Jesus enthralled people when He talked to them because He learned the Scriptures from His Father. Enthralling people with His teaching began when Jesus taught in the Temple in Jerusalem at age twelve. Luke 2:47 says, "Everyone who heard Him was amazed at His understanding and His answers." In John 7:17-

18 Jesus says, "If anyone chooses to do God's will, he will find out whether my teaching comes from God or whether I speak on my own. He who speaks on his own does so to gain honor for himself, but he who works for the honor of the one who sent him is a man of truth; there is nothing false about him."  In John 8:28 Jesus says, "When you have lifted up the Son of Man, then you will know that I am the one I claim to be and that I do nothing on my own but speak just what the Father has taught me."  In John 12:49 Jesus says, "For I did not speak of my own accord, but the Father who sent me commanded me what to say and how to say it."  In John 7, the chief priests and Pharisees sent the temple guards to arrest Jesus.  After listening to Jesus speak, verses 45-46 say, "Finally the temple guards went back to the chief priests and Pharisees, who asked them, 'Why did not you bring him in?'  The guards declared, 'No one ever spoke the way this man does!'"

The Jewish teachers of Jesus' day did not speak with authority.  Five times in Matthew 5 during the Sermon on the Mount Jesus refutes their teaching by saying, "You have heard it said. . .but I say to you."  Matthew 7 concludes, "When Jesus had finished saying these things, the crowds were amazed at His teaching, because He taught as one who had authority, and not as their teachers of the law." Jesus talks about God with authority because He knows God and He is God.  Jesus talks about Heaven with authority because He came from Heaven.  Jesus talks about angels with authority because He created angels, knows angels, and commands angels.  Jesus talks about God's Word with authority because He knows the Word of God and is the Word of God (John 1:1).  We can speak with that authority, too. We know the Father, we know the Son, and we have His Word.

In the next chapter, I will apply these study methods to a topic of Scripture: Can a Christian drink alcohol and wine?

## For Review and Discussion

- Define interpretation.

- How do "approved" and "not ashamed" relate to Bible study?

- Explain the communication process.

- What are the problems we face understanding the communication of the Bible?

- How is the Bible different from all other books?

- How is the Bible not different from all other books?

- How do you evaluate an Internet site?

- Define bias.

- What biases do political liberals exhibit?

- What biases do political conservatives exhibit?

- Explain the difference between covenant theology and dispensational theology?

- Explain selection bias.

- Was the church built on Peter? Defend your answer. Does this answer differ from the answer to question 8 in chapter 2? Why, or why not?

- Define bias by omission. Is this always a bad thing?

- How do you determine the value of a book?

- Explain Bloom's Taxonomy and its application to Bible study.

- Do a textual study of 1 Corinthians 13:8-13.

## ENDNOTES

1. Cooper, David L. "The Golden Rule of Interpretation." Duluth Bible. <http://www.duluth bible.org / g_f_j/ Golden_Rule.htm>.

2. Robertson, George. "Funny and True—The NASA Pen." Unsolved Mysteries. 19 April 2004. <http://www. unsolvedmysteries.com/usm379365.htm>.

3. Lenski, R. C. H. The Interpretation of St. Paul's Epistles to the Colossians, to the Thessalonians, to Timothy, to Titus and to Philemon. Minneapolis: Augsburg Publishing House, 1937, p. 798.

4. Green, Hollis. Oxford Graduate School "Philosophy of Education" class lecture notes, July 1994.

5. Kurtz, Howard. "New Vertigo." The Washington Post. 1 April 2005. <http://www.freepress.net/ news/print. php?id=7538>.

6. Maier, Gerhard. Biblical Hermeneutics. Wheaton, IL: Crossway Books, 1994, p. 22.

7. Jensen, Irving L. Enjoy Your Bible. Minneapolis: World Wide Publications, n.d, p.16.

8. Information paraphrased from Campbell, Susan and Kimberley Donnelly. Information Literacy." York College of Pennsylvania. 21 February 2005. <http:// www.ycp.edu/library/ifl/etext/ethome. html>.

9. Vanyek, Sherri. "White Papers and Reports." Association of College & Research Libraries. 2003. <http://www.ala.org/ala/acrl/acrlpubs/ whitepapers/ whitepapersreports.htm>.

10. Network Solutions. 23 September 2004. <http:// www.networksolutions.com/en_US/whois/index. jhtml>.

11. Milbank, Dana. "Scalia Showing His Softer Side." The Washington Post. 15 March 2005. <http:// www.washingtonpost.com/wp-dyn/articles/ A35096-2005 Mar14.html>.

12. Federer, William. "Neo-Nazis Kill Terri Schiavo." <u>Free Republic</u>. 31 March 2005. <http://www.freerepublic. com/ focus/fnews/1374810/posts>.

13. Ryrie, Charles Caldwell. <u>Dispensationalism Today</u>. Chicago: Moody Press, 1965, p. 18.

14. Enns, Paul. <u>Moody Handbook of Theology</u>. Chicago: Moody Press, 1989, p. 93.

15. Clarke, Adam. <u>Adam Clarke's' Commentary on the New Testament</u>. CD-ROM. Disc 2. Hiawatha, IA: Parson's Technology, 1999.

16. Morgan, G. Campbell. <u>Studies in the Four Gospels</u>. Old Tappan, NJ: Fleming H. Revel, Company, 1927, p. 211.

17. Walvoord, John F. and Roy B. Zuck, eds. <u>The Bible Knowledge Commentary</u>: New Testament. Wheaton, IL: Victor Books, 1985, p. 57.

18. Hendricksen, William. <u>New Testament Commentary: Matthew</u>. Grand Rapids, MI: Baker Book House, 1973, pp. 646-647.

19. Barnes, Albert. <u>Barnes' Notes on the New Testament</u>. CD-ROM. Disc 2. Hiawatha, IA: Parson's Technology, 1999.

20. Kearsley, Greg. "Taxonomies." Psychology. 2004. <http://tip.psychology.org/taxonomy.html>.

21. Warren, Rick. Personal Bible Study Methods: 12 Ways to Study the Bible on Your Own. Lake Forest, CA: The Encouraging Word, 1981, p. 45.

22. Teuber, Andreas. "The Freedom of Thought or 'A Pencil is the Best of Eyes.'" Brandeis University. <http://people.brandeis.edu/~teuber/thinking.html>.

23. Warren, p. 14.

24. Wald, Oletta. The Joy of Discovery in Bible Study. Minneapolis: Augsburg Publishing House, 1975, pp. 18-19.

25. Sears, Alan. "Where is that in the Constitution?" Townhall. 31 March 2005. <http://www.townhall.com/columnists/GuestColumns/Sears20050331.shtml>.Ibid.

26. Ibid.

What we hope to do with ease,

We must first learn

To do with diligence.

Samuel Johnson

(1709-1784)

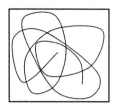

CHAPTER SEVEN

# Alcohol and Wine

I will apply the information from the previous chapter to a topical study about wine and alcohol. As critical thinkers, we must abandon what we think the Bible says or what our pastor's or denomination's position is on this subject. We must be teachable and allow the Scriptures to speak for themselves.

## Introduction

The German poet Johann Voss (1751-1826) said, "Who does not love wine, women, and song remains a fool his whole life long."[1] I hear that "amen" deep within your brain. Although you may think Voss is a moron (he is certainly not a Mormon), I believe he captures the essence of the biblical teaching about wine, women, and song. Amen? What does the Bible say about drinking adult beverages?

## Do a Word Study:
## Where does the Word Appear in the Bible?

The word "wine" occurs twenty-six times in the Bible. The Hebrew language has nine different words for wine describing color and taste. Four different words for wine are used in the New Testament. The word "liquor" occurs three times; "strong drink," made from dates, occurs twenty-one times and had a high sugar and alcohol content. All biblical words refer to fermented beverages.

## Research the Historical Context

The ancients knew nothing about grape juice. Wine fermented in Israel in three-to-four days, long before the wine was drinkable. Louis Pasteur (1822 to 1895) was the first person to stop the fermentation process,[2] thereby making the production of grape juice possible for the first time. New wine fermented quickly in Jesus' time. They could not stop the fermenting process, hence Jesus' warning in Matthew 9:17 not to put new wine in old wineskins. "Old wineskins had already been stretched to capacity by fermenting wine within them; if they were then filled with unfermented wine, it would likewise expand, and the old wineskins, already stretched to the limit, would burst."[3] Read the Church fathers. You will find hundreds of references to wine, but not one mention of grape juice because there was no such thing.

Archeologists have discovered that beer was the preferred drink of the Israelites, although beer is not mentioned in Scripture. Wine was the common beverage at meals. In the Old Testament, alcoholic beverages were consumed straight, unmixed and undiluted. The Greeks thought drinking undiluted alcohol was barbaric. By New Testament times, wine was cut by water 2- or 3-to-1. The wine of that day had such high alcohol content you could set it on fire with a small flame.[4] "The Romans flavored their wine with lead, which may be part of the reason they are not the force they used to be."[5]

## Exegete the Passages and Categorize Them into Sub-topics

What does the Bible say about alcohol, wine, and liquor? The Jews saw wine as a good gift from a good God. Having wine meant God was blessing you. Isaac blessed Jacob and asked God to bless him with wine. Genesis 27:28 says, "Now may God give you of the dew of heaven, and of the fatness of the earth, and an abundance of grain and new wine."

God promised the Jews if they obeyed Him, He would bless them with wine. Deuteronomy 7:13 says, "He will love you and bless you and multiply you; He will also bless the fruit of your womb and the fruit of your ground, your grain and your new wine and your oil, the increase of your herd and the young of your flock, in the land which He swore to your forefathers to give you." Proverbs 3:9-10 says, "Honor the LORD from your wealth and from the first of all your produce; so your barns will be filled with plenty and your vats will overflow with new wine."

God gives us wine to make us happy. Psalm 104:14-15 says, "He causes the grass to grow for the cattle, and vegetation for the labor of man, so that He may bring forth food from the earth, and wine which makes man's heart glad, so that he may make his face glisten with oil, and food which sustains man's heart." Ecclesiastes 9:7 adds, "Go then, eat your bread in happiness and drink your wine with a cheerful heart; for God has already approved your works."

God removes wine from people as punishment. Joel 1:5 and 10 says, "Awake, drunkards, and weep; and wail, all you wine drinkers, on account of the sweet wine that is cut off from your mouth. The field is ruined, the land mourns; for the grain is ruined, the new wine dries up, fresh oil fails." Zephaniah 1:13 adds, "Moreover, their wealth will become plunder and their houses desolate; yes, they will build houses but not inhabit them, and plant vineyards but not drink their wine." Haggai 1:9-11 says, "You look for much, but behold, it comes to little; when you bring it home, I blow it away. Why?' declares the LORD of hosts, 'Because of My house which lies desolate, while each of you runs to his own house. Therefore, because of you the sky has withheld its dew and the earth has withheld its produce. I called for a drought on the land, on the mountains, on the grain, on the new wine, on the oil, on what the ground produces, on men, on cattle, and on all the labor of your hands."

Wine is a good gift from a good God. James 1:17 says, "Every good thing given and every perfect gift is from above, coming down from the Father of lights, with whom there is no variation or shifting shadow." J. Dwight Pentecost of Dallas Theological Seminary said, "A blessing that God gave to man was the juice He put in that plump grape. It was there as one of God's blessings. But how Satan has taken that and perverted and distorted and used it to accomplish his own purposes."[6]

Jews used wine for celebrations. Wine was used to celebrate victory in war. Genesis 14:18 says, "Melchizedek king of Salem brought out bread and wine; now he was a priest of God Most High." Wine was used to celebrate David becoming king. 1 Chronicles 12:40 says, "Moreover those who were near to them, even as far as Issachar and Zebulun and Naphtali, brought food on donkeys, camels, mules and on oxen, great quantities of flour cakes, fig cakes and bunches of raisins, wine, oil, oxen, and sheep. There was joy indeed in Israel."

The Israelites used wine and liquor in worship offerings to God. The priests in the tabernacle and the temple used wine in the daily offerings. Numbers 28:4-7 commands to offer one lamb in the morning and the other at twilight, "also a tenth of an ephah of fine flour for a grain offering, mixed with a fourth of a hin of beaten oil. It is a continual burnt offering which was ordained in Mount Sinai as a soothing aroma, an offering by fire to the LORD. Then the drink offering with it shall be a fourth of a hin for each lamb, in the holy place you shall pour out a drink offering of strong drink to the LORD."

A libation, or drink offering, was poured on the ground in worship of God. A wine libation was part of the offering of first fruits. Leviticus 23:10-14 says, "Speak to the Israelites and say to them: 'When you enter the land I am going to give you and you reap its harvest, bring to the priest a sheaf of the first grain you harvest. He is to wave the sheaf before the LORD so it will be accepted on your behalf; the priest is to wave it on the day after the Sabbath. On the day you wave the sheaf, you must sacrifice as a burnt offering to the LORD a lamb a year old without defect, together with its grain offering of two-tenths of an ephah of fine flour mixed with oil—an offering made to the LORD by fire, a pleasing aroma—and its drink offering of a quarter of a hin of wine. You must not eat any bread, or roasted or new grain, until the very day you bring this offering to your God. This is to be a lasting ordinance for the generations to come, wherever you live.'"

Wine was part of the Jewish priest's salary. Deuteronomy 18:3-5 says, "Now this shall be the priests' due from the people, from those who offer a sacrifice, either an ox or a sheep, of which they shall give to the priest the shoulder and the two cheeks and the stomach. You shall give him the first fruits of your grain, your new wine, and your oil, and the first shearing of your sheep. For the LORD your God has chosen him and his sons from all your tribes, to stand and serve in the Name of the LORD forever."

Wine was part of the Jewish tithe. Wine was used during a party in the Tabernacle or Temple. Deuteronomy 14: 22-26 says, "You shall surely tithe all the produce from what you sow, which comes out of the field every year. You shall eat in the presence of the LORD your God, at the place where He chooses to establish His Name, the tithe of your grain, your new wine, your oil, and the firstborn of your herd and your flock, so that you may learn to fear the LORD your God always. If the distance is so great for you that you are not able to bring the tithe, since the place where the LORD your God chooses to set His Name is too far away from you when the LORD your God blesses you, then you shall exchange it for money, and bind the money in your hand and go to the place which the LORD your God chooses. You may spend the money for whatever your heart desires: for oxen, or sheep, or wine, or strong drink, or whatever your heart desires; and there you shall eat in the presence of the LORD your God and rejoice, you and your household."

The Lord thinks highly of wine. Wine is equated with the joy of salvation. Isaiah 55:1 says, "Ho! Every one who thirsts, come to the waters; and you who have no money come, buy and eat. Come, buy wine and milk without money and without cost."

Jesus drank wine. Luke 7:33-34 says, "For John the Baptist has come eating no bread and drinking no wine, and you say, 'He has a demon!' The Son of Man has come eating and drinking, and you say, 'Behold, a gluttonous man and a drunkard, a friend of tax collectors and sinners!"' Note Jesus' contrast. John did not eat, Jesus ate; John drank no wine; Jesus drank something that people accused him of being a drunkard. Of course, Jesus was not a drunkard, but people do not accuse you of being a drunkard because you drink water. The contrast is clear—John drank no wine, Jesus drank wine.

Jesus made high-alcohol content wine. John 2:7-10 says, "Jesus said to them, 'Fill the water pots with water.' So they filled them up to the brim. And He is saying to them, 'Draw some out now and take it to the headwaiter.' So they took it to him. When the headwaiter tasted the water which had become wine, and did not know where it came from (but the servants who had drawn the water knew), the headwaiter is calling the bridegroom, and is saying to him, 'Every man serves the good wine first, and when the people have drunk freely, then he serves the poorer wine; but you have kept the good wine until now.'"

Jesus' wine was high-quality wine, a "Christ Perignon" if you please. Jesus did not make grape juice. People in the New Testament era never tasted grape juice. The headwaiter is impressed with the quality of the wine. The vino was not diluted with water, either. Jesus made the good stuff. If Jesus had made grape juice, the people at the party would have been highly disappointed, but they were pleased that the host had kept the best until last.

Jesus promises to drink wine with us in the Kingdom. Matthew 26:29 says, "But I say to you, I will not drink of this fruit of the vine from now on until that day when I drink it new with you in My Father's kingdom." God will serve quality wine in the kingdom. Isaiah 25:6 says, "The LORD of hosts will prepare a lavish banquet for all peoples on this mountain; a banquet of aged wine, choice pieces with marrow, and refined, aged wine."

God says wine has medicinal value. Wine eases the pain of death and suffering. Proverbs 31:6-7 commands, "Give strong drink to him who is perishing, and wine to him whose life is bitter." Wine calms stomach ailments, particularly indigestion. In 1 Timothy 5:23, Paul commands Timothy, "No longer drink water exclusively, but use a little wine for the sake of your stomach and your frequent ailments."
Recent scientific studies bear out the medicinal use of wine. Two glasses of wine per day, considered moderate drinking, results in a 31% reduction in dying from cardio-vascular disease and cancer. Moderate drinking decreases physical and mental deterioration in elderly people and decreases the odds of macular degeneration of the eyes.

The world's leading epidemiologist, Emeritus Professor of Medicine at Oxford University Sir Richard Doll, and his coworkers (Doll et al., 1994) summed up the longest (13 years) study of a population, 12,000 male British doctors. The study showed that moderate drinkers had the lowest death rates and the lowest vascular death rates. As a matter of fact, this study also showed that moderate drinkers had fewer deaths from all causes including cancer, than either abstainers or heavy drinkers (Holmgren, 1995). Britain leads the world in heart disease mortality, and yet it was concluded that moderate drinkers were about 40% less likely to suffer heart attack than nondrinkers or those in the upper ranges of ethanol consumption.[7]

Caution!  Heavy drinking does severe bodily damage.

## Look for Specific Commands in These Passages

God does not condemn drinking, but He does condemn drunkenness.  God warns against drinking to excess. Youths who overeat and over drink are to be stoned to death. Deuteronomy 21:18-21 says, "If any man has a stubborn and rebellious son who will not obey his father or his mother, and when they chastise him, he will not even listen to them, then his father and mother shall seize him, and bring him out to the elders of his city at the gateway of his hometown.  They shall say to the elders of his city, 'This son of ours is stubborn and rebellious, he will not obey us, he is a glutton and a drunkard.' Then all the men of his city shall stone him to death; so you shall remove the evil from your midst, and all Israel will hear of it and fear." United States law forbids youths to do any drinking of alcoholic beverages (as well as stoning your drunken child).

Gluttony and drunkenness lead to poverty. Proverbs 23:20-21 says, "Do not be with heavy drinkers of wine, or with gluttonous eaters of meat; for the heavy drinker and the glutton will come to poverty, and drowsiness will clothe one with rags." You can sin just as much at Sunday dinner as you can at a bar on Saturday night.

Others will take advantage of you when you are drunk. Proverbs 23:29-35 says, "Who has woe? Who has sorrow? Who has contentions? Who has complaining? Who has wounds without cause? Who has redness of eyes? Those who linger long over wine, those who go to taste mixed wine. Do not look on the wine when it is red, when it sparkles in the cup, when it goes down smoothly; at the last it bites like a serpent and stings like a viper. Your eyes will see strange things and your mind will utter perverse things. And you will be like one who lies down in the middle of the sea, or like one who lies down on the top of a mast. 'They struck me, but I did not become ill; they beat me, but I did not know it. When shall I awake? I will seek another drink." These verses do not command us not to drink, but they do command us not to get drunk.

You are stupid if you get drunk. Proverbs 20:1 says, "Wine is a mocker, strong drink a brawler, and whoever is intoxicated by it is not wise."

Drunkenness leads to not worshipping God, which leads to God's judgment. Isaiah 5:11-12 says, "Woe to those who rise early in the morning that they may pursue strong drink, who stay up late in the evening that wine may inflame them! Their banquets are accompanied by lyre and harp, by tambourine and flute, and by wine; but they do not pay attention to the deeds of the LORD, nor do they consider the work of His hands."

God's judgment falls on those who get others drunk to take advantage of them. Habakkuk 2:15 says, "Woe to you who make your neighbors drink, who mix in your venom even to make them drunk so as to look on their nakedness!"

God does not want Christians getting drunk. We are to be controlled by the Holy Spirit, not by wine. Ephesians 5:18 says, "Do not get drunk with wine, for that is dissipation, but be filled with the Spirit." God killed Christians who got drunk on the communion wine. "If it was unfermented grape juice...how much grape juice would someone have to consume to get intoxicated? If you find out, let me know?"[8] Elders are not to get drunk. 1Timothy 3:3 says elders should not be "addicted to wine or pugnacious, but gentle, peaceable, free from the love of money." However, it does not say that elders cannot drink. Deacons are not to get drunk. 1 Timothy 3:8 says, "Deacons likewise must be men of dignity, not double-tongued, or addicted to much wine or fond of sordid gain." However, it does not say that deacons cannot drink. Older women are not to get drunk. Titus 2:3 says, "Older women likewise are to be reverent in their behavior, not malicious gossips nor enslaved to much wine, teaching what is good." However, it does not say that older women cannot drink. 1 Peter 4:3 says, "For the time already past is sufficient for you to have carried out the desire of the Gentiles, having pursued a course of sensuality, lusts, drunkenness, carousing, drinking parties, and abominable idolatries."

So, what is the conclusion? God gave wine as a good gift to His people. Wine should not be abused. To teach that God says Christians cannot drink alcohol is not doing your best study. It is fraud and dishonoring to the Lord—that teaching lies about what God says, and He cannot be and is not pleased with it. God is watching. If this is the teaching of the Bible, where did the idea of abstinence from drinking alcohol come from?

## Confront a Contrary View

Saying that the Bible teaches abstinence resulted from allowing a cultural problem to re-interpret Scripture. Alcoholism in America grew following the War for Southern Independence. 620,000 people died in that war, with 100,000's of people injured. The human mind cannot tolerate seeing that type of carnage, so many soldiers turned to alcohol following the war to ease their "battle fatigue," or post-traumatic stress. It is estimated that about 75% of American men became alcoholics. The responsibility to care for the families of these men fell on local churches.

Miraculously, for the first time in 3,000 years, some American preachers discovered the Bible teaches abstinence from drinking alcohol. They did that by taking many of the previous verses I quoted out of context. These preachers made the verses sound like God opposed alcohol by quoting only parts of the verses, like a sermon I once heard that explained why so many "bootlegging Kennedy's" have been murdered, "Woe to you who give your neighbor strong drink. God's woe is upon you if you give your neighbor alcoholic beverages." Whoa! The context (Habakkuk 2:15) does not allow this interpretation or application. In context, God's woe is upon you if you are trying to get your neighbor drunk to take advantage of him or her. God only opposes drunkenness.

Temperance unions were formed pushing abstinence, groups like the Christian Women's Temperance Union and the Anti-Saloon League. Churches joined the battle. Pastors and women conspired to take alcohol away from men and were successful with Prohibition in 1919. Men got angry and began to the see the church as a place for women and out to take away their pleasures. Men began a process of not going to church that has lasted to the present day. Scriptures were re-interpreted to teach abstinence and "tee totaling."

The social problems of drinking alcohol in modern America must not be read back into the culture of biblical times. However, Homer Kent, former President of Grace Seminary said, based on the social evils in modern America regarding alcohol, "To us, Paul would undoubtedly say, 'No wine at all.'"[9] I find that statement presumptuous. Kent goes to great lengths to explain it is true wine was the common beverage of the day in the New Testament era, but that it is wrong for a Christian to drink alcohol today. The Bible nowhere forbids drinking wine except for someone taking a Nazarite vow. What right has Kent to re-interpret Scripture and then imply that the Holy Spirit did not get His command right allowing some drinking of alcohol?

Our culture cannot dictate our interpretation of Scripture. What God's Word meant in A. D. 58 it means today. The Holy Spirit does not superintend the writing of Scripture for one period of church history and then change His views for other eras of church history. For one Christian to tell another Christian what he or she should do when the Bible is silent on an issue is spiritual abuse (Romans 14:1-12).

The minister of a city church enjoyed a drink now and then, but his passion was for peach brandy. One of his congregants would make him a bottle each Christmas. One year, when the minister went to visit his friend, hoping for his usual Christmas present, he was not disappointed, but his friend told him that he had to thank him for the peach brandy from the pulpit the next Sunday.

In his haste to get the bottle, the minister hurriedly agreed and left. So the next Sunday the minister suddenly remembered that he had to make a public announcement that he was being supplied alcohol from a member of the church.

That morning, his friend sat in the church with a grin on his face, waiting to see the minister's embarrassment. The minister climbed into the pulpit and said, "Before we begin, I have an announcement. I would very much like to thank my friend, Joe, for his kind gift of peaches . . . and for the spirit in which they were given!"

## Present Both Sides of an Argument

Drinking alcohol is an issue of Christian liberty. Every Christian must make his or her own decision to drink or not to drink alcohol. However, consider these statistics before you make your decision. There are 23 million alcoholics in the United States, or nearly 1-in-10 people. Some Christians are alcoholics. Fifty percent of homes in the United States are adversely affected by alcohol. More people die from alcohol-related deaths than deaths resulting from illegal drugs and cigarettes combined. Most arrests are due to alcohol; most workplace accidents are alcohol related.

To drink or not to drink alcohol must be a carefully-weighed decision. Romans 14:20-21 and 23 says, "Do not tear down the work of God for the sake of food. All things indeed are clean, but they are evil for the man who eats and gives offense. It is good not to eat meat or to drink wine, or to do anything by which your brother stumbles. But he who doubts is condemned if he eats, because his eating is not from faith; and whatever is not from faith is sin."

If you are a mature Christian and you decide to drink alcohol, you cannot flaunt your decision in front of weak Christians who have made rules not to drink alcohol. There is a difference between weak Christians and legalistic Christians. Weak Christians believe it would be wrong for them to drink alcohol, so they have made rules to stay away from alcohol. It is biblical to make rules for yourself as long as you do not then think obeying the rules make you more spiritual than other Christians.

If weak Christians see you drinking alcohol, they would be encouraged wrongly to drink as well, violating their conscience, causing them to sin against their conscience. Conversely, legalistic Christians believe their rules make them spiritual and, if you want to be spiritual, you must obey their rules, too. Legalists try to control you. If you drink alcohol, it will not cause the legalist to drink alcohol. Just tell him you will have to agree to disagree, and have a clean conscience as you imbibe.

Whatever a brother or sister in Christ decides to do with respect to drinking alcohol, support his or her decision. Romans 14:22 and 15:1-2 says, "The faith which you have, have as your own conviction before God. Happy is he who does not condemn himself in what he approves. Now we who are strong ought to bear the weaknesses of those without strength and not just please ourselves. Each of us is to please his neighbor for his good, to his edification." If you decide not to drink alcohol, keep it to yourself. Do not tell others you do not drink unless they ask (even if they ask, "That is a personal decision" is a biblical response), and do not tell others they must follow your example. If you were or are an alcoholic, or if you are fearful you may become one, you have no choice—do not drink alcohol. You are a weak Christian in this area of Christian liberty and you need stringent rules.

"I do not drink alcohol." Have it as your own conviction.

If you decide to drink alcohol, do it privately. Keep it to yourself. Have it as your own conviction. There is a difference between doing things in secret and doing things in private. Husbands and wives have sex, but they do it in private, not in secret. The same is true of alcohol because a cavalier attitude may destroy a weaker brother.

NOTE!! I am not saying it is permissible to drink alcohol. I am saying the Scriptures do not teach abstinence. If you or someone close to you has a problem with alcoholism, then the Bible teaches abstinence for you.

If you have a problem with alcohol, there is deliverance. An alcoholic is a person who finds alcohol essential to life. He or she consumes alcohol until drunk. The alcoholic likes the affects of the alcohol. Life becomes a series of opportunities to obtain alcohol to help "cope" with life, relax nerves, unwind, or gain control in life. Alcoholics try to hide their addiction, resulting in loss of friendships and economic problems.

Alcoholism is a choice and a disease. It starts with the choice to drink. It becomes a disease when you are chemically addicted. Alcoholism is treatable. Seek a doctor. Confess your sin to God and those you have hurt. You are responsible to rectify past mistakes and not take the next drink. God can grant deliverance.

God gave wine as a gift that is not to be misused to hurt ourselves or to hurt others. Make your decision wisely about its use. This may not be a popular American view of alcohol, but it is the biblical one, and that pleases God. As critical thinkers, men and women of faith, we must not and cannot be afraid to let the Scriptures speak the truth, whether we like what it says, or not.

## Conclusion

You may say, "Wow, that is a lot of work to do textual and topical studies!" You are correct, but that is what it means to do your best and please God with your study. The time we invest in study is time we spend worshiping God. For too many Christians, they read a text of Scripture, skip observation and interpretation, steps one to five of Bloom's Taxonomy, and jump right to application. You cannot properly apply what you have not properly studied. Then people wonder why they are not getting anything out of their Bible study.

Devotional commentaries usually do not give any better information than the reading/application approach. They tend not to be exegetically researched and miss God's point for the passage. The Holy Spirit therefore cannot use these devotionals to transform your mind because only a correct interpretation of the Scriptures can do that.

You may believe this will take a lot of time, and you will not get very far through the Scriptures. True, but you will learn much more following the observation, interpretation, and application format than by listening to sermons and lessons, or by doing the reading/application approach, or the devotional approach. Sermons and lessons have their place, but they cannot displace or replace personal study. Work hard at your study of God's Word. Do your best.

All Christians at one time or another get their interpretation or application of Scripture wrong. In the next chapter we will examine how to discover illogic in our own and other people's arguments.

## For Review and Discussion

- What surprised you most about this study of alcohol and wine?

- Why did it surprise you?

- Discuss your views about a Christian drinking alcohol.

- Do a topical study about gambling in the Bible.

## ENDNOTES

1. Voss, Johann Heinrich. "Quotable Quotes." Wrath of Grapes. 1996. <http://www.wrathofgrapes.com/winequot.html>.

2. Bellis, Mary. "Inventors: Louis Pasteur." About. <http://inventors.about.com/library/inventors/blpasteur.htm>.

3. Keener, Craig S. The IVP Bible Background Commentary: New Testament. Downers Grove, IL: InterVarsity, 1993. Oak Harbor: Logos, 1997.

4. Elwell, Walter A., ed. Baker Encyclopedia of the Bible, Volume 2. Grand Rapids, MI: Baker Book House, 1988, pp. 2145-2148.

5.  Bryson, Bill. <u>A Short History of Nearly Everything</u>. New York: Broadway Books, 2003. pp. 252-253.

6.  Pentecost, J. Dwight. <u>Your Adversary the Devil</u>. Grand Rapids, MI: Zondervan Publishing House, 1969, p. 59.

7.  Blevins, Janice R. and Justin R. Morris. "Health Benefits of Wine and Grape Juice." <u>University of Arkansas</u>. 1997, p. 2. <http://www.uark.edu/depts/ ifse/grapeprog/articles/ht7-3wg.pdf>.

8.  Perkins, Bill. <u>6 Rules Every Man Must Break</u>. Carol Stream, IL: Tyndale House Publishers, 2007, p.34

9.  Kent, Homer A. <u>The Pastoral Epistles</u>. Chicago: Moody Press, 1958, p.138.

He that cannot reason is a fool.

He that will not is a bigot.

He that dare not is a slave.

Andrew Carnegie

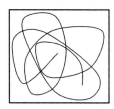

CHAPTER EIGHT

# Interpretation Impediments and Application Obstacles

When we hear sermons, read commentaries, or have discussions with others, emotions, authority figures, and illogical reasoning masquerading as logic can sway us. We need to understand illogic, or logical fallacies, and avoid being trapped by them.

## Fallacy Inefficacy

A fallacy is:

> An error in reasoning that either results from faulty logic, or from some distortion or distraction created by the language of the argument. Fallacies have three common forms.
>
> (1) Providing reasoning that requires erroneous or incorrect assumptions
>
> (2) Distracting us by making information seem relevant to the conclusion when it is not
>
> (3) Providing support for the conclusion that depends on the conclusion already being true.[1]

Fallacies, unless you examine them closely, are persuasive. Unfortunately, even though fallacy identification started with Aristotle in the fourth century B. C., fallacies are often a common component of Christian arguments and arguments against Christians and against Christianity. I know I have been guilty of fallacious arguments on innumerable occasions. I may even have committed some fallacies in this book. I am sure someone will find them and point them out to me, or use an inadvertent fallacy I have stated to make an argument to try to discredit everything I say (doing that is a fallacy, too—see straw man). Our goal cannot be to trick people into believing what we say (which is what fallacies do); our goal must be to present logical, well-reasoned arguments.

I will use familiar passages of Scripture and typical church conversations as my examples of fallacious thinking. The fallacies are listed in alphabetical order so you can access them quickly when you need them.

### Ad Hominen
The *ad hominen* (which is Latin for "against the person") fallacy occurs when you attack the person you are arguing with instead of debating the argument. The unstated point of the fallacy is that the verbal assault annuls the argument presented by your opponent. The attacker uses words like religious right, religious fanatic, right-winger, conservative, ultra-conservative, homophobe, racist, neo-Nazi, fascist, liberal, and left-winger. The attacker wrongly thinks name-calling undermines the other person's argument. Although the names the "attackee" is being called may be true, the names do not invalidate the argument. Either the argument is right or wrong regardless of who says it.

The *ad hominen* fallacy fails to address the reasoning and evidence presented by the opponent's argument. Here are some examples.

I have heard Christians say, "Do not listen to Dr. James Dobson, he's a behaviorist." This attack may identify one of Dr. Dobson's biases, but it does not undermine his reasoning. What Dr. Dobson says about raising a child should be judged by its truthfulness, not by Dr. Dobson's psychological belief system. Either what he says is right or it is wrong regardless of his personal biases.

Some Christians say, "I will not listen to Dr. Dobson because he fellowships with Methodist preachers." This *ad hominen* attack is called "guilt by association" and is totally irrelevant to what Dr. Dobson says. It is an evil argument.

Have you heard this one? "Do not believe Betty. She has been caught lying several times." Who has not lied—and been caught? (If you just said you do not lie, you just lied again.) If that were the criteria, we would never believe anyone, especially ourselves. Granted, a person with a history of lying may give you pause to consider more thoroughly what he or she said, but it does not mean the person always lies.

Betty's argument must be judged by its logic, reasoning, and supporting evidence, not by past behavior. If Betty ran up to you and said your daughter was drowning in the pool in the backyard, a critical thinker would run to the pool to investigate, not continue on with the yard work because Betty has lied in the past. Every argument Betty gives must be investigated on its own merits.

"How can you listen to what he says about how a church should operate? He is divorced." Does sin in one area of our life disqualify us from speaking about Christian belief and practice? If it did, no one could speak about anything.

It is appallingly sad to see how quickly Christians are willing to write someone off who has committed sin in the past. They need to look more closely in the mirror. We are sinners saved by grace, but we are sinners (James 4:8; 5:19-20). We need to forgive, and we all need to be forgiven and given another chance. We need to forgive ourselves as well. We can call ourselves some nasty names because of the sin we have done in the past. If we confessed our sin, God has forgiven us. We need to accept His forgiveness regardless of what we have done and stop berating each other and ourselves. Let's stop shooting our wounded. The only one who benefits from that is Satan.

God gives second chances. After Jonah sinned and fled to Tarshish, God gave him a second chance to go to Nineveh. A year after King David committed adultery with Bathsheba and murdered her husband Uriah, David repented. God forgave David and allowed him not only to be king of Israel, but also to continue writing Scripture. After Peter denied Jesus three times, the Lord specifically commissioned him to "Feed my sheep." In fact, every major character in the Bible sinned and God gave them more work to do for Him. God gives people second chances. Can we, His children, do any less?   Do not hold people's past peccadilloes, blatant blunders, and serious sins against them in an *ad hominen* attack.  Give every sinner a chance to make an argument and contribute to the discussion; that way you can participate, too.  "He did this; she did that."  That kind of talk is demonic—it is Satan who is the accuser of the brethren (Revelation 12:9-10), and when we do *ad hominen* attacks, we are the Devil's mouthpieces.

Another type of *ad hominen* attack is called the "*circumstantial ad hominen.*"  Assume Father Perkins, a Roman Catholic priest, has presented an argument against abortion.  Allen replies by saying, "He's a Catholic priest.  The Catholic Church is officially opposed to abortion.  What would you expect him to say?!"  Allen claims that Father Perkins' "reasons" for opposing abortion are mere rationalizations.  Since there was no examination of the argument presented, it is fallacious.

Or, assume that Jen, who for many years had argued against euthanasia, presents an argument favoring euthanasia in very specific circumstances.  Doug replies to the argument by saying, "Ten years ago Jen published a paper called 'Euthanasia? Never!' in which she provided very strong arguments against euthanasia.  Now she's arguing that euthanasia is okay. Since she's defended inconsistent positions, we cannot believe anything she says."  Again, Doug attacks the person rather than the argument presented, so it is an instance of the fallacy of personal attack.[2]

Can you imagine living in a world where you can never grow or change your mind, and what you said in the past will always be held against you? In politics, we call these people "flip-floppers," hoping to destroy their chances of winning elections. People change; even politicians do so without just trying to win an election.

One other form of an *ad hominen* argument is not harmful, but it is not logical either. "Do you need a plumber? Don't call Andy Weaver. He's not a Christian." What you need is a plumber, not a Christian. Just because Andy is not a Christian does not make him a bad plumber or mean I will not get good service. Either Andy is a good plumber, or he is not. It is a stupid stewardship of my money to pay a poor plumber. We should not reverse this and hire Bill because he's a Christian. I have fallen for this fallacious argument enough to know I should be using other criteria to make my decision.

## Appeal to Ignorance

The appeal to ignorance occurs when you either believe a statement is true because you have no evidence it is false, or you believe a statement is false because you can find no evidence it is true. This fallacy simply is shifting the burden of evidence to the other person. Here are examples I have heard. "Just because no one in the Bible used the phrase, 'the Lord led me,' doesn't prove people living in the New Testament era never used the phrase." However, our only source for authoritative instruction about how to live the Christian life is the Word of God. We not follow doctrines not found in the Scriptures. If my strongest argument for a doctrine is, "Just because no one in the Bible used the phrase, 'the Lord led me,' doesn't prove people living in the New Testament era never used the phrase," I better seriously question the way I make biblical decisions. I have heard people argue that the Bible is not against homosexuality because Jesus never condemned it.[3]  He also never condemned child molestation, but that does not mean He endorses it.  The Old Testament Law says (Leviticus 20:13), "If a man lies with a man as one lies with a woman, both of them have done what is detestable. They must be put to death; their blood will be on their own heads." Jesus said in Matthew 5:17-19, "Do not think that I have come to abolish the Law or the Prophets; I have not come to abolish them but to fulfill them. I tell you the truth, until heaven and earth disappear, not the smallest letter, not the least stroke of a pen, will by any means disappear from the Law until everything is accomplished. Anyone who breaks one of the least of these commandments and teaches others to do the same will be called least in the kingdom of heaven, but whoever practices and teaches these commands will be called great in the kingdom of heaven." Jesus said you may not break the Law of God, which includes homosexuality.  Jesus said He did not abolish the Law, which includes homosexuality.  Jesus believed homosexuality was a sin because Jesus believed the Law (If "A," then "B").

My friend Greg Hake created this syllogism:  If a man having sex with another man is detestable to God, and since Jesus is God who cannot go against His own Law (if A), Jesus teaches men not to have sex with another man (then B).  To endorse homosexuality as legitimate for today because Jesus did not specifically teach against it is to misunderstand the Person of Christ and the permanence and authority of the Word of God. This statement about homosexuality is not only the Appeal to Ignorance fallacy, but it is also heresy to say Christ does not agree with the Law of God, His own Law.

Former Democrat presidential John F. Kerry condemned Republicans for inserting a religious "orthodoxy of view" into politics. To support his claim he used an appeal to ignorance: "I went back and reread the whole New Testament the other day. Nowhere in the three-year ministry of Jesus Christ did I find a suggestion at all, ever, anywhere, in any way whatsoever, that you ought to take the money from the poor, the opportunities from the poor and give them to the rich people."[4] The fact that Jesus did not make this statement neither supports nor opposes the position. Jesus also did not say to take money from the rich and give it to the poor. The Law, which Jesus came to fulfill says, "Do not pervert justice; do not show partiality to the poor or favoritism to the great, but judge your neighbor fairly" (Leviticus 19:15). God says it is a perversion of justice to favor the poor.

Here's an appeal to ignorance statement from a mental giant (just ask them; they will tell you), "You cannot prove to me there is a God, so there is no God." Has the objector thoroughly investigated all of the evidence for the existence of God? This is not a fallacious argument only if the person investigated all of the evidence and if God does not exist. Otherwise, it is a fallacy. God's verdict on this form of the appeal to ignorance fallacy—fool! (You thought me calling you ignorant was bad!) Ask them to draw a circle and put in their dot representing their knowledge (see chapter 2).

Could God's existence be found in the white space?  Do they know everything?

## Appeal to Tradition

The appeal to tradition fallacy is committed when the premise for an argument is true because it has been around for a long time.  This fallacy rears its ugly head when someone proposes change—from the time a church service starts to going to two worship services.  It has several forms.  "The King James Version was good enough for St. Paul; it is good enough for me" (I am not making up this one, or any of them for that matter).  "We've always done it that way."  "If it ain't broke, do not fix it (my motto is 'If it ain't broke, break it')."  "The late Pastor Popper would never have done it that way."  "The late Pastor Popper did it this way" (though dead, he still speaketh).  "We tried it before; it will never work."  However, just because something has been believed for a long time or it did not work before is no reason to believe what you are believing or do what you are doing.  The context of the decisions has changed.  Perhaps the options and their possibility of success have changed as well.  People have believed for years Columbus was one of the few men of his day who believed the Earth was round.  Should we continue to teach that lie simply because people have believed it for a long time?  A lie, an untruth, can live indefinitely.  We need to kill and bury them.

## *Argumentum Ad Populum* or Appeal to the People

The fallacy of appealing to the people occurs when you say you believe something because it is what most Christians believe.  That most Christians believe something may give weight to an argument, but as we saw in chapter two with the story of the Magi, most Christians believing something does not guarantee its validity. Conversely, to propose an argument is false simply because it is not what most Christians believe is another form of this fallacy. "Agreement with popular opinion is not necessarily a reliable sign of truth, and deviation from popular opinion is not necessarily a reliable sign of error."[5]

For example, a Christian may say, "You should believe God has chosen someone specifically for you to marry because most Christians believe that to be true." However, it does not matter primarily what most Christians think; what matters is what the Bible says.

Another form of this fallacy is called the appeal to numbers. This fallacy has swept through the American church. "God must be being blessing our church. Look how many people go here." The first part of the statement may be true, but the second part is fallacious. You need to determine why the people are coming. Division 1 College football games draw large crowds, but God is not blessing them. They attract crowds because they put on a good show and are not boring. Some churches attract a crowd for the same reason. Besides, God's blessing can be on small churches, too. The Bible nowhere says the size of the congregation is a measuring device for the blessing of God—to do so is to commit the appeal to numbers fallacy.

A similar argument relates to how much money is collected at the church each week. A lot of money is not a sign of the blessing of God. The Bible nowhere promises that as a measuring instrument of a church's success.

## *Argumentum Ad Consequentiam*
## or Appeal to Consequence

The appeal to consequence fallacy occurs when you say something is false because you do not want to believe it. "You can let your pocketbook sit on the chair while you go to the bathroom. No one in this church will steal it." This is the false belief no sinners exist in this church. If I had a pocketbook, which I do not, I would rather hear, "You can let your pocketbook sit on the chair while you go to the bathroom. I will guard it for you." I have also heard students say, "I don't lock my dorm room door. This is a Christian college." Crime rates may be lower on Christian college campuses than other college campuses, but crimes are committed there. The fallacy states living at a Christian college guarantees nothing bad will happen. The odds may be low something will happen, but there are no guarantees. Christians sin and non-Christians may gain access to the property.

'"That cannot be Senator Smith in the videotape going into her apartment. If it were, he'd be a liar about not knowing her. He's not the kind of man who would lie. He's a member of my congregation.' Smith may or may not be the person in that videotape, but this kind of arguing should not convince us that it is someone else in the videotape"[6].

Appeal to consequence is the fallacy of choice for many evolutionists. They want creationism to be false, not because they can give reams of evidence to support evolution, but because if creation is true, they worry they would have to abandon their life's work and would have to concede the existence of God. The latter would also make them accountable to God, and for many evolutionists, the reason to be one is to find evidence to support their materialistic atheism. For example, evolutionist E. M. S. Watson said, "Evolution (is) a theory universally accepted not because it can be proved by logically coherent evidence to be true, but because the only alternative, special creation, is clearly incredible."[7]

John Maynard Smith, dean of British neo-Darwinists said in 1994:

> We take the side of science *in spite of* the patent absurdity of some of its constructs, *in spite of* its failure to fulfill many of its extravagant promises of health and life, *in spite of* the tolerance of the scientific community for unsubstantiated just-so stories, because we have a prior commitment, a commitment to materialism. It is not that the methods and institutions of science somehow compel us to accept a material explanation of the phenomenal world, but, on the contrary, that we are forced by our a priori adherence to material causes to create an apparatus of investigation and a set of concepts that produce material explanations, no matter how counterintuitive, no matter how mystifying to the uninitiated. Moreover, that materialism is absolute, for we cannot allow a Divine Foot in the door.[8]

Here is an evolutionist who is honest about their agenda and presuppositions. I admire his candor.

## Bifurcation or False Dilemma

The bifurcation fallacy is committed when you tell others they only have two options to choose between, when more options are available.  Your dad may have said to you, "Either go to college or you will be worthless all of your life."  Granted, going to college may increase your chances of being successful in life, but it does not guarantee success.  Besides, many people succeed in life that never went to college.  A bifurcation fallacy previously alluded to stated, "Either you believe God created the universe in six, 24-hour days, or you believe in evolution." That is not true.  You simply believe God gradually created life forms over eons of time as the planet was ready for them.  Rarely are there only two options when you make a decision.

Some Christians subtly use bifurcation in evangelism. Telling stories about someone who was "almost persuaded' to believe the gospel, but decided to wait, got in his car, and died in a wreck with a truck, is a scare tactic to manufacture the work of the Holy Spirit and manipulate someone into the kingdom.  The false dilemma is, "Do you want to get saved now or go to hell."  Ask people if they want to believe in Christ, but do not manipulate them. Trust the Holy Spirit to do His work.  No one will die before believing in Christ for salvation who is part of God's elect. Salvation is a process, not an event.  It takes time for a person to consider the claims of the gospel.

A pastor friend told me about the first time he went door-to-door presenting the gospel.  He was teamed with an experienced "evangelist."  They knocked on a house door and a man answered. The evangelist asked if they could come into the home and talk about the gospel. The man politely said, "No, thank you." The evangelist yelled, "Well, go to hell if you want to!" and stormed off the porch. People who use bifurcation in evangelism seem more interested in scalps for their belt than souls for God's kingdom.

Despite his best sales pitch, a life-insurance salesman was unable to get a couple to sign up for a policy. "'I certainly do not want to frighten you into a decision,' he said, standing up to leave. 'Please sleep on it tonight, and if you wake up in the morning, let me know what you think.'"[9]

In 2002, a suburban Atlanta school board put stickers on a science textbook that read, "This textbook contains material on evolution. Evolution is a theory, not a fact, regarding the origin of living things. This material should be approached with an open mind, studied carefully, and critically considered." As usual, the ACLU sued. U.S. District Judge Clarence Cooper ruled the sticker was a violation of the supposed separation between church and state. He committed the bifurcation fallacy by declaring the stickers send "a message that the school board agrees with the beliefs of Christian fundamentalists and creationists. The school board has effectively improperly entangled itself with religion by appearing to take a position. Therefore, the sticker must be removed from all of the textbooks into which it has been placed."[10] The sticker said nothing about religion. The judge assumed the sticker had to be advocating Christian fundamentalism because, I conclude from his reasoning, no scientist would want critical thinking on the subject of origins and you either totally agree with

Darwin (which most scientists do not), or you believe in special creation by the God of the Bible.

Are these really the only two options that people posit? Of course not. However, the left in America cannot make that distinction. Paul Krugman, opining in the New York Times about President Bush's statements about evolution said, "Today's Republican Party—increasingly dominated by people who believe truth should be determined by revelation, not research—does not respect science, or scholarship in general."[11]  Most Christians love science and discovery; we just do not believe science and discovery always result in absolute truth or the belief in evolution.

## Equivocation

The fallacy of equivocation is committed when someone uses the same word in an argument, using two different meanings, implying the word means the same thing in both instances.  The word changes meaning in the argument or can be taken two different ways.

It was the pastor's first Sunday at church.  A woman in the congregation gave him a cherry pie.  He took it home, bit into it, and gagged on its awful taste.  He immediately grabbed the pie and threw it in the trash.  He thought, "What am I going to tell this woman?"  The next Sunday, the woman asked the pastor how he liked the pie.  He said, "A pie like that does not last long around our house." The equivocation in this story is the dual meaning of, "A pie like that does not last long," what the pastor actually meant, and how he hoped the woman would take the comment.

A typical anti-Christian equivocation is:

- Because humans are fallible, everything they do contains errors.
- Humans wrote the Bible.
- The Bible has errors.

The equivocation is the absence of the superintending work of the Holy Spirit on the writers of Scripture. True, humans make errors, but not humans controlled by God.

Another anti-Christian equivocation is:

- Jesus Christ is a man.
- God is not a man.
- Jesus Christ is not God.

The equivocation is found in the first premise use of the word "man." Jesus was more than a mere man—He was God in the flesh. Christ cannot be separated from His Deity. Whenever we speak of Christ, we do so acknowledging He is both God and man. The word "man" when referring to Jesus does not mean the same thing as it does for everyone else.

Another anti-Christian equivocation is:

- Christians say it is wrong to discriminate against them for being Christians.
- But I have seen Christians in a grocery store—they discriminate when they buy lettuce. They choose only fresh lettuce, not the brown lettuce.
- If Christians discriminate, how can it be wrong to discriminate against them?

The equivocation is the dual meaning of the word "discriminate." In the first premise, "discriminate" means to be prejudiced against someone. It means to treat the person poorly because of the group to which he or she belongs. "Discriminate" in this sense is unethical and immoral. In the second premise about lettuce, "discriminate" means to make a wise judgment, a choice. It carries no ethical or moral connotations.

Politicians use equivocation. For many years, the right has been calling liberal judges who legislate from the bench "judicial activists." Recently the left has started calling judges who try to make decisions based on what the Constitution says "judicial activists." Judicial activists unconstitutionally make law. However, the New York Times says judicial activism means to "invalidate laws passed by Congress." Invalidating unconstitutional laws passed by Congress is the legitimate purpose of the court system.

Ann Coulter said:

> If Congress passed a law prohibiting speech criticizing [President] Bush, or banning blacks from owning property, or giving foreigners the right to run for president—all those laws could be properly struck down by the Supreme Court. That's not 'judicial activism,' it is 'judicial.'

> Invalidating a law that prohibits killing unborn children on the preposterous grounds that the Constitution contains an extra-double-secret right to abortion no one had noticed for 200 years—

that's judicial activism.  When conservative judges strike down laws, it is because of what's in the Constitution.  When liberal judges strike down laws (or impose new laws, such as tax increases), it is because of what's in The New York Times.

The left's redefinition of judicial activism to mean something it is not allows liberals to claim they oppose judicial activism and to launch spirited denunciations of conservative judges as the real 'judicial activists.'  This is the Democrats' new approach to winning arguments: Change the definition of words in mid-argument without telling the guy you're arguing with.  Chairman Mao would approve. Thus, The New York Times prissily informed its readers: 'There is a misconception that so-called activist judges who 'legislate from the bench' are invariably liberal.  In fact, conservative judges can be even more eager to overrule decisions made by elected officials.'

That statement has as much intellectual content as saying: 'There is a misconception that so-called activist judges who 'legislate from the bench' are invariably liberal.  In fact, conservative judges can be even more eager to play tennis.'

The very act of redefining 'judicial activism' to mean invalidating any law passed by elected officials is precisely the sort of Alice-in-Wonderland nonsense we are talking about.  Liberal judges redefine the Constitution's silence on abortion to mean 'abortion is a precious constitutional right.' Liberal flacks in the media redefine judicial activism to mean 'striking down laws.'

The Times' definition isn't even coherent. If it were 'judicial activism' to strike down laws—any laws, ever—there would be no point to having a Supreme Court.[12]

Redefining a term is not making an argument; it is a smokescreen to fool whoever is not paying attention.

## Etymological

The etymological fallacy occurs when someone wrongly believes the meaning of a word can be determined by its origin. "The word for power in the Greek is dunamis. We get our word dynamite from it. The gospel is the dynamite power of God." Because we use a word derived from a Greek word does not give a basis to interpret the Greek word. Anyway, what does the statement mean: "The gospel is the dynamite power of God?" D. A. Carson confronted this anachronism. "Dynamite blows things up, tears things down . . . destroys things. The power of God concerning which Paul speaks . . . aim[s] for the wholeness and perfection implicit in the consummation of our salvation."[13] The point the teacher was trying to make about dynamite is how powerful God is, but dynamite is weak compared to the transformational power of God.

Although many commentators define words from their root meanings, root meanings more than not are meaningless. A word is defined by its context, not root origin. We would not determine much meaning from a housefly derived from "house" that "flies" or a pineapple is an "apple" from a "pine" tree.[14]

## Group Think

The group think fallacy takes two forms. First, the fallacy occurs when allegiance is assigned to a belief because the group I belong to believes it, and my group cannot be wrong. "My denomination or my church believes _____, so it must be right." The second form of the fallacy occurs when you have doubts about what your group believes or is planning to do, but you do not press discussion on the issue because you fear you will alienate yourself from the group. Those who offer opposing or differing points of view in churches can be quickly ostracized or marginalized.

## Hasty Generalization

The hasty generalization fallacy is committed when you jump to a generalized conclusion from insufficient data. "The first two people I ran into when I visited Community Church didn't say hello to me. I turned around and walked out. They're an unfriendly church." Two people do not make a church. Besides, how do you know they were not visitors, too?

"John MacArthur said it, so it must be true." It may be true, but I have heard John MacArthur admit he makes exegetical mistakes. We all do. We need to seek data from more than one person before we make a decision.

A popular form of hasty generalization is saying because something happened in the Bible, it should happen the same way today. The popular view concerning the existence of speaking in tongues today is based on this argument. You will often hear the argument supported by Hebrews 13:8, "Jesus Christ is the same yesterday and today and forever." However, in context, Hebrews 13:8 does not declare Jesus' programs do not change. A better translation of the verse is, "Jesus is the Christ, the same yesterday and today and forever." The writer's point is the Hebrews' leaders in the past taught Jesus is the Christ, the Messiah, He is the Christ now, and He will forever be the Christ—so do not change your message about Him. God's message does not change in the church era, but His methods change.

Description of an event in the Bible does not mean a prescription for something to occur today. 2 Samuel 17:23 says, "When Ahithophel saw that his advice had not been followed, he saddled his donkey and set out for his house in his hometown. He put his house in order and then hanged himself." Prescription would say, "If you give counsel and it is not followed, hang yourself." It makes as much sense as saying when you get saved, you will know it because a cloven tongue of fire will rest on your head and you will speak in tongues (Acts 2:4-5). Interestingly, many Christians push for speaking in tongues as normal activity but not the tongues of fire. It seems inconsistent to me, but then fallacies tend to be inconsistent.

## No True Scotsman
This fallacy occurs as a way to rescue yourself from a hasty generalization. A hasty generalization is,
"All Christians tell the truth," says Pete.

"Stein is a Christian, and he committed perjury."
"Well, then Stein is not a true Christian."

Stein is "no true Scotsman." Not sinning is not the prerequisite for being a true Christian. Sinning is inconsistent with what we say we believe, but we are all inconsistent. By this logic, no one could be a true Christian.

### Non Sequitur
A *non sequitur* (meaning "does not follow") occurs when the conclusion is supported by weak or irrelevant data. "If we go to two church services, we won't know everyone. If we don't know everyone, that will destroy our fellowship. If you love this church, vote against going to two church services." Chances are, few people can stand up in any congregation and tell the names of everyone present and give a biography about them, yet the fellowship is not destroyed now. Why would two services make it any worse? I know of no church that has two church services whose fellowship is destroyed. You only have time to get to know a certain number of people regardless of how many church services are available for you to attend. The premises for this inductive argument are irrelevant.

Dr. Duane Litfin, my homiletics professor at Moody, assailed a *non sequitur* application of Mark 4:36-39, "Leaving the crowd behind, they took him along, just as he was, in the boat. There were also other boats with him. A furious squall came up, and the waves broke over the boat, so that it was nearly swamped. Jesus was in the stern, sleeping on a cushion. The disciples woke him and said to him, 'Teacher, do not you care if we drown?' He got up, rebuked the wind and said to the waves, 'Quiet! Be still!' Then the wind died down and it was completely calm." Many sermons have been preached on this passage.

Most teachers interpret correctly that Jesus has authority over His creation. Jesus speaks and the howling wind immediately ceases to blow and the churning sea instantly become smooth as glass. However, in the application of this passage, Litfin said the teachers go askew when they say, "Jesus calms the storms of our lives." Does He? Do the storms of life always calm? Does the Lord protect Christians from financial crisis or debilitating injuries? Do situations in life always get better? Do Christians not get sick and die? Do our children not get sick and die? The application is a *non sequitur*. Nothing in the passage supports this falsehood. The passage deals with the power of God over creation, not with God soothing our lives from problems. Calming our storms does not follow from God calming the storm at sea.

### Post Hoc, Ergo Propter Hoc
The Latin phrase means, "after this, therefore because of this." It means A caused B. A happened first, so it caused B to occur. However, if A did not cause B, the *post hoc* fallacy has been committed. For example, why do Christians wear black to funerals? Is it really a symbol of mourning? Not originally, but that is how we rationalized wearing it. In Europe, Christians used to believe the spirit of the deceased followed you home from the cemetery. If you wore black (some painted themselves black), the spirit could not see you and would not follow you home (hence the continued tradition of some who go home by

a different route than they went to the cemetery). It must work because the spirits do not show up at the house—hence *post hoc* . Wear bright colors to a funeral for a Christian. Do not mourn that person's death; celebrate her life and the fact that while she is absent from her body, she is present with the Lord. Her spirit will not follow you home.

Why do Christians put tombstones on graves and not just markers? Why does a tombstone getting kicked over make front-page news? In Europe, Christians believed the tombstone held the departed person's spirit in the ground, and the heavier the tombstone, the better. To kick over a tombstone meant to let the spirit get out of the grave and haunt people. Believe Abraham who said in Luke 16:19-31 the dead do not come back as spirits. Be a good steward of your money and just buy a marker so future generations can visit the site.

Why do we say "God bless you" when someone sneezes? German Christians believed when a person sneezed, evil spirits were expelled from the body. Saying "*gesundheit,*" (God bless you) kept the demons from re-entering the body. Do you believe that?

Have you ever wondered why people in some cultures do rain dances? Because it seems to work—if you dance long enough, it will rain. Superstitions are *post hoc* arguments, whether not walking under a ladder to prevent bad luck or not stepping on a crack so you do not break your mother's back.

Why do brides wear "something old, something new, something borrowed, something blue?"     Simple, they love emulating prostitutes.  Would you like more information?  Temple prostitutes at the oracle of Delphi in ancient Greece would wear these combinations at the initiation rite to become a "minister" at the temple. How does a bride wearing these items help insure a successful marriage?  Hence, this is a *post hoc*  fallacy.

## Quoting out of Context

This fallacy is committed when you quote someone, but what you say they said is not what they meant.  Preachers using the alcohol passages to teach abstinence I discussed in the last chapter is an example.  Let's look at how Christians take God out of context.  For fun, get out some paper and a pen and write what most Christians teach the following passages mean.

1. Genesis 3:6.  "When the woman saw that the tree was good for food, and that it was a delight to the eyes, and that the tree was desirable to make one wise, she took from its fruit and ate; and she gave also to her husband with her, and he ate."

When Eve was talking to the serpent, what was Adam doing?

2.  Genesis 3:16.  "To the woman He said, 'I will greatly multiply your pain in childbirth, in pain you will bring forth children; yet your desire will be for your husband, and he will rule over you.'"

3. Genesis 31:49. "May the LORD watch between you and me when we are absent one from the other." (You often see this verse on a locket Christian teens that are dating wear, often symbolizing a broken heart that each wears half.)

4. Romans 8:14. "For all who are being led by the Spirit of God, these are sons of God."

5. Colossians 3:15. "Let the peace of Christ rule in your hearts, to which indeed you were called in one body; and be thankful."

6. Romans 8:28. "And we know that God causes all things to work together for good to those who love God, to those who are called according to His purpose."

7. Matthew 18:20. "For where two or three have gathered together in My Name, I am there in their midst."

8. 1 Corinthians 2:9. "Things which eye has not seen and ear has not heard, And which have not entered the heart of man, All that God has prepared for those who love Him."

9. Philippians 4:19. "And my God will supply all your needs according to His riches in glory in Christ Jesus."

10. 1 John 4:4. "You are from God, little children, and have overcome them; because greater is He who is in you than he who is in the world."

Now let's look at these verses in context.

1.  Genesis 3:6.  When eve was talking to the serpent, what was Adam doing? "Eating Yourself Out of House and Home," or "On the Eve of Destruction."  The traditional interpretation says Adam was away picking fruit or cultivating the garden while the Serpent talked to Eve.  I and other teachers I have heard excoriated Eve for not running to get Adam to verify what the Lord had really said.  We mildly praised Adam for loving Eve enough to join in her death after hearing the story by eating the fruit, too, like he is a quasi-romantic hero.  However, the person we should have excoriated is Adam.  Look closely at the verse—she gave also to her husband with her.

The word "with" means with.  Adam was standing right next to Eve while this discussion took place, and the coward said or did nothing, plunging the human race into sin.  Adam should have argued with the Serpent or stopped Eve from picking the fruit, but he said or did nothing.  He willfully, passively, quietly participated in Eve's sin.  Adam heard the lies Satan told and watched his wife pick the fruit and eat it, yet he neither said nor did anything to stop her or to confront Satan.  When God confronted Adam about his sin, Adam foolishly blamed Eve and God—"the woman You gave me" (verse 12), while Eve blamed the Serpent.  God controlled the Serpent's testing of Eve so Adam was with her when it happened, eliminating any possible excuse for what happened.  I admitted I was wrong and re-taught this passage.

Notice also the text does not use the word apple, and "forbidden fruit" has nothing to do with sex, two more erroneous beliefs people have that are not in the context.[15]  The problem was not the apple; it was the pair.

2. Genesis 3:16. The common interpretation of this verse is that husbands will make their wives subservient, keeping them pregnant and barefoot. However, the same phrase interpreted here as, "*yet your desire will be for your husband, and he will rule over you*" occurs in the Hebrew of Genesis 4:6-7. "Then the LORD said to Cain, "Why are you angry? Why is your face downcast? If you do what is right, will you not be accepted? But if you do not do what is right, sin is crouching at your door; *it desires to have you, but you must master it*." So, God did not curse women by making them subservient to men. God created men and women as equals, and then cursed women with the desire to rule over their husbands *(your desire will be to rule over your husband)*, but women must master that desire *(but you must master it)*. Many New Testament commands to women concern what it means to act as an equal partner in marriage, not the superior one.

3. Genesis 31:49. These lockets are given by lovers to remind each other of their commitment to each other and to remind them of how much the other person loves them. However, the context of the verse will not allow this application. When I see Christian teens wearing this I say, "Oh, I'm sorry. You can't trust each other, I see." Genesis 31:43-53 says:

> Laban answered Jacob, "The women are my daughters, the children are my children, and the flocks are my flocks. All you see is mine. Yet what can I do today about these daughters of mine, or about the children they have borne? Come now,

let's make a covenant, you and I, and let it serve as a witness between us."

So Jacob took a stone and set it up as a pillar. He said to his relatives, "Gather some stones." So they took stones and piled them in a heap, and they ate there by the heap. Laban called it Jegar Sahadutha, and Jacob called it Galeed.

Laban said, "This heap is a witness between you and me today." That is why it was called Galeed. It was also called Mizpah, because he said, "May the LORD keep watch between you and me when we are away from each other. If you mistreat my daughters or if you take any wives besides my daughters, even though no one is with us, remember that God is a witness between you and me."

Laban also said to Jacob, "Here is this heap, and here is this pillar I have set up between you and me. This heap is a witness, and this pillar is a witness, that I will not go past this heap to your side to harm you and that you will not go past this heap and pillar to my side to harm me. May the God of Abraham and the God of Nahor, the God of their father, judge between us."

Jacob and Laban told each other they could trust each other only as far as they could see each other. "Since I usually can't see you, and therefore I can't trust you, I am asking God to watch you and to watch my back to keep you from doing harm to me." What a wonderful sentiment for Christian lovers.

4. Romans 8:14. This verse is often used to say God will tell you what to do when you make decisions about whom to marry, which house or car to buy, which job to take, ad infinitum. The context does not bear this out. Romans 8:2, 5, 7-9, and 13 says:

> Because through Christ Jesus the law of the Spirit of life set me free from the law of sin and death. Those who live according to the sinful nature have their minds set on what that nature desires; but those who live in accordance with the Spirit have their minds set on what the Spirit desires. The sinful mind is hostile to God. It does not submit to God's law, nor can it do so. Those controlled by the sinful nature cannot please God.
>
> You, however, are controlled not by the sinful nature but by the Spirit, if the Spirit of God lives in you. And if anyone does not have the Spirit of Christ, he does not belong to Christ. For if you live according to the sinful nature, you will die; but if by the Spirit you put to death the misdeeds of the body, you will live, for all who are being led by the Spirit of God, these are sons of God.

God is drawing a contrast in this pericope between being controlled by our old sinful nature to sin and being controlled by the Holy Spirit not to sin. There is nothing in these verses talking about general life decisions. Those who are led by the Holy Spirit are those who obey the Word of God and do not sin. We are either being controlled by our sinful nature or by the Holy Spirit. The context does not allow for general decision-making.

5. Colossians 3:15. This verse is often used in conjunction with Romans 8:14 to help you determine if you made the right decision about whom to marry, ad infinitum. If you made a right decision, you will feel peaceful about it. Unfortunately, you guessed it, the context will not allow this misinterpretation. Colossians 3:8-15 says:

> But now you must rid yourselves of all such things as these: anger, rage, malice, slander, and filthy language from your lips. Do not lie to each other, since you have taken off your old self with its practices and have put on the new self, which is being renewed in knowledge in the image of its Creator. Here there is no Greek or Jew, circumcised or uncircumcised, barbarian, Scythian, slave or free, but Christ is all, and is in all.

> Therefore, as God's chosen people, holy and dearly loved, clothe yourselves with compassion, kindness, humility, gentleness and patience. Bear with each other and forgive whatever grievances you may have against one another. Forgive as the Lord forgave you. And over all these virtues put on love, which binds them all together in perfect unity.

> Let the peace of Christ rule in your hearts, since as members of one body you were called to peace. And be thankful.

The Christians in Colossae were fighting with each other—there was anger, rage, malice, slander, and filthy language directed at each other. They refused to forgive each other. They were divided due to a lack of love. Paul calls for an end to the war they declared on each other and to let the peace of Christ reign in their hearts, and ultimately in their Church.[16]  So, this peace is not an inner feeling of well-being. It is the absence of war and fighting.

6. Romans 8:28. The popular interpretation of this verse is that no matter how bad things are in your life, God has an ultimate purpose to make it all work out for you. However, the context refutes that argument.  Romans 8:28-30 says, "And we know that in all things God works for the good of those who love him, who have been called according to his purpose. For those God foreknew He also predestined to be conformed to the likeness of his Son, that He might be the firstborn among many brothers. And those He predestined, He also called; those He called, He also justified; those He justified, He also glorified."

Paul explains "the good" in verses 29-30. Note verse 29 begins with the word "for," indicating an explanation of verse 28 will follow. The "good" is God worked out all the events of our pre-salvation life to bring us to the place where we would accept Christ as our Savior. Once we are saved, the "good" is that God will mature us in our faith and ultimately take us to Heaven. To say Romans 8:28 means, "No matter how bad things are in your life, God has an ultimate purpose to make it all work out of for you," trivializes the verse. It causes us not to think critically about what good God has done in saving us, even if situations do not work out to our liking, increasing our faith. We need to reflect on the circumstances God ran us through to lead us to salvation, recognizing He had to potentially, in effect, run through millions of scenarios to see what would cause us to say "Yes" to His offer of salvation—the ultimate good.

7. Matthew 18:20. I often hear this prayed at the beginning of prayer meeting. After the person prayed, I ask, "Uh oh, who's in trouble?'

Sometimes this verse is used to justify the meeting about to happen outside of a church context makes the place of the meeting a church. "You do not need structure, and elders, and pastors to be a church. For where two or three have gathered together in Jesus' Name, He is here in our midst. We are a Church." Others see this verse as a comfort since Christ is present.

Both of these interpretations violate God's context. Matthew 18:15-20 says:

> If your brother sins against you, go and show him his fault, just between the two of you. If he listens to you, you have won your brother over. But if he will not listen, take one or two others along, so that 'every matter may be established by the testimony of two or three witnesses.' If he refuses to listen to them, tell it to the church; and if he refuses to listen even to the church, treat him as you would a pagan or a tax collector.

"I tell you the truth, whatever you bind on Earth will be bound in heaven, and whatever you loose on Earth will be loosed in heaven.

"Again, I tell you that if two of you on Earth agree about anything you ask for, it will be done for you by my Father in heaven. For where two or three come together in my Name, there am I with them."

Jesus promises to be part of church discipline when it happens according to His instruction. The "anything you ask for" refers to excommunicating a sinning, non-repentant brother from the Church. Jesus will support that decision and will be with us as we make the decision and enforce it. Hence, "Uh oh, who's in trouble?'

8. 1 Corinthians 2:9. I have heard some flowery sermons on this text talking about how wonderful Heaven will be and about all the things we will learn when we get there. True, Heaven will be wonderful, but that is not what God was talking about here. Verse 10 gives a different context. "But God has revealed it to us by his Spirit." The point of this passage is—we know now what God wants us to know. We are to rejoice in what we know, not wish for more knowledge when we get to Heaven. To talk about Heaven is to miss the context and the wonders of what God has revealed to us here on Earth. Verse 9 talks about the wonders that will occur when we accept Christ as our Savior, not about the wonders we will see when we get to Heaven. When we were saved, God revealed these wonders to us.

9. Philippians 4:19. This verse is generally taught to mean God will meet every Christian's financial need. I wonder how well that interpretation of this verse works for Christians in Haiti? The context is not about an individual having needs met but about a church having its needs met. Verses 15-19 say:

> Moreover, as you Philippians know, in the early days of your acquaintance with the gospel, when I set out from Macedonia, not one church shared with me in the matter of giving and receiving, except you only; for even when I was in Thessalonica, you sent me aid again and again when I was in need. Not that I am looking for a gift, but I am looking for what may be credited to your account. I have received full payment and even more; I am amply supplied, now that I have received from Epaphroditus the gifts you sent. They are a fragrant offering, an acceptable sacrifice, pleasing to God. And my God will meet all your needs according to his glorious riches in Christ Jesus.

The point is quite simple in context. Since the Philippian Church met Paul's financial needs, God would repay them by meeting the financial needs of the Church. Churches that generously support staff, ministries, missionaries, and missions can expect God to meet their financial needs. This verse has nothing to do with individual Christians.

10. 1 John 4:4. Most commentators who commit the exegetical fallacy of this verse are close to getting it right, but are not quite on target. The common interpretation of

this verse is the Holy Spirit in us is greater than Satan who is in the world. That is of course a true statement, but that is not what John is talking about. 1 John 4:1-6 says:

> Dear friends, do not believe every spirit, but test the spirits to see whether they are from God, because many false prophets have gone out into the world. This is how you can recognize the Spirit of God: Every spirit that acknowledges that Jesus Christ has come in the flesh is from God, but every spirit that does not acknowledge Jesus is not from God. This is the spirit of the antichrist, which you have heard is coming and even now is already in the world.
>
> You, dear children, are from God and have overcome them, because the one who is in you is greater than the one who is in the world. They are from the world and therefore speak from the viewpoint of the world, and the world listens to them. We are from God, and whoever knows God listens to us; but whoever is not from God does not listen to us. This is how we recognize the Spirit of truth and the spirit of falsehood.

The ones who are in the world are the false-teaching antichrists. The Holy Spirit is in us to help us determine whether someone in the world is a false teacher. Granted, Satan empowers false teachers, but he is not the subject of these verses in context—false teachers are the subject. The point is that the truth in you is greater than the lie in the world.

## Red Herring

Escaped convicts used a red herring, a foul-smelling fish, to elude capture. The convicts would rub the fish across their trail to throw the bloodhounds off track that were stalking them. The red herring fallacy is committed when an arguer uses a similar tactic—switching the subject. An irrelevant issue is inserted into the conversation to end discussion about what was being discussed. Politicians are masters of the red herring. Instead of answering the question they were asked, they answer the question they wish they had been asked. "Topic A is being discussed; Topic B is introduced as though it is relevant to Topic A, but it is not: Topic A is abandoned."[17]

Homosexual marriage is a major topic of discussion in America as I write this chapter. President Bush, some Christian leaders, and some members of Congress are suggesting a Constitutional amendment to define marriage as solely the union between a woman and a man. This amendment is being considered because these leaders do not want judicial activists discovering homosexual marriage as a Constitutional right. Of course, pro-homosexual marriage-rights activists are mounting their argument. Elizabeth Birch, who was at the time of the Massachusetts Supreme Judicial Court ruling (February 2004) that declared it unconstitutional not to allow homosexuals and lesbians to marry said, "If not for courts, African-Americans would not have had the right to vote, women would not have the right to vote. The purpose of a constitution is to protect a minority group from the wrath of the majority."[18]

Birch raised several red herrings in this statement. The right to vote has nothing to do with marriage. Besides, the right to vote for everyone is specifically guaranteed in the Constitution, while homosexual marriage is not guaranteed. To make certain African-Americans and women had the right to vote, amendments were added to the Constitution. The courts did not ultimately decide these issues; the people of the United States decided them. Amendment XV, ratified February 3, 1870 says, "The right of citizens of the United States to vote shall not be denied or abridged by the United States or by any State on account of race, color, or previous condition of servitude."[19] Amendment XIX, ratified August 18, 1920 says, "The right of citizens of the United States to vote shall not be denied or abridged by the United States or by any State on account of sex."[20]

The purpose of the Constitution has never been "to protect a minority group from the wrath of the majority." The purpose of the Constitution is stated in its Preamble, "We the People of the United States, in order to form a more perfect Union, establish justice, insure domestic tranquility, provide for the common defense, promote the general welfare, and secure the Blessings of Liberty to ourselves and our posterity, do ordain and establish this Constitution for the United States of America."[21] This says nothing about minority rights being protected as the purpose of the Constitution. The Framers seem more worried about the rights of the majority than the minority.

The purpose of the U.S. Constitution and its twenty-seven amendments is to delineate the separation of powers between the three branches of government and to set limits on those powers. In response to Ms. Birch, Rich Lowry said, "Most of them (the amendments) explain things the government may not do, and this proposed 28th Amendment would do the same thing: it would make clear that the government shall not change the traditional definition of marriage as being between a man and a woman."[22]

So, how are Elizabeth Birch's historically inaccurate statements red herrings? Because Lowry and I spent a great deal of time refuting her argument about voting and the purpose of the Constitution—she diverted us from the issue of homosexual marriage. Her premises had nothing to do with the argument at hand. She diverted attention away from the discussion of homosexual marriage. God already answered that question in Matthew 19:4-5. "'Have not you read,' He replied, 'that at the beginning the Creator 'made them male and female,' and said, 'For this reason a man will leave his father and mother and be united to his wife, and the two will become one flesh.'"

Red herring arguments are most significant for Christians when they are raised while sharing the gospel. What you must determine is whether or not the person raising an objection to the gospel like, "If God is loving, how can He send a person to Hell?", has a legitimate hurdle to faith or whether the person is trying to change the subject from the gospel and just quarrel with you. If it is a legitimate objection impeding belief, answer it, obeying 1 Peter 3:15, "Always be prepared to give an answer to everyone who asks you to give the reason for the hope that you have.

But do this with gentleness and respect." If the person is throwing a red herring at you, do not quarrel with her or him. Instead, obey Matthew 7:6, "Do not give dogs what is sacred; do not throw your pearls to pigs. If you do, they may trample them under their feet, and then turn and tear you to pieces." Dogs and pigs fling red herrings; do not stoop to their level and give them an opportunity to malign Christ and the gospel. An appropriate response to a red herring, said respectfully is, "I see you don't want to discuss this, and that's fine."

## Slippery Slope

The slippery slope fallacy occurs when you say one decision will lead to a consequence, which will lead to another, which eventually leads to doom and destruction. The fallacy inherent in this is two-fold. First, you cannot predict with accuracy what will be the outcome of future events. Second, even if outcome two or three occurs, it does not mean that steps cannot be taken to avert the ultimate outcome of doom and destruction being prophesied. Those familiar with the Viet Nam war era remember the slippery slope "Domino Theory," which stated America had to keep South Viet Nam from turning communist, because if it did, Laos, Cambodia, and all Southeast Asia would turn communist. South Viet Nam fell to communism, but Southeast Asia did not fall slide down that slippery slope.

Some Christians use slippery slope arguments to keep change from occurring. Sadly, some get upset if people "not like us" start attending church. "Why, the next thing you know, we will not even recognize our church or be welcome here." Really? The comfortableness you now feel and the power you now wield may be diminished, but do the other things have to happen?

"If we allow the singles group to show a PG-rated movie, next they'll want to show PG-13 movies, then R-rated movies, then X-rated movies. The next thing you know, the singles will be having orgies in the sanctuary. So, I vote they can't show a PG-rated movie." Does showing a PG-rated movie mean there will eventually be orgies in the sanctuary? Nothing could be done to prevent that?

"If we allow our teens to attend a contemporary Christian concert, next they will want to go to a Kid Rock concert, then they will start doing drugs. So no, I vote they cannot attend a contemporary Christian concert." Does allowing the teens to attend the contemporary Christian concert mean they will end up on drugs? Nothing could be done to prevent that?

The argument against Matthew 16:18 that Peter cannot be the rock upon which Christ builds the church is a slippery slope argument. "If we say the ordinary meaning of this text that Christ built the church on Peter, then it will give legitimacy to the Roman Catholic Church doctrine saying Peter is the first Pope. If that happens, Protestant Christianity will be undermined and Protestants may start honoring the Pope. To avoid all of that, we will misinterpret the passage." Do we have to misinterpret Scripture to keep Protestants from embracing the Pope or giving Roman Catholics ammunition for their position?

## Straw Man

The straw man fallacy is committed by ascribing an easily refuted position to your opponent, one the opponent did not say and would not support, and then attack the easily refuted position believing you have defeated the opponent's actual position. The straw man is constructed because it is easier to knock down than the opponent's actual argument. If the misrepresentation is on purpose, then you are lying. When an author or speaker says someone said something, ask for documentation so you can check what the person actually said. Let the person speak for himself.

A classic straw man argument was crafted by Bill Moyers, formerly of CBS News and PBS, who spoke at Harvard University in December 2004 in response to receiving the Global Environmental Citizen Award. He said:

> As difficult as it is, however, for journalists to fashion a readable narrative for complex issues without depressing our readers and viewers, there is an even harder challenge—to pierce the ideology that governs official policy today. One of the biggest changes in politics in my lifetime is that the delusional is no longer marginal. It has come in from the fringe, to sit in the seat of power in the Oval Office and in Congress. For the first time in our history ideology and theology hold a monopoly of power in Washington. Theology asserts propositions that cannot be proven true; ideologues hold stoutly to a world view despite being contradicted by what is generally accepted as reality. When ideology and

theology couple, their offspring are not always bad but they are always blind. And there is the danger: voters and politicians alike, oblivious to the facts.

Remember James Watt, President Reagan's first Secretary of the Interior? My favorite online environmental journal, the ever engaging Grist, reminded us recently of how James Watt told the U.S. Congress that protecting natural resources was unimportant in light of the imminent return of Jesus Christ. In public testimony he said, "After the last tree is felled, Christ will come back." (NOTE: Moyers has admitted this never occurred and has apologized to Watt.)

Beltway elites snickered. The press corps did not know what he was talking about. But James Watt was serious. So were his compatriots out across the country. They are the people who believe the Bible is literally true – one third of the American electorate, if a recent Gallup poll is accurate. In this past election several million good and decent citizens went to the polls believing in the rapture index. That's right—the rapture index. Google it and you will find that the best-selling books in America today are the twelve volumes of the left-behind series written by the Christian fundamentalist and religious right warrior, Timothy LaHaye. These true believers subscribe to a fantastical theology concocted in the 19th century by a couple of immigrant preachers who took disparate passages from the Bible and wove them into a narrative that has captivated the imagination of millions of Americans.

Moyers then describes the "bizarre" beliefs about the Tribulation and adds, "I am not making this up." He says according to Christians, "A war with Islam in the Middle East is not something to be feared, but welcomed—an essential conflagration on the road to redemption." He adds that, "Millions of Christian fundamentalists may believe that environmental destruction is not only to be disregarded but actually welcomed – even hastened – as a sign of the coming apocalypse." What is worse, "Nearly half the U.S. Congress before the recent election...are backed by the Religious Right." He asks, "Why care about the Earth when the droughts, floods, famine and pestilence brought by ecological collapse are signs of the apocalypse foretold in the Bible? Why care about global climate change when you and yours will be rescued in the rapture? And why care about converting from oil to solar when the same God who performed the miracle of the loaves and fishes can whip up a few billion barrels of light crude with a word?" He quips, "No wonder Karl Rove goes around the White House whistling that militant hymn, 'Onward Christian Soldiers.' He turned out millions of the foot soldiers on November 2, including many who have made the apocalypse a powerful driving force in modern American politics. I can see in the look on your faces just how hard it is for the journalist to report a story like this with any credibility."[23]

At Harvard University Bill Moyers said that Christians, particularly the Bush administration, want war and environmental collapse because they believe in the prophesied Tribulation. He uses this lie to then discredit the policies of the Bush administration. This is a classic straw man fallacy.

Mona Charen confronted Moyer's illogic:

> Someone needs to get this man some Prozac. His imagination is torturing him. I checked in with Michael Cromartie, author of many books about American Protestantism. He said rapture thinking was much more pronounced during the Cold War. Today, it is greatly diminished. I also followed Moyers' suggestion and looked at Rapture Index on the web. Adorning the site were numerous ads showing the faithful how to make contributions to victims of the tsunami. So if these rapture types believe that the end times are upon us, why would they help tsunami victims? For that matter, as Cromartie points out, why would they support conservative candidates for public office?[24]

Keep your pearls away from Moyers.

Fallacies are a key component of false teaching. James W. Sire, formerly a Senior editor at InterVarsity Press, concluded from examining a liberal Protestant book by Archie Matson:

> Matson began to twist biblical texts out of shape either to show how they supported his occult world view or how they contradicted other biblical texts. His caricature of traditional biblical interpretation infuriated me: 'The idea that every word is literally true is so obviously false that we need not belabor the matter.' This is, of course, a cheap shot at the sophisticated attempt of traditional biblical scholars to get at the original meaning of the texts.

> As I read Matson further, I began to see that he had
> what could not unfairly be called a methodology of
> misreading . . . Matson set up straw men (like the
> literal view of interpreting Scripture), used innuendo,
> argued in a circle, failed to take into account
> other relevant biblical texts, engaged in name-
> calling, misrepresented the biblical data, charged
> contradictions in the Bible that are clearly not there,
> and drew wild, speculative conclusions.[25]

What Sire derived from Matson is what happens in most
books and articles attacking Christianity. Fallacies rule in
cult literature.

## Confronting the Fallacies

Non-Christians seem determined to attack Christians
and Christianity with fallacies and lies. If I believe their
attack is damaging the credibility of the Bible or may sway
seekers away from God, I respond. I wrote the following
articles with a non-Christian audience in mind. You may
recognize some of the premises. I wrote the first editorial
to my fellow faculty members, the second was submitted to
the Journal of Higher Education, and the third was written
to my local newspaper. (A school board in the county in
which I reside decided to read a statement saying some
people question Darwinism and believe in Intelligent
Design. The story created outcries from the political left
locally and nationwide.)

## Critical Thinking, Truth, Logical Fallacies, and Left Hands

The discussion facilitator at yesterday's diversity seminar

made some critical thinking and theological errors. Since I teach the former and have degrees in the latter, I want to address these matters. I would challenge a student who made such an argument, and I will challenge the credentialed that do so as well. Lecturers with Ph.D.'s are accountable for what they say just as well as anyone else, if not more so, since they are supposed experts in the field.

The presenter said the "Devil is in the left hand." The Doctor even said this occurs in the Book of Leviticus. The Bible nowhere says this. Based on this error, the speaker said the phrase "the right hand of God," therefore, provides grounds for rejecting the moral arguments of the Bible because the Bible discriminates against left-handed people. Allow me to disassemble this argument piece-by-piece.

The Book of Leviticus has two references to the left hand, both of which have nothing to do with the Devil. The Bible has eleven references to the left hand. Not one of them is negative.

In Genesis 48:13, Jacob blessed Joseph's younger son by placing his right hand on him, indicating he was the next spiritual leader in the family. At the same time he blessed the older son by placing his left hand on him.

One of the great heroes of Israel was the judge Ehud, "a left-handed man." He used his left-handedness to win a great battle and became, in my opinion, the patron saint of proctologists (Judges 3).

Proverbs 3:16 says wisdom holds in her left hand riches and honor for all who will take it. This is a figure of speech known as personification.

The phrase "the right hand of God" is another figure of speech known as anthropormphism, attributing human characteristics to God so humans can understand Him better. In the ancient Middle East, if someone sat at the king's right hand, it meant this person had a special place of honor, power, and authority. The left hand was also good, being second only to the person on the right hand. This is why James' and John's mother asked Jesus, when He entered the kingdom, to have her sons sit next to Him, one on His left and one on His right. God does not discriminate against left-handed people.

The idea that the Devil lives in the left hand came from medieval philosophy, not the Bible. We carry this superstition into our culture, which is why parents used to try to make their babies use their right hand if they were left handed. If someone is awkward and lacks social grace, we call her gauche, French for left hand. If someone is evil and deceptive, we call him sinister, Latin for left hand. If someone is talented, however, we call this person dexterous, Latin for right hand. It is western culture that discriminates against lefties, not biblical culture.

What the speaker did yesterday was to read Medieval and western culture back into biblical culture, an anachronism if I ever saw one.

Her argument was what we call a straw man fallacy in

critical thinking terminology.   You misrepresent your opponent (The Bible discriminates against left-handed people), say how wrong that is, then say that the Bible's treatment of left-handed people disqualifies everyone from using the Bible to discuss homosexuality and lesbianism since the Bible is obviously discriminatory.  This is illogical reasoning that would have been awarded the grade "F" in my critical thinking class, and is unwarranted in a discussion about diversity.

We need facts to make reasoned conclusions about this important subject of diversity, not subjective and illogical opinions, even if those who express these opinions have Ph.D.'s.  No one is above the law of logic.  I do not believe, as the speaker said, she chose the left-handed discussion as an innocuous way to introduce the discussion about homosexual and lesbian issues.  It seemed to me she designed her handout to limit discussion of this topic, trying to eliminate those who would try to interject moral beliefs into the argument.

## To the Editor:

Please ensure more scholarly thinking is used in the essays you publish.  In "Words, Science, and the State of Evolution" (The Review, November 29, 2002), Lawrence M. Krauss said, "It is important to stress that there is no such controversy about evolution.  In a recent electronic survey of the more than 10 million articles that have appeared in over 20 major science journals during the past 12 years, Leslie C. Lane, a biologist at the University of Nebraska at Lincoln, found 115,000 articles that used the keyword 'evolution,' and most of those articles referred to biological evolution. 'Intelligent design,' often promoted by religious groups as the alternative to evolution, appeared as a keyword in 88 articles."

Lack of articles by those who believe in intelligent design does not mean there is "no such controversy about evolution." Editors and their biases determine which articles get published. Krauss needs to demonstrate that articles are not being submitted by those who believe in intelligent design, and that the volume of articles being written correlates to controversy.

Whether one believes in intelligent design or not, this is shoddy research.[26]

## Evolutionism

In a Letter to the Editor, Steven Z____ said the Church in 1616 opposed Galileo's teaching of the Copernican theory that the world was round. He claimed the church of that day taught the Earth was flat. This is factually and historically incorrect. Galileo and Copernicus were not concerned about a flat Earth because the church was not teaching a "flat-Earth" view. The controversy was about the Earth being the center of the universe. Let's look at the facts.

Aristotelian philosophy reigned in medieval Europe up through the Renaissance. Aristotle taught that the Earth was the center of the universe (geocentric). Planets (perfect circles) moved in perfect circles around the Earth.

Galileo, using the newly discovered telescope, found that the moon was not perfectly round. He also confirmed Copernicus' theory, based on mathematics, that the Earth revolved around the sun, not vice versa. The authorities of and scientists of Galileo's day did not oppose him because they believed in a flat Earth; the Catholic Church did not oppose Galileo because he was contradicting the Bible; they opposed Galileo because, like most scholars of the day, they were adhering to Aristotle's geocentric beliefs.

No educated medieval or Renaissance person believed in a flat Earth, not even in the Europe of 1492. According to Encarta Encyclopedia and the World Book Encyclopedia, the church and scholars of Columbus' day opposed him because he "greatly underestimated the circumference of the Earth." Columbus believed it was closer to get to the Indies sailing west than it was to sail around the horn of Africa. The Council of King John II of Portugal rejected Columbus' calculations about the Earth's circumference. The Greek philosopher Eratosthenes, in the third century B.C., estimated the circumference of the Earth to be 25,000 miles, and most educated people believed this latter number, including this Council. The Council recommended finding a route around Africa. The Spanish Court reached the same conclusion around 1490.

With extraordinarily few exceptions, no educated person in the history of Western Civilization from the third century B.C. onward believed the Earth was flat. The Bible, (you know, that unscientific book) in the eighth century B.C., is the oldest text to state that the Earth is spherical (Isaiah 40). Pythagoras, in the sixth century B.C., postulated a round Earth. Aristotle, Euclid, and Aristarchus wrote about a spherical planet. This belief does not change with the advent of Christianity. Tens of thousands of Christian theologians, poets, artists, and scientists taught the spherical view throughout the early, medieval, and modern church.

No one before the 1830's believed medieval people thought the Earth was flat. Storyteller Washington Irving (1783-1859) invented the idea in 1828 in his historical fiction novel about Columbus. Irving wanted to paint Christians as dolts who oppose science. His desires live on in people like Mr. Z_____. Although Mr. Z_____ does not clearly state his premises, he was implying Christians today are dolts, following in the footsteps of their doltish flat-Earth predecessors, because they also oppose science, namely evolutionism.

As a professor of logic, I tell my students that a critical thinker is someone who attempts to arrive at a conclusion through honestly evaluating a position and its alternatives with respect to the available evidence and arguments. True science tests theories and data that may invalidate a theory. Proponents of evolutionism want to do none of these logical, scientific endeavors. Their religious/philosophical paradigm of atheistic naturalism (all nature is a closed system of material cause and effect that cannot be influenced by anything "outside") is afraid to test macroevolutionism because, according to them, the only alternative is religious creationism, which is contrary to their religion of naturalism.

Contrary to Mr. Z____'s statement, there is a plethora of evidence challenging most evolutionary beliefs. Many people would be happy if just the contradictory information was included in teaching about evolution. Macroevolutionism, however, is a religious dogma that is taught to secondary students as scientific fact. Proponents also teach that macroevolution has little or no scientific opposition. Proponents of exclusive macro evolutionary teaching have no room for contrary evidence. Evolutionism, as taught in secondary education, is therefore not science; it is indoctrination into the religion of naturalistic atheism.

The Supreme Court has violated the establishment clause of the First Amendment by promoting naturalistic atheism and by silencing contrary theories and evidence. This is tyranny. Opposing tyranny would be the "purpose" for taking this issue back to the courts, Mr. Z____.

Evolutionism is not the only model available. The theory of intelligent design examines the scientific evidence and reaches conclusions contrary to macroevolution that do not have to adhere to any religious view of creation, or any mention of God, let alone "biblical creationism." This would not violate the First Amendment.

The Dover School Board should consider adding collateral reading to their science textbooks, such as Michael Behe's Darwin's Black Box. Let the students study the alternatives as homework, under the tutelage of their parents, and reach their own conclusions. If evolution is the truth, why fear students researching the evidence thoroughly?

## Conclusion

Fallacies, unless you examine them closely, are persuasive. Unfortunately, fallacies are often a common component of Christian arguments and arguments against Christians and against Christianity. It is not necessary to memorize what the fallacies are called, but it is helpful to see when someone is trying to manipulate the argument by using them. Critical thinkers do not intentionally use logical fallacies and must guard against doing so.

Fallacies are not the only things that cause us problems in arguments and decision-making; sometimes God's laws cause us problems. What do we do if two of God's laws conflict with each other? We will unearth this dilemma next chapter.

**And then she understood the devilish cunning of**
**The enemies' plan. By mixing a little truth with it**
**They had made their lie far stronger.**

**C. S. Lewis**

# For Review and Discussion

- Define fallacy.

- Define an *ad hominen* fallacy and give an example of your own.

- Describe a time when you needed to be given a second chance.

- Who do you need to contact to give a second chance?

- Define the appeal to ignorance fallacy and give an example of your own.

- Define the appeal to tradition fallacy and give an example of your own.

- Define the appeal to the people fallacy and give an example of your own.

- Define the appeal to consequence fallacy and give an example of your own.

- Define the bifurcation fallacy and give an example of your own.

- Define the equivocation fallacy and give an example of your own.

- Define the etymological fallacy and give an example of your own.

- Define the group think fallacy and give an example of your own.

- Define the hasty generalization fallacy and give an example of your own.

- Define the no true Scotsman fallacy and give an example of your own.

- Define the *non sequitur* fallacy and give an example of your own.

- Define the *post hoc, ergo propter hoc* fallacy and give an example of your own.

- Define the quoting out of context fallacy and give an example of your own.

- Of the ten passages quoted out of context, which one surprised you the most?  Why?

- Define the red herring fallacy and give an example of your own.

- Define the slippery slope fallacy and give an example of your own.

- Define the straw man fallacy and give an example of your own.

- Describe your reaction to what Bill Moyers said.

- Write a letter to the editor of your local newspaper.

## ENDNOTES

1.  Browne, M. Neil and Stuart Keeley. <u>Asking the Right Questions: A Guide to Critical Thinking</u>, 6th edition. Upper Saddle River, NJ: Prentice Hall, 2001, p. 84.

2.  Flage, Daniel E. <u>The Art of Questioning: An Introduction to Critical Thinking</u>. Upper Saddle River, NJ: Prentice Hall, 2004, p. 333.

3.  Leo, John. "Sex for Dummies." <u>USNews</u>. 23 May 2005. <http://www.usnews.com/usnews/opinion/article/ 050523/23john.htm>

4.  Branom, Mike. "Kerry sounds like he's still on campaign trail at Orlando event." <u>CBS News</u>. 27 May 2005. <http://cbs4.com/apbroadcastsports/FL--Kerry-Florida-ds/resources_news_html>.

5.  Dowden, Bradly. "The Internet Encyclopedia of Philosophy." <u>California State University Sacramento</u>. 2004. <http://www.iep.utm.edu/f/fallacies.htm #Appeal%20to%20the%20People>.

6.  Ibid.<http://www.iep.utm.edu/f/fallacies.htm #Appeal%20to%20Consequence>.

7.  Watson, D.M.S. "Adaptation." Nature 124:233, 1929.

8.  Johnson, Phillip E. Objections Sustained: Subversive Essays on Evolution, Law & Culture. Downers Grove, IL: InterVarsity Press, 1998, pp. 71-72.

9.  Adair, Jody. "A Good Sales Pitch." Sojourners of the Lord.    <http://www.clean-funnies.com/html/f18. htm>.

10. CNN. Law Center. "Judge: Evolution Stickers Unconstitutional." 14 January 2005. <http://www. cnn.com/2005/LAW/01/13/evolution.textbooks. ruling/>.

11. Bowers, Michael . "A Nonbeliever Takes Sides with the Believers." Free Republic. 10 April 2005.    <http:// www.freerepublic.com/focus/f-news/1380871/ posts>.

12. Coulter, Ann. Townhall.com. "Actually, 'Judicial Activism' Means 'E=mc2.'" 14 September 2005. <http://www.townhall.com/columnists/anncoulter/ ac20050914.shtml>.

13. Carson, D. A. Exegetical Fallacies. Grand Rapids, MI: Baker Book House, 1996, p. 34.

14. Ibid, p. 30.

15. For a further discussion, see <u>The Silence of Adam</u> by Larry Crabb.

16. For a further discussion of numbers 4 and 5, see Gary Friesen's <u>Decision Making and the Will of God</u>.

17. Browne and Keeley, p. 96.

18. "Massachusetts Court Rules Ban on Gay Marriage Unconstitutional."CNN. 4 February 2004.<http://www.cnn.com/2003/LAW/11/18/samesex.marriage.ruling>.

19. Mount, Steve.    "The U.S. Constitution Online." <u>Usconstitution</u>.  30 March 2004. <http://www.usconstitution.net/const.html #Am15>.

20. Ibid.<http://www.usconstitution.net/const.html#Am19>.

21. Ibid.<http://www.usconstitution.net/const.html #Preamble>.

22. Lowry, Rick.  "Forcing Our Hand."  <u>Townhall</u>.  27 February, 2004. <http://www.townhall.com/ columnists/richtucker/printrt20040227.shtml>.

23. Moyers, Bill. "Acceptance Remarks by Bill Moyers for the Global Environmental Citizen Award." Harvard University.  1 December 2004.  <http://www.med.harvard.edu/chge/ Moyerstranscript.pdf>.

24. Charen, Mona. "Moyers and the Party of Gloom." Townhall. 4 February 2005. <http://www.townhall.com/columnists/monacharen/mc20050204.shtml>.

25. Sire, James W. Scripture Twisting: 20 Ways the Cults Misread the Bible. Downers Grove, IL: InterVarsity Press, 1980, pp. 11-12.

26. Shelley, Brian J. "To the Editor." The Chronicle of Higher Education. 24 January 2005. <http://proquest.umi.com/pqdweb?index>.

There is only one way to find out if a man is honest—
Ask him.  If he says 'yes' he's not honest.

Groucho Marx


Life is the art of drawing sufficient conclusions

From insufficient premises.

Samuel Butler

(1835 -1902)

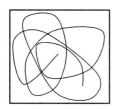

CHAPTER NINE

# What Do You Do When God's Laws Conflict with Each Other?

### To Tell the Truth

On the Kentucky frontier of 1804, church members gathered one Sunday morning for worship at their local Baptist Church. The pastor posed a hypothetical question during his sermon. "Suppose you have ten children and your home were attacked by Indians. You hid your children as best you could, but they found nine of them and killed them. Further, suppose one of the Indians asked you, 'Do you have anymore children?' What would you say?"

I doubt the pastor was trying to do church planting, but the next week there were two Baptist Churches in that rural area of Kentucky, one was affectionately known as the "Truthful Baptist Church," the other was known as the "Lying Baptist Church."

How would you have answered the Indian's question? Would it honor God to say, "Yes, I have another child?" If the Indian then killed the tenth child, would you bear any legal guilt before God for the murder? If you said you had no more children, would you be lying?  Would you later have to repent?  Would repentance mean tracking the Indian and confessing you lied to him?  Which church would you have attended the following Sunday?

## Abraham and His Cherry Tree

In Genesis, Abraham faced a similar situation on two occasions.  God said to Abraham, "Leave your country and go to a land that I will show you.  I will make of you a great nation.  In you all the families of the earth will be blessed.'

Abraham traveled 1,100 miles when God appeared to him again and said He would give Abraham the land of Canaan.

Before Abraham and his wife Sarah left Mesopotamia, he asked her to tell everyone she was his sister, not his wife.  She was his sister.  They had different mothers but the same father.  You may think that strange, but he was born only one hundred years after the great Flood of Noah.  There was not much choice but to marry relatives.

Abraham asked Sarah to say she was his sister because of the culture.  Sarah was a gorgeous woman.  When they entered Canaan she was 65 years old, but she probably looked like she was in her early 30's.  In that culture, it was wrong to take and marry a married woman.  So, if you wanted the woman, you would kill the husband and take the wife.

He knew when the tribal kings saw Sarah that he was a dead man, so he asked her to say she was his sister. That would save his life, the kings would treat him well, Sarah would be spared humiliation and grief from his murder, and it would give them time to escape.

When they got to Canaan they found the land decimated by a famine. There was no artificial irrigation. So, they traveled south to Egypt for a temporary stay until the famine ended. As they journeyed through Egypt, Abraham saw the admiring and lustful glances directed toward his beautiful wife. He figured he would be killed and Sarah would end up in some king's bed.

He couldn't say she was his wife; he would be murdered. He could not say she was his servant. She would have suffered an even worse fate—they would have just taken her and raped her. The best solution was to say she was his sister. So, he said, "Sarah, you're a beautiful woman. When the Egyptians see you they will kill him if they know you are his wife. Please say you are his sister so that he will be treated well for your sake." Sarah, the godly woman she was, agreed.

The situation in Egypt was worse than Abraham thought. Pharaoh's servants saw Sarah and praised her prettiness to him. They thought she would make an excellent addition to his harem. Believing she was his sister, the servants took Sarah and held her in Pharaoh's harem.

Sarah was spared humiliation and grief, and Pharaoh treated Abraham well. Pharaoh gave Abraham sheep, cattle, donkeys, camels, and male and female servants. This was the dowry for a future marriage that was paid to the bride's brother. But how was he going to get Sarah out of there before the wedding?

Sarah and he both prayed to the Lord deep into the night for many sleepless nights. God honored their story about her being his sister and answered their prayers for deliverance from the marriage. The Lord struck Pharaoh and his house with great plagues because he wrongly took Abraham's wife. The Egyptians were superstitious people and the plagues were ominous to them. Somehow Pharaoh found out Sarah was not just his sister, but his wife. He sent for Abraham.

Pharaoh said, "What have you done to me? Why did not you tell me she was your wife? Why did you say 'She is my sister,' so that I took her to become my wife. Take your wife and go!" They were given a military escort from Egypt and were allowed to keep everything Pharaoh gave them. God blessed them because they honored Him by saying Sarah was his sister. Isn't that just like God?

Back in Canaan, Abraham grew closer to the Lord. As time passed, they moved into the Negev, the desert region south of Canaan. They went to Gerar, a city that controlled a lucrative caravan route. Abraham wanted to do business there. God rejuvenated their bodies in preparation to produce children, and Sarah was lovely as ever. Again Sarah's beauty caught everyone's attention.

The same fears of murder and marriage materialized, so they pursued the same strategy. They had much to fear from these people. They lived close to Sodom and Gomorrah, which God had just destroyed. When the two angels, disguised as men, entered Sodom to rescue Lot, the men and boys of the city surrounded Lot's house and demanded the two men be brought outside to have homosexual relations with all of the male population of the city. If that is what they did to strangers, what would these people in the Negev do to Abraham and Sarah?

Again they said Sarah was Abraham's sister. Abimelech, king of the area, sent men and took Sarah. They waited on the Lord to deliver them again. He did. God appeared to Abimelech in a dream. He said to Abimelech, "Behold, you are a dead man because of the woman you have taken, for she is married." Abimelech objected. He had not had sexual relations with Sarah. "Lord, will you destroy an innocent nation? Did Abraham not say to him, 'She is my sister,' and did not she say, 'He is my brother?' We have done this with a clear conscience and clean hands." The Lord replied, "Yes, I know you did this with a clear conscience, and so I made you sick to keep you from sinning against me. That is why I did not let you touch her. Now return the man's wife, for he is a prophet, and he will pray for you and you will live. But if you do not return her, you may be sure that you and all yours will die."

Early the next morning Abimelech summoned all his officials, and when he told them what had happened, they were terrified. Rightly so. The smell of Sodom's sulfur was still pungent in the memories of their nostrils.

Then Abimelech summoned Abraham and said, "What have you done to them? How have he wronged you that you have brought such great guilt upon my kingdom and him? You have done things to him that should not be done. Why did you do this?"

Abraham replied, "I said to myself, 'There is surely no fear of God in this place, and they will kill him because of my wife.' Besides, she really is my sister, the daughter of my father though not of my mother; and she became my wife. And when God had me wander from my father's household, I said to her, 'This is how you can show your love to him: Everywhere they go, say of him, 'He is my brother.'"

Then Abimelech brought sheep, cattle, and male and female slaves, and gave them to Abraham. He gave him 1,000 pieces of silver, 25 pounds worth. He said this vindicated Sarah from any wrongdoing and absolved him of guilt. Then Abraham prayed for Abimelech and God healed him. His wife and slave girls were also healed so that they could have children again.

The Lord was especially gracious to them. Sarah became pregnant, and they had a son, Isaac. Isn't that just like God?

Was Abraham a liar? Plenty of people think poorly of Abraham for these two episodes in his life. Some say God tested him with the famine, and that he failed miserably. They say he should have stayed in Canaan, but that seems unwise and unnecessary. Others say he did not love Sarah because true love would have made him willing to sacrifice his life for her, but I do not understand how dying needlessly proved that. One person said Abraham repented for my sin, although he admitted it was unrecorded. Some say Abraham should have apologized to Pharaoh and Abimelech for lying and being a selfish coward, and he should have told them that no child of Adam has ever sinned as much against grace. One said Abraham had no fear of God. Another said Abraham was only concerned for himself and not for Sarah. Others said he should have learned from the first sin not to do it again.

Abraham did not sin. He did not lie. He would not have lied even if Sarah were not his half-sister. God never said the famine was a test, before, during or after these events occurred. Abraham loved Sarah. He was more concerned for her welfare than for his own. Abraham never silently repented of sin—he never sinned. That's why his repentance is unrecorded. It was not to Sarah's advantage if Abraham had died or if she became another man's wife against her will. What kind of husband stands back and let's terrible things like this happen to 'prove' he loves his wife?

Abraham had no need to apologize. He did not apologize. Sarah and he feared God—that's why Abraham had Sarah say she was his sister; that is why she agreed to say it. Abraham knew God would get them out of this, particularly the second time. He did so once before. God promised them a son. Things had to work out. Abraham was trusting God.

Look how God treated him. God never said Abraham lied or sinned. In both instances God vastly increased his wealth. Just before the Abimelech incident, God appeared to him and three times called Abraham His friend. God told Abimelech that Abraham was a prophet, the first person ever called that. The word means one who stands out in front to represent God. If Abraham had not prayed for Abimelech, he would have died. God honored Abraham and blessed him for what he did.

What do you think? Did Abraham lie to Pharaoh and Abimelech? Did he need to repent? Was he like George Washington in the myth about cutting down the cherry tree who needed to repent for telling a lie?

## The Lesser of Two Evils

Sometimes God's laws are difficult to follow because of the consequences.

- The telephone rings at work. The boss says, "If that is Bill Murphy, tell him I'm not in." You may lose your job if you do not obey your boss. What do you do?

- You know the project is not designed as well as it should be, but you are scheduled to sell it to the Board of Directors at 2:00 p.m. What do you do?

- Your phone at home rings at 7:30 a.m. and wakens you. You pick up the receiver to hear, "Did I wake you?" You cringe because it is okay the person called, but you do not want them to feel badly because they wakened you. What do you do?

- The federal government bans Christian worship: do you attend an underground church?

- The government decides to take your children when they are two-years-old because you are a Christian. Do you let them?

- The government decides to tax the church. Should your church pay?

- You and your family are hungry and you have no food or money? May you steal to feed them? May you not pay income taxes to feed them?

- Christians in China are told not to have more than one child. Should they obey the government?

- Do you strike if you believe your union is wrong?

We are constantly faced with moral and ethical dilemmas. Sometimes God's laws are difficult to follow; at other times God's laws come into conflict with each other, or at least they seem to do so, and seem impossible to follow. No matter what you do it seems wrong. God commands us to encourage others and commands us not to lie. Then your wife asks you, "Do I look fat?" It is decision time—will you be an encourager or not talked to for three days? Ricky, age ten, advised, "Tell your wife that she looks pretty even if she looks like a truck."[1]

Many of the conflicts between God's laws are much more serious than that, like the ones Abraham faced and the Kentucky church experienced.

- Would you fund a missionary who was smuggling Bibles into a Muslim country in disobedience to the Muslim government?

- Would you hide Jews in your home if you had lived in Germany during World War II like Corrie Ten Boom did, in defiance of the government?

- If a Muslim terrorist pointed a gun at your wife, husband, or child's head and said, "Denounce Christ or I pull the trigger," what would you do?

- Is it lying to keep a light on in your house to deceive burglars into wrongly thinking you are home?

- Does a wife have to stay, in the name of submission, with a husband who beats her?

People in the Bible faced situations where God's laws conflicted. We face situations like that as well. We can learn from their encounters. Critical thinking can help us in these situations.

## Defining Our Terms

As we saw in chapter one, logic was part of the philosophical category of epistemology, which tries to answer the question "What is truth?" We now will deal with another philosophical category—axiology, which tries to answer the questions "What is valuable and what is good?" There are two branches of axiology: one branch is called ethics and investigates what is right and what is wrong; the other branch is aesthetics, which sets standards for artwork and tries to determine art's meaning in human experience. We will concern ourselves with ethics in this chapter and aesthetics in the next chapter. Ethics examines what a person should do in a given circumstance. The "should" is determined by our:

- Values—the worth and importance we assess to people, places, and things.

- Norms—what we consider typical rules of conduct, but are unwritten and peculiar to a region or culture.

- Laws—formal standards of right and wrong, some instituted by God, and others instituted by the government.

An example of our values would be spending time with our family. Our values may differ. You may think a picture of my wife is nice; to me, it is precious.

Liberals' values are often driven by their feelings. They want homosexual marriage because they feel sorry for them, or they push for animal rights because they attribute human feelings to animals. "But far more conservative positions are based on 'What is right?' rather than on 'How do I feel?' That is why a religious woman who is pregnant but does not wish to be is far less likely to have an abortion than a secular woman in the same circumstances. Her values are higher than her feelings."[2]

An example of a norm is expecting people to bathe and use deodorant. Americans find body odor offensive, but that is not true in all cultures.

One norm I have seen in churches in North America and Europe is prayer posture. The Bible describes many bodily positions for prayer, among them a person's head raised to Heaven, kneeling, hands raised to Heaven, and lying prostrate on the ground. In evangelical western culture, most churches have adopted bowing your head and closing your eyes as the only acceptable way to pray. However, of the many bodily positions mentioned in the Bible, the stance not found there is bowing your head and closing your eyes. Ironically, not to pray in this presumed pious posture is to have your spirituality called into question. Bowing your head and closing your eyes are a cultural norm, not a biblical model or mandate.

The boss and the Bill Murphy phone call, the Board of Directors meeting, and the 7:30 a.m. phone call made us uncomfortable because God's laws were conflicting with our values and norms—we do not want to look unprepared or hurt other's feelings. The situations Abraham and the Kentucky church faced were conflicts within the laws of God themselves—in these cases, the sanctity of life and telling the truth—we are commanded not to murder and not to lie.

## Being Absolutely Certain

In the Christian evangelical tradition, three main views concerning absolute truth (see chapter 2) have emerged. I will define each and show how people who hold each position would have answered the Indian about the existence of a tenth child.

## Unqualified Absolutism

Unqualified Absolutism says God's absolute laws never conflict with one another.[3] The supposed conflict is only illusionary. Covenant theologians tend toward this position. Augustine, John Murray, and Charles Hodge advocated this view. In studying their premises for this argument, it seems to me that people who hold this position see the sovereignty of God as His overarching attribute. In response to the Kentucky Indian, you tell him you have one more child, but you do not tell him where the child is hidden. (I suppose the Indian would ask further questions like, "Is the child in the house or under the bed"—then what?) You leave the situation up to the sovereignty of God to protect the tenth child. However, if you trust the sovereignty of God, why hide the children in the first place? According to Unqualified Absolutism, if the Indian finds the child and kills the child, it is not your responsibility. It was God's sovereign plan.

I see this position as a denial of reality and indefensible—God's laws do conflict. You have to do mental gymnastics to say they do not clash.

## Conflicting Absolutism

Conflicting Absolutism says God's absolute laws come in conflict with one another, so you break the lesser of the two evils.[4] You are guilty of sinning, so you confess it later. Martin Luther took this position.

In response to the Kentucky Indian, you knowingly lie and tell the Indian you do not have a tenth child, then confess the sin to God later. I cannot support a position that says sinning is the right thing to do. If Jesus was tempted in every way like we are tempted (Hebrews 4:15), He had to face conflicting laws, which means if this is the biblical position, then Jesus would have had to sin. The position is logically impossible. (If "A," then "B")

## Graded Absolutism

The third position, Graded Absolutism, or Hierarchicalism, says God's absolute laws can come in conflict with one another, but they are ranked in a hierarchy so that it is not sin to violate breaking a lower law if necessary to keep a higher law.[5] This is the position espoused by Samuel Rutherford, Francis Schaeffer, and Norman Geisler, President of Southern Evangelical Seminary.

How would a Hierarchicalist answer the Kentucky Indian? Because the sanctity of human life, particularly the child that God entrusted to your care, is more valuable than telling the truth, you tell the Indian you do not have another child. You have not lied; therefore you do not need to repent. You protected a higher law of God—saving a life. You have not violated a lower law—lying.

Unqualified Absolutists seem to come unglued when they hear the Graded Absolutist position. Unqualified Absolutists accuse Hierarchicalists of relativism and supporting situation ethics, beliefs Graded Absolutists find abhorrent and repugnant.[6] Other examples of their disgust and disdain for the Graded Absolutist position are statements like, "Did God give the Ten Ascending Priorities?" and, "It takes a lazy approach to the ethical questions raised by historical portions of Scripture." [7] Can you feel the love? I have witnessed Unqualified

Absolutists try to rip my church apart.  Adhering to the Graded Absolutist position means you will have to have a backbone to defend it, as is the case for most critical thinking.

## Norman's Norms

Norman Geisler has argued the biblical position well that some sins are greater than others:

> Not all moral laws are of equal weight.  Jesus spoke of the 'weightier' matters of the law (Matthew 23:23) and of the 'least' (Matthew 5:19) and the 'greatest' commandment (Matthew 22:36).  He told Pilate that Judas had committed the 'greater sin' (John 19:11). Despite a rather widespread evangelical distaste for a hierarchy of sins (and virtues), the Bible does speak of the 'greatest' virtue (1 Corinthians 13:13) and even of 'greater' acts of a given virtue (John 15:13).

> The common myth that all sins are equal is often based on erroneous interpretations of James 2:10, which does not speak of the equality of all sins but rather of the unity of the law: 'Whoever . . . fails in one point has become guilty of all of it' (RSV).  It does not say he is equally guilty of all, nor that all infractions bring equal guilt (compare James 3:1).

> Others have supposed wrongly that simply because Jesus said that one can lust and even murder 'in his heart' (Matthew 5:28) that this means it is equally evil to imagine a sin as it is to do it.  In the same

sermon, Jesus rejected this view, indicating there are at least three levels of sins with corresponding judgments (5:22). Indeed, the whole concept of degrees of punishment in hell (Matthew 5:22; Romans 2:6; Revelation 20:12) and Graded levels of reward in heaven (1 Corinthians 3:11-12) indicates that sins come in degrees. The fact that some Christian sins call for excommunication (1 Corinthians 5) and others for death (1 Corinthians 11:30) also supports the general biblical pattern that all sins are not equal in weight. In fact, there is one sin so great as to be unforgivable (Mark 3:29).[8]

Geisler succinctly defines the biblical view of sin. Although all sins bring death, some sins bring more severe temporal, and at times, eternal punishment.

If Graded Absolutism is the biblical position, what is the hierarchy? If two laws of God conflict, which is the greater law? Let's look at some instances in Scripture where laws conflicted, how the people involved made critical thinking decisions, how God responded to their decisions, and then construct a hierarchy from what we find.

## King-Size Defiance

The king of Egypt told the Hebrew midwives Shiphrah and Puah, "'When you help the Hebrew women in childbirth and observe them on the delivery stool, if it is a boy, kill him; but if it is a girl, let her live.' The midwives, however, feared God and did not do what the king of Egypt had told them to do; they let the boys live. Then the king of

Egypt summoned the midwives and asked them, 'Why have you done this? Why have you let the boys live?' The midwives answered Pharaoh, 'Hebrew women are not like Egyptian women; they are vigorous and give birth before the midwives arrive'" (Genesis 1:15-21).

The king told the midwives to murder the boys. He was the law of the land whom they were to obey. The midwives do not tell the truth about Hebrew women's birthing habits. Notice they did not slit the boys throats and leave their life up to the sovereignty of God; they did not tell the truth that they were letting the boys live; they did not repent of sin. Instead, God said what they did was in fear, or honor, of Him. God blessed the midwives. "So God was kind to the midwives and the people increased and became even more numerous. And because the midwives feared God, He gave them families of their own." Warren Wiersbe said the midwives were right not to kill the babies, but then he added, "While God did not approve of the excuses the midwives gave Pharaoh (although their words may have been true), He did bless them for their faith."[9]

The Text does not say God did not approve of the excuses. The Bible says God was kind to the midwives, but not until after they told the king the Hebrew women were vigorous. Besides, the words were not true. They were not too late to get to the birthing mothers. God's Word says, "They let the boys live." The midwives' critical thinking skills resulted in faith, and God was pleased with what they did and said in respect of Him. The midwives were not guilty of lying or disobeying the government because they protected a higher-value law—the sanctity of life."

The king of Egypt tried another tactic. "Then Pharaoh gave this order to all his people: 'Every boy that is born you must throw into the Nile, but let every girl live'" (Exodus 1:22). Israelite Amram and his aunt/wife Jochebed had a son together after the Pharaoh's edict was given. The parents did not throw the baby in the river and hope he learned to swim by the sovereignty of God. They did not ask God to forgive them for disobeying the king. Instead, in defiance of Pharaoh and in honor of God, Jochebed hid the boy three months. "But when she could hide him no longer, she got a papyrus basket for him and coated it with tar and pitch. Then she placed the child in it and put it among the reeds along the bank of the Nile" (Exodus 2:1-3).

God did not get angry at Amram and Jochebed for disobeying the king. Instead, God blessed them. Isn't that just like God? Pharaoh's daughter found the baby, hired Jochebed to nurse the child, then raised the baby, Moses, as her own child. God blessed the world through a child the king ordered killed. Amram and Jochebed's critical thinking skills resulted in faith, and God was pleased with what they did. Hebrews 11:23 says, "By faith Moses' parents hid him for three months after he was born, because they saw he was no ordinary child, and they were not afraid of the king's edict." God declared disobedience to the king an act of faith, a faith based in critical thinking skills. Amram and Jochebed were not guilty of disobeying the government because they protected a higher-value law—the sanctity of life.

## The Oscar for Best Actor Goes to . . .

King Saul hunted David to kill him. David, "the man after God's own heart," went to Gath of the Philistines to hide. The servants of Achish, king of Gath, did not like the idea David was among them and complained to the king about him. "David took these words to heart and was very much afraid of Achish king of Gath. So he pretended to be insane in their presence; and while he was in their hands he acted like a madman, making marks on the doors of the gate and letting saliva run down his beard" (1 Samuel 21:10-13). What did David dread? He feared Achish would kill him, making Saul's job easier. David did not just trust the sovereignty of God; he acted like a crazy person and saved his life.

David was not through with Achish. He stroked the king's ego, asking for the town of Ziklag to live in because, "Why should your servant live in the royal city with you?" (1 Samuel 27:5). David used Ziklag as a staging area to attack Israel's enemies. In verse 8 we read, "Now David and his men went up and raided the Geshurites, the Girzites and the Amalekites. (From ancient times these peoples had lived in the land extending to Shur and Egypt.) Whenever David attacked an area, he did not leave a man or woman alive, but took sheep and cattle, donkeys and camels, and clothes. Then he returned to Achish." David and his men attacked the region of the Gaza strip to just east of the Nile River in Egypt. However, when Achish (the man who David feared would kill him) asked David where he had raided, David said, "Against the Negev of Judah' or 'Against the Negev of Jerahmeel' or 'Against the Negev of the Kenites.' He did not leave a man or woman alive to be brought to Gath, for he thought, 'They might inform on us and say, 'This is what David did.'' And such was his practice as long as he lived in Philistine territory. Achish trusted David and said to himself, 'He has become so odious to his people, the Israelites, that he will be my servant forever'" (1 Samuel 27:10-12).

David said he raided in the land of southern Judah. Achish thought David was a loyal subject and was not concerned about killing David anymore. David did not tell the truth and trust the sovereignty of God to see what would happen. He did not confess his sin to God or Achish. Graded Absolutism worked and God rewarded David for using it.

## Scarlet for the Harlot

When the time came for the children of Israel to conquer Canaan, General Joshua sent two undercover agents into Jericho (Joshua 2:1-23). They stayed in the home of Rahab the prostitute, who lived in an apartment on the city wall. Someone told the mayor the Jewish spies were in Rahab's house, so he ordered Rahab to turn the infiltrators over to him. Rahab was hiding the Israeli spies on her roof under flax stalks. She said, "Yes, the men came to me, but I did not know where they had come from. At dusk, when it was time to close the city gate, the men left. I do not know which way they went. Go after them quickly. You may catch up with them." The spies were thrilled with what she did and promised to save her life and the lives of her family. They did not ask her to repent for lying. They did not trust the sovereignty of God and not hide under flax stalks on the roof. They did not run to the mayor and say Rahab was a liar, entrusting their lives to God's sovereignty. Instead, they gave Rahab a red thread to dangle from her window as a sign that her life would be spared. She used a rope to lower the spies from her window, and they escaped.

Rahab did not turn the spies over to the mayor, trusting in the sovereignty of God to protect them. She did not confess to God that she lied. The Lord was not displeased with Rahab. Instead, God blessed her. Isn't that just like God? Joshua ordered his troops not to harm Rahab or her family when they conquered Jericho (Joshua 6:17 and 25) because she disobeyed the mayor and protected the spies.   Rahab's great-great grandson was King David, which means her descendant was Jesus, the Messiah. Now that's a blessing from God!  The Lord saved Rahab because of what she did in hiding the spies by telling the mayor they left the city, "In the same way, was not even Rahab the prostitute considered righteous for what she did when she gave lodging to the spies and sent them off in a different direction?" (James 2:25).  Rahab's critical thinking skills resulted in faith and God was pleased with what she did.   Hebrews 11:31 says, "By faith the prostitute Rahab, because she welcomed the spies, was not killed with those who were disobedient." She was not guilty of lying or disobeying the government because she protected a higher-value law—the sanctity of life.

Not everyone agrees with me (but that is all right; the sun will come up tomorrow). Walvoord and Zuck said:

> Was Rahab wrong to lie since her falsehood protected the spies?  Are there some situations in which a lie is acceptable?

After all, some say, this was a cultural matter, for Rahab was born and raised among the depraved Canaanites among whom lying was universally practiced. She probably saw no evil in her act. Further, if she had told the truth the spies would have been killed by the king of Jericho. But such arguments are not convincing. To argue that the spies would certainly have perished if Rahab had been truthful is to ignore the option that God could have protected the spies in some other way. To excuse Rahab for indulging in a common practice is to condone what God condemns. Paul quoted a prophet of Crete who said that Cretans were inveterate liars, and then added, 'This testimony is true. Therefore, rebuke them sharply, so that they will be sound in the faith' (Titus 1:13). The lie of Rahab was recorded but not approved. The Bible approved her faith demonstrated by good works (Hebrews 11:31), but not her falsehood.[10]

Note closely what Walvoord and Zuck said, "The lie of Rahab was recorded but not approved. The Bible approved her faith demonstrated by good works (Hebrews 11:31), but not her falsehood." You cannot say what she said was disapproved by God. That is an argument from silence. These authors are saying the good thing she did was hide the men on the roof, but that, however, did not demonstrate her faith. Her faith was demonstrated when she told the mayor the spies left the city, and he sent his men to capture them. She diverted the predators from the prey. Rahab would not have made the "Hall of Faith" in Hebrews 11 if she had simply covered the spies with flax and, following the Unqualified Absolutist position, said the spies were on her roof. The spies would have been killed. Hebrews 11:31 says, "By faith the prostitute Rahab, because she welcomed the spies." Welcomed does not just mean she invited them into her home, or that she hid them on the roof; to welcome people into your home in middle-eastern culture meant you guaranteed their life and safety, just as Jael did with Sisera in Judges 4 (see chapter 1). Her welcome included saying the spies were at her home, but they left the city. God called everything she did "faith," and blessed her for it. Isn't that just like God?

Walvoord and Zuck accused Rahab of lying, but God did not accuse her of that. She was not guilty of lying—she was responsible to uphold a higher law of God—the sanctity of life. She was exempt from not telling the truth. She did not need to repent and ask forgiveness for lying because she did not lie—she protected life.

Walvoord and Zuck also said, "To argue that the spies would certainly have perished if Rahab had been truthful is to ignore the option that God could have protected the spies in some other way." However, Rahab did not know that. Even though Walvoord and Zuck are far from being covenant theologians, this is an argument based in trusting the sovereignty of God. However, God in His sovereignty has given us a brain that can do critical thinking.

Where do you draw the line to determine when to let a given situation up to God's sovereignty? Do I not take the medicine or get the surgery the doctor recommends because it may go against God's sovereignty.  Should I just wait and see if He heals me?  Should I not try to deceive would-be thieves by turning a light on, especially on a timer, when I am not home?  When King Saul pursued David to kill him, David hid.  He did not stand in the open, entrusting his life to the sovereignty of God.  We wear seat belts and obey traffic lights in heavily traffic-congested areas not because it is the law primarily, but we are protecting ourselves.  Are we not trusting God when we wear seat belts?  We do not walk alone down dark streets at night in major cities, unarmed, trusting our safety to the sovereignty of God.  Granted, these are not moral issues, but the principle is the same—we protect ourselves by avoiding those situations.  We do not stand in the middle of the street letting the consequences up to the sovereignty of God.  God has given us brains to think about the consequences of what we say and do, and using those brains is how we honor and trust God's sovereignty.

God does not produce miracles on demand to keep us from human dilemmas.  If you refuse the surgery or the medicine, you may have rejected God's sovereign way of healing you, and you may die.  God does not kill the mugger coming up behind you on the dark street—His sovereign plan was for you to think and avoid that situation.  If you stand in the middle of the street, a car will hit you because you did not use God's sovereign gift of a brain.  Do I drive with my eyes closed, expecting God to sovereignly guide me?  Should I not lock the doors of my car or my house—is that not an indication that I do not trust the sovereignty of God.  These would be foolish notions, but no more foolish than telling an Indian who just murdered nine of your children that you have another child or that God's spies are hiding on your roof.  The Lord wants us to critically think through these situations and keep ourselves well and safe, not flirt with death and destruction.  God not only does not produce miracles on demand to keep us from human dilemmas, He does not produce miracles on demand to keep us from moral dilemmas (or our stupidity).

If God intended to sovereignly intervene in these biblical situations, He could have made certain the accountability phase never occurred.  Abraham had to answer Pharaoh's and Abimelech's questions about Sarah.  If God planned to sovereignly intervene, He could have not allowed news about Sarah to reach Pharaoh and Abimelech's ears, but He did not do that.  Abraham had to face them both.  God could have sovereignly not allowed Pharaoh to order the death of Hebrew boys, or the Lord could have killed Pharaoh, but God did not do either.  The midwives had to face Pharaoh and give an account concerning why they were not murdering the children.  God could have sovereignly kept the presence of the spies in Jericho a secret, but He did not.  He could have killed the mayor, but He did not.  Rahab had to face the mayor and answer his questions.  Besides, God blessed them only after they obeyed the higher law.  God did not sovereignly intervene in these situations.

Satan tempted Jesus with a "trust God's sovereignty" scenario.  Satan took Jesus to the top of the Temple.  Satan says in Matthew 4:5, "If you are the Son of God, throw yourself down.  For it is written: 'He will command his angels concerning you, and they will lift you up in their hands, so that you will not strike your foot against a stone.'" Satan was telling Jesus to trust the sovereignty of God. Jesus objected, "It is also written: 'Do not put the Lord your God to the test.'" Responding to the Indian, "I have another child," and telling the mayor "The spies are on the roof," are putting the Lord to the test.

Moral issues are not the only exemptions to the law of God. For example, it would be a sin to approach someone and cut off his foot. However, if the person has gangrene, the right thing to do would be to amputate the foot to save the person's life. Should we prosecute the doctor? Of course not—the higher standards of mercy, justice, and love must be followed, exempting the doctor from prosecution. The doctor did what was right; she does not need to repent or apologize for removing the festering foot.

Killing someone is wrong and worthy of the death penalty. Numbers 35:16-21 says, "If a man strikes someone with an iron object so that he dies, he is a murderer; the murderer shall be put to death. Or if anyone has a stone in his hand that could kill, and he strikes someone so that he dies, he is a murderer; the murderer shall be put to death. Or if anyone has a wooden object in his hand that could kill, and he hits someone so that he dies, he is a murderer; the murderer shall be put to death. The avenger of blood shall put the murderer to death; when he meets him, he shall put him to death. If anyone with malice aforethought shoves another or throws something at him intentionally so that he dies or if in hostility he hits him with his fist so that he dies, that person shall be put to death; he is a murderer. The avenger of blood shall put the murderer to death when he meets him."

However, there is an exemption to this given in the next four verses, "But if without hostility someone suddenly shoves another or throws something at him unintentionally or, without seeing him, drops a stone on him that could kill him, and he dies, then since he was not his enemy and he did not intend to harm him, the assembly must judge between him and the avenger of blood according to these regulations. The assembly must protect the one accused of murder from the avenger of blood and send him back to the city of refuge to which he fled. He must stay there until the death of the high priest, who was anointed with the holy oil." If you inadvertently kill someone, you are exempt from the death penalty. There are exemptions to the laws of God in human interactions; there are exemptions when there is moral conflict as well. Telling someone to trust in the sovereignty of God begs the question—the person is saying there is a way to do right without real moral conflict and expect God to work a miracle. If God does not intervene, your child gets murdered. You put the Lord your God to the test. You are culpable for the murder of that child God gave you to protect.

Telling the Indian you have one more child may save you from a sin of commission, but what about the sins of omission—of mercy, love, and justice. Jesus said in Matthew 23:23, "Woe to you, teachers of the law and Pharisees, you hypocrites! You give a tenth of your spices—mint, dill, and cumin, but you have neglected the more important matters of the law—justice, mercy and faithfulness. You should have practiced the latter, without neglecting the former. You blind guides! You strain out a gnat but swallow a camel." To paraphrase Jesus,

"You would tell the truth, 'I have one more child,' but you let someone murder your son.  You blind guides!"

Besides these reasons previously mentioned, God taught and used Graded Absolutism.  It is time for the heavy artillery.

## Holy Cow

God reached the end of His patience with King Saul.  Saul had disobeyed the Lord time and again, and God wanted a new king to rule Israel.  God ordered Samuel (1 Samuel 16:1) to, "Fill your horn with oil and be on your way;  I am sending you to Jesse of Bethlehem.  I have chosen one of his sons to be king."  But Samuel objected, "How can I go?  Saul will hear about it and kill me."  Now the story gets interesting.  God did not tell Samuel to trust His sovereignty.  He did not tell Samuel, "Saul will never know."  He did not say, "Lie, and ask for forgiveness later." Instead, the Lord said, "Take a heifer with you and say, 'I have come to sacrifice to the LORD.'  Invite Jesse to the sacrifice, and I will show you what to do.  You are to anoint for me the one I indicate" (verses 2-3).

Charles Ryrie said, "The Lord did not suggest deception, but simply told Samuel to take care of the anointing while he was in Bethlehem on official business."[11]  Walvoord and Zuck copy Ryrie.[12]

I agree—to a point; God does not suggest deception; He gives Samuel a way to protect his life with a cow. The official business Samuel would be conducting in Bethlehem was not a sacrifice as Ryrie, Walvoord, and

Zuck implied (I guess trying to protect the integrity of God), but the business of anointing a king (the purpose of the oil). The sacrifice was secondary, not primary. If the main point was a sacrifice, Samuel could have done that where he was. God's purpose in sending Samuel to Bethlehem was not to sacrifice a cow; it was to anoint David king of Israel—that was the truth, but that was not what God told Samuel to tell King Saul if he asked. We have no record that Saul even asked, yet this is what God told Samuel to do just in case. God could have told Samuel. "I will make sure Saul does not find out," but the Lord makes no such promise. Unless we are to draw a principle from this passage (which I believe to be Graded Absolutism), why even record it in Scripture at all? The cow adds nothing to the story because Saul does not confront Samuel as far as we know. God practiced Graded Absolutism.

## You Take the High Road

Jesus did something similar to the cow story in John 7:1-13. In verses 1-9 we read, "After this, Jesus went around in Galilee, purposely staying away from Judea because the Jews there were waiting to take his life. But when the Jewish Feast of Tabernacles was near, Jesus' brothers said to him, 'You ought to leave here and go to Judea, so that your disciples may see the miracles you do. No one who wants to become a public figure acts in secret. Since you are doing these things, show yourself to the world.' For even His own brothers did not believe in Him. Therefore Jesus told them, 'The right time for me has not yet come; for you any time is right. The world cannot hate you, but it hates me because I testify that what it does is evil. You go to the Feast. I am not going up to this Feast, because for me the right time has not yet come.' Having said this, He stayed in Galilee."

The passage begins with, "After this." The "this" is Jesus telling the twelve disciples one of them would betray Him to death (John 6:70-71). Based on Judas' plot and the Jews in Judea wanting to kill Him, Jesus stayed in Galilee. His death would occur on His timetable, not theirs. Note He did not boldly walk through Judea trusting the sovereignty of God; He used wisdom and critical thinking, avoiding a dangerous situation, like us when we avoid dark city streets. Jesus' brothers mocked Him and told Him to go to Jerusalem and make a spectacle of Himself to get more followers. Knowing their mocking disbelief could cause Him trouble in Jerusalem, putting God to the test, Jesus told His brothers He was not going to the Feast. Based on this information, Jesus, who is God, will not go to the Feast of Tabernacles, right? Not exactly. Verse 10 says, "However, after his brothers had left for the Feast, He went also, not publicly, but in secret." Did Jesus change His mind? Did He lie? Did He have to track His brothers and apologize to them? Did He fail to trust the sovereignty of God?

The New International Version, following the lead of the King James Version, tried to circumvent the literal translation of this text by adding the word "yet" to verse 8, "I am not yet □ going up to this Feast," the "□" being added by the publisher to indicate the lack of textual support for the word "yet." The New American Standard Bible rightly does not insert the word "yet." (I guess someone added "yet" to a later manuscript who did not understand Hierarchicalism, trying to protect the integrity of Jesus.)

Albert Barnes avoided the whole issue saying, "We have here a signal instance of our Lord's prudence and opposition to parade. . . . He chose to forego these advantages rather than to afford an occasion of envy and jealousy to the rulers, or to appear even to excite a tumult among the people."13  The Text does not allow for an opposition to parade, but an opposition to a premature death.  Walvoord and Zuck tackled the issue head on:

> I am not yet going up to this Feast is clearly the thought in light of verse 10.  However, most Greek editions of the New Testament omit the word "yet," because it is considered a difficult reading, but it is more likely in the original.  If Jesus said, "I am not going up to the Feast," was He lying since He did go to the Feast (v. 10)?  No, He simply meant that He was not going up to the Feast "right then," as they suggested.  Jesus then for a time stayed in Galilee, doing the tasks of ministry which the Father had ordained.[14]

Paraphrasing, Walvoord and Zuck said, "There is little to no manuscript support for the word yet, but we are counting on it being in the original manuscript no one has seen in nearly 2,000 years." (I guess Walvoord and Zuck were again trying to protect the integrity of God.)  How convenient.  Can we use that argument for other texts we do not wish to follow or verses we do not like what they say?  Can we add words wherever we like?

Graded Absolutism provides the most logical, textually consistent explanation for these verses.  Jesus was avoiding a premature death His brothers could have caused, so He told them He was not going to the Feast. He did not lie; He was protecting a higher law of God— dying when the Father wanted Him to die and not putting the Father to the test.  Jesus was tempted in all ways like we are.

## They Passed on Passover

A great revival occurred during the reign of King Hezekiah after years of apostasy in Judah and Israel.  He wanted to re-instate the worship of YHWH.   The key annual Jewish Feast was Passover, which God commanded to be celebrated in the first month, Nisan.  However, "The king and his officials and the whole assembly in Jerusalem decided to celebrate the Passover in the second month. They had not been able to celebrate it at the regular time because not enough priests had consecrated themselves and the people had not assembled in Jerusalem" (2 Chronicles 30:2-3).   Using critical thinking skills and following the principle of Graded Absolutism—i.e., actually *celebrating* the Passover is more important than *when* you celebrate it, the king invited the whole nation to Jerusalem in the month of Ziv, the second month.  Verse four says, "The plan seemed right both to the king and to the whole assembly."

What did God think of this hierarchically-motivated decision that did not adhere to His command to meet in March?  As always, God blessed the Graded Absolutist decision.  Verse 12 says, "Also in Judah the hand of God was on the people to give them unity of mind to carry out what the king and his officials had ordered, following the word of the LORD."  Even though God said Passover was to be observed during the first month (and a certain day in that month), and they were celebrating Passover in the second month, God said they were "following the word of the LORD." Hezekiah prayed for the people, "and the LORD heard Hezekiah and healed the people" (verse 20). The chapter concludes in verses 25 to 27, "The entire assembly of Judah rejoiced, along with the priests and Levites and all who had assembled from Israel, including the aliens who had come from Israel and those who lived in Judah. There was great joy in Jerusalem, for since the days of Solomon son of David king of Israel there had been nothing like this in Jerusalem. The priests and the Levites stood to bless the people, and God heard them, for their prayer reached heaven, His holy dwelling place."

That the Jews celebrated the Passover was more important than when they celebrated it, even though the when was a law of God. The people did not need to repent for celebrating the Passover in the wrong month. The Jews did not wait for revelation from God or wait until the next Nisan. They celebrated late, and God loved it. Isn't that just like God?

## Worship Me or I'll Fire You
The revival during King Hezekiah's reign did not last long. The Jews abandoned the worship of YHWH, and in 586 B.C., God sent them into captivity in Babylon. Nebuchadnezzar, the king of Babylon, ordered a statue to be built of himself in his honor in a valley surrounded by mountains (Daniel 3). The king assembled all his government workers and officials before the idol, and commanded everyone to bow when the band played. Among the throng were Jewish

captives Shadrach, Meshach, and Abed-Nego. Suddenly, the hills were alive with the sound of music. More than 99% of these sycophants fell. You would have thought that someone had yelled "Incoming!"

As these government officials cowered like dogs and the dust settled, three lonely figures were still standing, defiantly—Shadrach, Meshach, and Abed-Nego. Bowing to this statue was abhorrent to them. They knew Exodus 20:4-5, "You shall not make for yourself an idol, or any likeness of what is in heaven above or on the earth beneath or in the water under the earth. You shall not worship them or serve them; for I, the LORD your God, am a jealous God, visiting the iniquity of the fathers on the children, on the third and the fourth generations of those who hate Me."

They could have rationalized this away. "When in Babylon, do as the Babylonians do." "We can just pretend to bow down, but in our hearts we are really standing up." "The king has been so good to us. It would be ungrateful not to bow." "We are being forced against our will to bow. God will forgive us." "No one back in Jerusalem will ever know whether we bow or not." "Everyone else is bowing down." "If we do not bow, we'll be killed." When you want to compromise, you can always find an excuse, but since they intended to obey God, they did not need any excuses.

The three Jewish captives refused to bow, and news of their rebellion reached the king. Nebuchadnezzar was dumb-founded and enraged. "His furnace was hot, but he was hotter."[15] "This is the thanks I get for capturing you and let you serve me?" Nebuchadnezzar was furious and ordered Shadrach, Meshach, and Abed-Nego to answer to him for their crime. He must have lowered his own thermostat because he decided to give the three another chance. "Maybe you did not understand, so I will give you another chance, bow or burn (verses 14-15)." The pressure was on. Not to bow in the valley absent the king was one thing, but to defy the king to his face next to his furnace was quite formidable.

Shadrach, Meshach, and Abed-Nego replied to the king in verses 16 to 18, "O Nebuchadnezzar, we do not need to defend ourselves before you in this matter. If we are thrown into the blazing furnace, the God we serve is able to save us from it, and He will rescue us from your hand, O king. But even if he does not, we want you to know, O king, that we will not serve your gods or worship the image of gold you have set up."

They did not know what was about to happen, and they did not care. The only power the king had over them was the power of death, and since they were not afraid to die, he had no power at all. The king could not intimidate them because they were ready to die if need be. What can you do with men like that?

Observe the excellence of their faith. They recognized obeying God might not be pleasant to them. Even so, they did not make their own obedience contingent on God doing what they wanted. They knew God could save them. They did not know if He would save them. They determined to obey the Lord either way.

So many Christians want to make deals with God. "Lord, I'll stand up for you as long as (pick one) (A) I do not lose my job, (B) my friends do not make fun of me, (C) I still get that promotion, (D) I do not get in trouble with my boss, (E) I can still have a successful career." But God does not make deals with anyone. He calls us to be faithful and we are called to leave the results with Him. He does not promise us an easy road if we decide to be faithful to Him, and that's why these three young men said, "But if not . . . " They knew God could save them, but they also knew He might have higher purposes in mind that would require their death. They knew they were pawns in God's life chess match. Therefore, they did not try to back God into a corner or test Him by demanding the Almighty work a miracle on their behalf. They accepted God's will in advance without knowing or worrying about how the situation would work out.

Shadrach, Meshach, and Abed-Nego used critical thinking skills that resulted in faith in their great God. Hebrews 11:26 says they quenched the fury of the flames by faith. They used critical thinking skills—"God can save, but even if not, we will not bow to your idol or to you." Their convictions were not for sale. Not at any price, not even their own lives. They did not bow. They did not bend. "We are in Babylon, but we will not do what you do."[16]

While all the other government officials decided to bow, not burn, the three would rather burn than bow. Nebuchadnezzar obliged them because they rained on his parade. The king had the flames made hotter. They probably poured on oil. The flames were so hot that the strong men who were heating the furnace were cremated on the spot.

As Shadrach, Meshach, and Abed-Nego were cast into the furnace, they were not expecting deliverance. As far as they knew, they were about to perish in the flames. That raises a question. Why did God let things go this far?

Nebuchadnezzar asked, "What god can deliver from my hands?" He was about to find out. Instead of three men, he sees four. Instead of being bound, they are free. Instead of burning, they are playing. Instead of trying to get out, they are content to stay in. Shadrach, Meshach, and Abed-Nego did not forswear, founder, falter, flinch, fib, freeze, fear, faint, fade, or fail. They were unbending, unbound, unburned, unbeaten, and unbreakable. But we know their God, so it is not unbelievable. God delivered Shadrach, Meshach, and Abed-Nego from the king's hands. Isn't that just like our God?

"Now wait," you may object. "Shadrach, Meshach, and Abed-Nego do not try to spare their lives like the people in the previous examples had done." This is true, but the situation is different. In the former examples, the sanctity of life trumped telling the truth. Here, the worship of God, the greatest commandment, trumps the sanctity of life. We can build a deductive syllogism:

The sanctity of life is a higher law than telling the truth.

- The worship of God is a higher law than the sanctity of life.

- Therefore, the worship of God is a higher law than telling the truth.

"If we are thrown into the blazing furnace, the God we serve is able to save us from it, and He will rescue us from your hand, O king. But even if he does not . . . " They did not bow; they did not bend; they did not burn. Situations that entail the greatest commandment are where we commit ourselves to the sovereignty of God. We may have to die to keep the greatest commandment, but as Esther said as she planned to go in unannounced before her husband, King Ahasuareus, "If I perish, I perish" (Esther 4:16). Honoring God is the most important thing we do. Jesus warns us to be prepared for death. Revelation 2:10 says, "Do not be afraid of what you are about to suffer. I tell you, the devil will put some of you in prison to test you, and you will suffer persecution for ten days. Be faithful, even to the point of death, and I will give you the crown of life." There is a reward in Heaven for those who are martyred for keeping the greatest commandment. If given the chance, be a man and do not miss it.

Polycarp was the Bishop of Smyrna (to whom Revelation 2:10 was addressed). "Prior to his martyrdom in A. D. 160, Polycarp uttered these noble worlds to his heathen judges who wanted him to renounce his faith. He said, 'Eighty-six years have I served the Lord, and He never wronged me; how then can I blaspheme my King and Savior?'"[17]

Trust God when called upon to honor His Name; He knows what He is doing. No matter what happens, God is in control. In situations like these is where we can do nothing but depend on God's sovereignty.

## They Just Kept Lion There

In Daniel 6, Shadrach, Meshach, and Abed-Nego's friend Daniel found himself in a similar situation as his buddies. Another king, Darius the Mede, ruled Babylon. Some government leaders conspired against Daniel and asked Darius to pass a law that no one be allowed to petition any god or government leader except King Darius for 30 days. Humbly, Darius signed the legislation. The story continues in verses 10 to 15:

> Now when Daniel learned that the decree had been published, he went home to his upstairs room where the windows opened toward Jerusalem. Three times a day he got down on his knees and prayed, giving thanks to his God, just as he had done before. Then these men went as a group and found Daniel praying and asking God for help. So they went to the king and spoke to him about his royal decree: 'Did you not publish a decree that during the next thirty days anyone who prays to any god or man except to you, O king, would be thrown into the lions' den?'

> The king answered, 'The decree stands—in accordance with the laws of the Medes and Persians, which cannot be repealed.'

> Then they said to the king, 'Daniel, who is one of the exiles from Judah, pays no attention to you, O king, or to the decree you put in writing. He still prays three times a day.' When the king heard this, he was greatly distressed; he was determined to rescue Daniel and made every effort until sundown to save him.

Then the men went as a group to the king and said to him, 'Remember, O king, that according to the law of the Medes and Persians no decree or edict that the king issues can be changed.'

These government officials trapped the king and Daniel. Darius had no choice but to throw Daniel in the lion's den. However, God sovereignly spared Daniel. Isn't that just like God? In verses 21 to 22 Daniel says, "O king, live forever! My God sent His angel, and He shut the mouths of the lions. They have not hurt me, because I was found innocent in His sight. Nor have I ever done any wrong before you, O king."

Notice carefully what Daniel said—"I am innocent before God and before you," even though Daniel disobeyed the law of government. By obeying the greater law of God to worship Him in prayer, Daniel was not guilty of not obeying the lower law of obeying the government. This is a key passage—you are innocent of breaking a lower law if you are obeying a higher law. Daniel did not need to repent for praying; he broke the lower law of disobedience to the government. He was innocent, but it did mean He had to trust the continuance of his life to the sovereignty of God. Worshiping God was more important than the sanctity and continuance of his life. Obeying God in these circumstances may have severe consequences, including death, but obey God we must.

## God Over Government

Paul is quite clear in Romans 13:1-2, "Everyone must submit himself to the governing authorities, for there is no authority except that which God has established.

The authorities that exist have been established by God. Consequently, he who rebels against the authority is rebelling against what God has instituted, and those who do so will bring judgment on themselves." However, when the government intrudes on the worship of God or the salvation of humans, the government must be disobeyed because worship and evangelism are more important than any government edict.

## Apostolic Absolutism

The apostles followed Graded Absolutism. In Acts 4:1-3, the Jewish authorities in Jerusalem arrested Peter and John for preaching the gospel in the Temple and threw them in jail. Rome gave the Jewish religious leaders the authority to legislate and enforce civil law in Jerusalem.[18] They ordered Peter and John, "Not to speak at all in the Name of Jesus" (Acts 4:18). Obeying the higher law of evangelism, Peter and John replied in verses 19 and 20, "Judge for yourselves whether it is right in God's sight to obey you rather than God. For we cannot help speaking about what we have seen and heard." They had a backbone—Peter and John get an A in critical thinking.

God honored their decision to evangelize the lost over obeying the government. After being released from custody, the Christians gathered together and prayed, committing their lives to the worship of God and to the proclamation of the gospel. Verse 31 says, "After they prayed, the place where they were meeting was shaken. And they were all filled with the Holy Spirit and spoke the word of God boldly." Graded Absolutism again ruled the day. However, the Jews did not like being disobeyed.

The religious leaders again arrested the apostles for preaching and tossed them in jail. However, God sent an angel to unlock the prison cell and release the apostles. Isn't that just like God? The Lord honored their decision not to obey the government in favor of obeying His higher law of evangelism. The Jews said to the apostles, "We gave you strict orders not to teach in this Name. Yet you have filled Jerusalem with your teaching and are determined to make us guilty of this man's blood." Peter and the other apostles replied, "We must obey God rather than men!" The apostles argued using Graded Absolutism as their guide.

The Council ordered the apostles to be flogged for their "disobedience," commanded them to speak no more in the Name of Jesus, and released them from prison. In disobedience to the Council and in obedience to the higher law of God, "We must obey God rather than men!," they returned to evangelism.

## Wheat Whining

"At that time Jesus went through the grain fields on the Sabbath. His disciples were hungry and began to pick some heads of grain and eat them. When the Pharisees saw this, they said to Him, 'Look! Your disciples are doing what is unlawful on the Sabbath.'

He answered, "Have not you read what David did when he and his companions were hungry? He entered the house of God, and he and his companions ate the consecrated bread—which was not lawful for them to do, but only for the priests. Or have not you read in the Law that on the Sabbath the priests in the temple desecrate the day and yet are innocent? I tell you that one greater than the temple is here. If you had known what these words mean, 'I desire mercy, not sacrifice,' you would not have condemned the innocent. For the Son of Man is Lord of the Sabbath'" (Matthew 12:1-8).

It was a norm in Jesus' day to pick grain and eat it as you walked through someone's field. However, the rabbis said you were working in violation of the fourth commandment if you picked grain on the Sabbath, particularly threshing and winnowing by removing the kernels from the grain. Jesus made several Graded Absolutist points in this passage. The rabbinical laws about the Sabbath—it is work to pick grain and eat it—did not have to be obeyed because they were a misinterpretation of what God intended when He wrote the laws. God's intended meaning supersedes human interpretation and application (see chapter 7). Jesus declared Himself and His disciples "innocent" in verse seven, yet they were disobeying their religious leaders.

Next, David did something "worse" on the Sabbath—he and his partners ate bread in the Tabernacle that God commanded to be eaten only by the priests. It was not lawful to eat this bread, but they were innocent because people being hungry and feeding them (showing love and mercy) is more important than the law of consecrating bread to the priests. David did not steal this bread; Ahimilech the priest offered it to David and his men after David asked for something to eat. One law was more important than the other. Third, God said no one was to work on the Sabbath, but priests worked in the Tabernacle on the Sabbath, and were innocent. One law was more important than the other.

Jesus promulgated this same principle in Matthew 12:9-14, "Going on from that place, He went into their synagogue, and a man with a shriveled hand was there. Looking for a reason to accuse Jesus, they asked Him, 'Is it lawful to heal on the Sabbath?' He said to them, 'If any of you has a sheep and it falls into a pit on the Sabbath, will you not take hold of it and lift it out? How much more valuable is a man than a sheep! Therefore it is lawful to do good on the Sabbath.' Then He said to the man, 'Stretch out your hand.' So he stretched it out and it was completely restored, just as sound as the other. But the Pharisees went out and plotted how they might kill Jesus." Jesus elevated God's authorial intent of a text above incorrect human interpretation and application of a passage. Note that although you may be right in God's eyes about how to handle a conflict between God's laws, those around you may not agree and attack you. Jesus had a backbone, but by His own choice, He would feel their wrath at the cross.

## When in Rome

When Peter wrote 1 Peter, he says in 5:13 the Church in Babylon, where he evidently was, sent their greetings. However, Peter was not in the literal Babylon; he was in Rome. "The secrecy with which Peter conveys greetings reflects not only the perilous times in which he and his readers lived, but also the desire to protect the church from possible harm."[19] By the time Peter penned this epistle, persecution had already begun in Rome under emperor Nero. Peter was not forthright about his location to protect his life. He did not give his location and trust the sovereignty of God.

## Two for Ten

One of the teachers of the law asked Jesus, "Of all the commandments, which is the most important" (Mark 12:28)? If the Unqualified position is true, Jesus would have answered, "All laws are equal," but He does not. Verses 29 to 31 say, "The most important one," answered Jesus, "is this: 'Hear, O Israel, the Lord our God, the Lord is one. Love the Lord your God with all your heart and with all your soul and with all your mind and with all your strength.' The second is this: 'Love your neighbor as yourself.' There is no commandment greater than these."

The greatest commandment summarizes the first four of the Ten Commandments:

- You shall have no other gods before me.

- You shall not make for yourself an idol in the form of anything in heaven above or on the earth beneath or in the waters below. You shall not bow down to them or worship them; for I, the Lord your God, am a jealous God, punishing the children for the sin of the fathers to the third and fourth generation of those who hate me, but showing love to a thousand generations of those who love me and keep my commandments.

- You shall not misuse the Name of the Lord your God, for the Lord will not hold anyone guiltless who misuses His Name.

- Remember the Sabbath day by keeping it holy. (God no longer requires Sabbath observance, so it is not part of the hierarchy).

Since these are the greatest commandments (If "A"), they supersede all other laws of God (then "B"). The first three commandments trump any other laws of God or man with which they would ever conflict. However, these three commandments can never conflict with one another. These are the only laws of God where your option is to obey them and trust in the sovereignty of God about the future length of your life or someone else's life. When the conflict before you involves one of the first three commandments, the greatest commandment according to Jesus, your job is to be faithful and let God take care of the results. Be faithful. Stand tall. Obey God. Live for Him. Do what you know is right and let God take care of what happens next.

When you stand up for Jesus, Jesus stands up with you (note Nebuchadnezzar saw four people in the flame, not three, and Jesus stood as Stephen was being stoned). Not just that He stands up for you (that is true), but He stands up with you, by your side. There is a blessing reserved for bold believers that cowardly Christians never know. Jesus stands with those who stand up for Him. That's all we need to know. The rest is up to God.

The second greatest commandment encompasses the last six of the Ten Commandments:

- Honor your father and your mother, so that you may live long in the land the Lord your God is giving you.
- You shall not murder.

- You shall not commit adultery.
- You shall not steal.
- You shall not give false testimony against your neighbor.
- You shall not covet your neighbor's house. You shall not covet your neighbor's wife, or his manservant or maidservant, his ox or donkey, or anything that belongs to your neighbor.

Other than the first four commandments, these six commandments trump any other laws of God or man with which they would ever conflict. Since God required the death penalty for violation of numbers five to seven, and did not require the death penalty for numbers eight to ten, if any one of numbers five to seven conflicts with any of numbers eight to ten, numbers five to seven must be considered more important than numbers eight to ten.

## Greater Sins

Jesus made it clear some sins were worse than others. In Matthew 12:31 Jesus said there is an unforgivable sin— blasphemy against the Holy Spirit. In John 19:9-11, we have this dialogue between Pilate and Jesus:

- 'Where do you come from?' Pilate asked Jesus, but Jesus gave him no answer. '

- Do you refuse to speak to me?' Pilate said. 'Do not you realize I have power either to free you or to crucify you?'

- Jesus answered, 'You would have no power over me if it were not given to you from above. Therefore the one who handed me over to you is guilty of a *greater sin.*'

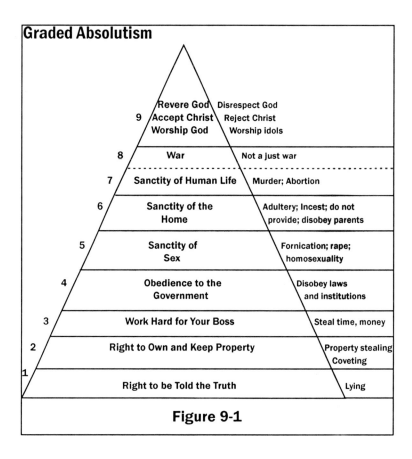

**Figure 9-1**

## Constructing the Hierarchy

Figure 9-1 is how I biblically construct the hierarchy. The apex of the pyramidal hierarchy (number 9) represents commandments one to three, there is a section with dashed lines for those instances when your nation is at war, but this level only applies at that time (I will discuss this later), and the other commandments are under a time of war. Note that lines do not separate the three commandments listed in the apex of the pyramid since these laws can never conflict with each other. For example, I will never have to choose between worshiping God and accepting Christ for salvation. Examples of sin you commit if you do not obey God are listed to the right of the pyramidal hierarchy. From Jesus' statement in Mark 12:29-31, the apex of the pyramidal hierarchy represents the greatest commandment to love God, the eight under layers represent the second greatest commandment to love your neighbor as you love yourself. I added "Work Hard for Your Boss" at number three based on Ephesians 6:5-8. "Slaves, obey your earthly masters with respect and fear, and with sincerity of heart, just as you would obey Christ. Obey them not only to win their favor when their eye is on you, but like slaves of Christ, doing the will of God from your heart. Serve wholeheartedly, as if you were serving the Lord, not men, because you know that the Lord will reward everyone for whatever good he does, whether he is slave or free." Since the government regulates business, I put "Work Hard for Your Boss" beneath the government.

Anytime a situation entails a lower law conflicting with a higher law, obey the higher law, and you are not guilty of breaking the lower law. Should Abraham have said that Sarah was his sister based on what he understood about his life being taken? The sanctity of life (number 7) is greater than (>) the right to be told the truth (number 1), or 7>1, so protect the sanctity of life. Abraham was not a liar since he was protecting a higher law.

## Caesar Said it is Safer to be Herod's Pig than His Son

King Herod ordered the Magi to return to him and tell the whereabouts of the Christ Child (Matthew 2:8). God warned the Magi in a dream not to return to Herod, a conflict of laws number 4 and 9.  Since 9>4, the Magi returned home another way and did not need to apologize to Herod.  This situation would also work 7>4, but the Magi did not seem to understand Herod's obsession with killing everyone he suspected was trying to usurp his throne, including his wife and two of his children.  No wonder all Jerusalem was upset when the Magi asked, "Where is He who is born King of the Jews?"

## Celebrity Roast

God ordered Abraham to murder his son as a sacrifice.  Since 9>7, Abraham planned to kill his son.  He would have scarified Isaac on that altar if God had not stopped him (Genesis 22:12).  From this passage we glean another hierarchical principle—God's latest commands ("Do not lay a hand on the boy.  Do not do anything to him.") trump His earlier commands ("Take your son, your only son, Isaac, whom you love, and go to the region of Moriah.  Sacrifice him there as a burnt offering on one of the mountains I will tell you about.").  Hence, we are not under law but under grace (Romans 6:15).

## Honest Indian

How would you answer the Indian about whether you have another child?  Again, 7>1, so you say, "No, I do not have another child."

The boss says, "If that is Bill Murphy, tell him I am not in."  You may lose your job if you do not lie.  What do you do?  It looks like number one is conflicting with number six (providing for the needs of your family).  After all, 6>1.

However, it only appears to be a conflict because in your mind you have crafted a Bifurcation, or False Dilemma Fallacy (see chapter 8). There are not just two options. Although you may not like the consequences, the biblical recourse is to tell the truth. You could tell Bill Murphy that the boss is unavailable right now and offer to take a message. Since there is no conflict, to say, "The boss is not in," is lying.

You know the project is not designed as well as it should be, but you are scheduled to sell it to the Board of Directors at 2:00 p.m. What do you do? Since there is no moral conflict, you tell the truth. You have a responsibility to work hard for your boss.

Your phone at home rings at 7:30 a.m. and wakens you. You pick up the receiver to hear, "Did I wake you?" You cringe because it is okay the person called, but you do not want them to feel badly because they wakened you, or you may not want them to think that you are lazy. What do you do? There is no conflict morally, so you tell the truth. You could just tell the person, "It's okay; I had to get up to answer the phone anyway."

Would you fund a missionary who was smuggling Bibles into a Muslim country in disobedience to the Muslim government? Since 9>4, you fund the missionary if that is your desire.

If a Muslim terrorist pointed a gun at your wife, husband, or child's head and said, "Denounce Christ or I pull the trigger," what would you do? Since 9>7, "I will not renounce Christ!" is the only answer. At that point you can only trust the sovereignty of God since one of the three parts of the greatest commandment is involved.

Is it lying to keep a light on in your house to deceive burglars, making them incorrectly think that you are home? Since 2>1, and if you are home, 7>1, turn on the light; even get a timer for it.

Does a wife have to stay, in the name of submission, with a husband who beats her? Since what he is doing is sin, and since beating your wife is an incorrect interpretation and application of submission, she does not have to stay with him. Since beatings can lead to death, and 7>6, she may leave. However, I can find no grounds for her to re-marry. She can re-marry only if he commits adultery or leaves her because he is a non-Christian.

The federal government bans Christian worship: do you attend an underground church? 9>4, so you attend (cf. Hebrews 10:25).

The government decides to take your children when they are two-years-old to rear them since you are a Christian. Do you let them? God gave those children to you to rear, not the state. 6>4, so hide, or do something to train and rear your own children.

The government decides to tax the church. Should your church pay? Your church pays because 4>2. This would violate the First Amendment to the U. S. Constitution, but taxing the church does not violate any biblical law. In Matthew 22:21, Jesus said, "Give to Caesar what is Caesar's, and to God what is God's."

You and your family are hungry and you have no food or money? May you steal to feed them? Hunger is not a moral conflict. You can ask other people to help you or you can do menial tasks to raise money for food. Proverbs 6:30-31 says, "Men do not despise a thief if he steals to satisfy his hunger when he is starving. Yet if he is caught, he must pay sevenfold, though it costs him all the wealth of his house." David and his band ate consecrated bread because they were hungry, but they first asked for food; they did not steal it.

Can you not pay income taxes to feed your hungry family? You must pay your taxes since there is no conflict. "Give to Caesar." 4>2.

Christians in China are told not to have more than one child. Should they obey the government? 6>4, so they should have as many as children as they want; but they must be willing to pay the consequences for disobeying a communist government.

I support a form of civil disobedience when the government conflicts with higher laws on the hierarchy (so did Shadrach, Meshach, Abed-Nego, Daniel, Peter, and Paul). Because of this, I find another reason to reject the Unqualified Absolutism position and find it untenable.

Do you strike if you believe your union is wrong? Since you work for the company, not the union, there is no moral conflict. You are to work hard for you boss, so you do not go on strike. What if you believe your union is right? I see no difference in your response. You work for the company, not the union.

Instances of two laws conflicting are rare. In my 50+ years on Earth, I have only faced it once. It is not a common problem in the Bible either, but these situations do occasionally, but rarely occur.

## More on the Sanctity of Human Life

Concerning the sanctity of human life, two lives are better than one. You may have to make decisions to save a greater amount of lives without being able to save all lives. Suppose Muslim terrorists have captured four people. You stumble upon them and see they are about to execute all four prisoners. One of the terrorists grabs you and hands you a gun. He says, "If you kill one of these prisoners, we will let the other three live. If you do not kill one of them, we will kill all of them." What would you do? Since three lives are more important than one life, I would pull the trigger, shaking and probably vomiting, to save as many lives as I could. "They may be lying to you," you object. True, but I do not know that. I do know if I do not pull the trigger they are all dead. I would do what I could to save as many lives as possible.

Another scenario concerning the sanctity of human life is: actual life is more important than potential life. If a pregnant woman has cancer and will not live if she does not have chemotherapy, but taking the chemotherapy will result in the death of the unborn child, what do you do? You cannot go wrong either way. You can decide to save the life of the mother or the mother may sacrifice her own life to let the baby live.

The pro-life movement has erred in regards to Hierarchicalism, contributing to the continued murder of unborn children. If pro-lifers would recognize that it is better to save most babies than none at all, laws could be enacted to stop most abortions. Pro-lifers cannot reach unanimity because of the issues of abortion in the cases of rape, incest, and saving the life of the mother, and therefore do not get any legislation passed through Congress, and we stop none of the abortions. I agree with most pro-lifers that it is murder to abort a baby because the mother was the victim of rape or incest. However, I believe it is better to allow abortions for the few cases of rape and incest than to have no laws restricting abortions for the convenience of the mother. Many pro-lifers take an all or nothing position, and get nothing but the destruction of millions of babies.

Senator Dick Durbin (D, IL), went to Washington believing in the pro-life position. He is now pro-choice. Tim Russert, on NBC News' "Meet the Press" asked Durbin what caused his change of heart. Durbin replied:

> Well, at that point, I can tell you I came to Congress not having seen what I think is the important part of this debate and not understanding, if you will, really what was behind it. You know, it is a struggle for me. It still is. I am opposed to abortion. If any woman in my family said she was seeking abortion, I'd go out of my way to try to dissuade them from making that decision. But I was really discouraged when I came to Washington to find that the opponents of abortion were also opponents of family planning. This did not make any sense to me. And I was also discouraged by the fact that they were absolute, no exceptions

for rape and incest, the most extraordinary medical situations. And I finally came to the conclusion that we really have to try to honor the Roe vs. Wade thinking, that there are certain times in the life of a woman that she needs to make that decision with her doctor, with her family and with her conscience and that the government shouldn't be intruding.[20]

The "all-or-nothing" approach gets pro-lifers nothing. Columnist Terence Jeffrey rightly concluded about Senator Durbin's remarks:

This is not only devoid of constitutional reasoning, it is devoid of all reasoning. Durbin effectively argues: Because some pro-lifers do not believe in family planning or rape or incest or other exceptions, the U.S. Constitution guarantees a right to abortion.[21]

Whether the argument is illogical or not, even anti-abortionists use it to oppose legislating the murder of millions of children.

Following the principle that two lives are better than one, we can enact legislation allowing for abortions in the cases of rape and incest (as well as saving the life of the mother) and outlawing abortion for all other reasons. We would eliminate at least 95% of the abortions, saving millions of lives. It is morally and ethically wrong not to support this legislation because a majority of Americans would support it, Congress would pass it, and we could save babies. Ironically, it is the pro-lifers who do not support this legislation, and the pro-abortion crowd keeps disposing of our precious children unrestricted, but at least we are "standing by our principles"—yet a baby is murdered every 20 seconds. After the law is passed we can work on persuading the public that abortion for rape and incest is wrong. Let's do some critical thinking about this.

## Isn't this Situational Ethics in Disguise?

Situationism says you are always obligated to act in love. The problem is, acting in love is subjective. The situation in which you find yourself determines what you do as you act in love toward others, and that by your own norms and values, not God's.

Graded absolutism rejects situationism as a means of action. "The situation does not determine what is right; God does. The situation simply helps us discover which of God's laws is the one applicable there."[22]

## Just in Case there is a Just War

The first cogent argument for determining a just war was presented by Thomas Aquinas (1225-1274) in The Summa Theologica, Question 40.[23] Vincent Ferraro, the Ruth C. Lawson Professor of International Politics at Mount Holyoke College summarized Aquinas' views of a just war:

- A just war can only be waged as a last resort. All non-violent options must be exhausted before the use of force can be justified.

- A war is just only if it is waged by a legitimate authority. Even just causes cannot be served by actions taken by individuals or groups who do not constitute an authority sanctioned by whatever the society and outsiders to the society deem legitimate.

- A just war can only be fought to redress a wrong suffered.  For example, self-defense against an armed attack is always considered to be a just cause (although the justice of the cause is not sufficient—see point #4).  Further, a just war can only be fought with "right" intentions: the only permissible objective of a just war is to redress the injury.

- A war can only be just if it is fought with a reasonable chance of success.  Deaths and injury incurred in a hopeless cause are not morally justifiable. The ultimate goal of a just war is to re-establish peace. More specifically, the peace established after the war must be preferable to the peace that would have prevailed if the war had not been fought.

- The violence used in the war must be proportional to the injury suffered.  States are prohibited from using force not necessary to attain the limited objective of addressing the injury suffered.

- The weapons used in war must discriminate between combatants and non-combatants. Civilians are never permissible targets of war, and every effort must be taken to avoid killing civilians.  The deaths of civilians are justified only if they are unavoidable victims of a deliberate attack on a military target.[24]

I add three more qualifications:

- Combatants must be distinguishable from noncombatants, based on the Geneva Conventions.

- There must be a withdrawal strategy.

- There must be a definition of victory before going to war.

For a war to be just, it must meet all ten criteria; if it does not meet all ten requirements, it is an unjust war. If the government declares an unjust war, it has usurped its authority and you are right not to participate in the conflict. However, if the war meets the just-war criteria, the war then assumes number 8 ranking on the pyramidal hierarchy. You are then obligated to fight in the war if called on to do so by the government. You must obey every lawful order given to you, and since 8>7, you are not guilty of murder or assault if you injure or take the life of any enemy combatant. (The same is true for police officers who have to use lethal force.) You need not ask God for forgiveness.

During World War II, the British secret service broke the Nazi's code and told Winston Churchill the Germans planned to bomb Coventry. Churchill could either warn the citizens of the town and save many lives at the expense of alerting the Germans the code had been broken, or do nothing, which would result in many dead British citizens, but be able to interpret what the Nazi's were planning to do, and possibly save many more lives. Churchill rightly chose the latter option.[25] Saving many lives is more important than saving a few lives.

Terrorists are waging an unjust war. Although the inept United Nations cannot define a terrorist,[25] the word is not hard to define. A terrorist is a person who does not wear a military uniform (in violation of the Geneva Conventions) and intentionally targets civilians with acts of war and vicious violence to cause fear in the general public. The terrorists' goal is that the fear will result in their desired political change. Terrorists wage an unjust war (If A) and should not be accorded the provisions of the Geneva Conventions (then B).

## Was Corrie Ten Boom Right?

Should you have hidden Jews in your home if you had lived in Germany during World War II? Yes you should have; it was an unjust war from Germany's standpoint, so war (position number 8) was removed from the hierarchy—7>1.

## Conclusion

The charge that Hierarchicalism is lazy thinking sounds ludicrous to me. It is a logical attempt to make sense of some difficult passages God does not explain clearly. It makes this chaotic, sin-soaked world a little saner to survive in.

In this chapter we dealt with one branch of axiology called ethics; in the next chapter we will investigate aesthetics, which sets standards for artwork and tries to determine art's meaning in human experience.

**Between two evils,**

**I always pick the one I never tried before.**

**Mae West**

## For Review and Discussion

- Did Abraham lie about Sarah being his sister?  Explain your answer.

- Would you have told the Kentucky Indian you had another child?  Explain your answer, including your view of lying in this case?

- List three of your values other than those listed in the text.

- Explain Unqualified Absolutism.

- Explain Conflicting Absolutism.

- Explain Graded Absolutism.

- To which of the three previous theories do you ascribe, and explain why.

- Explain whether Rahab's faith included saying the spies left town.

- Why does God not always sovereignly intervene to stop bad things from happening to us?

- What difference is there between an exception to a law and an exemption from a law?

- If a parent told the Kentucky Indian there was another child, and the Indian found and murdered the child, was the parent culpable?  Explain your answer.

- Was Samuel's purpose traveling to Bethlehem to sacrifice a cow?  Why did God tell him to do this? Explain a modern-day parallel situation.

- Why was God pleased with Israel during Hezekiah's reign for not obeying His command to celebrate Passover in March?

- During what types of moral dilemmas do you exactly tell the truth requested of you, then leave the results to the sovereignty of God?  Why then?

- Evaluate the Graded Absolutism hierarchy.  What are its strengths and weaknesses?

- Was Churchill right not to warn the people of Coventry the Nazis were coming?  Explain your answer.

# ENDNOTES

1. "How Do You Decide Whom to Marry?" Car Talk. 2005.<http://www.cartalk.com/content/read-on/2000/ 03.18.html>.

2. Prager, Dennis. "The Case for Judeo-Christian Values: Values vs. (Liberal) Feelings." Jewish World Review. <http://www.jewishworldreview.com/0205/prager.php3?printer_friendly>.

3. Reeves, Stanley, J. Auburn University. <http://www.eng.auburn.edu/~sjreeves/ cm/ethics.html>.

4. Ibid.

5. Ibid.

6. For a thorough rebuttal of the arguments against Hierarchicalism, see Norman Geisler's Christian Ethics, pp. 122-130.

7. Reeves.

8. Geisler, Norman L. Christian Ethics: Options and Issues. Grand Rapids, MI: Baker Book House, 1989, p. 116.

9. Wiersbe, Warren. Expository Outlines on the Old Testament. CD-ROM. Disc 3. Hiawatha, IA: Parson's Technology, 1999, n. p.

10. Walvoord, John F. and Roy B. Zuck, eds. The Bible Knowledge Commentary: Old Testament. Wheaton, IL: Victor Books, 1985, p. 331.

11. Ryrie, Charles Caldwell. The Ryrie Study Bible: New American Standard Translation. Chicago: Moody Press, 1976, p. 434.

12. Walvoord and Zuck, p. 448.

13. Barnes, Albert. Barnes' Notes on the New Testament. CD-ROM. Disc 2. Hiawatha, IA: Parson's Technology, 1999, n. p.

14. Walvoord, John F. and Roy B. Zuck, eds. The Bible Knowledge Commentary: New Testament. Wheaton, IL: Victor Books, 1985, p. 299.

15. Strauss, Lehman. The Prophecies of Daniel. Neptune, NJ: Loizeaux Brothers, 1969,   p. 97

16. Ibid, p. 100.

17. Walvoord, John and Roy B. Zuck, eds. The Bible Knowledge Commentary: New Testament. CD-ROM. Disc 2. Hiawatha, IA: Parson's Technology, 1999.

18. Class notes from Dr. Robert Willey, Book of Acts course, Lancaster Bible College.

19. Kistemaker, Simon J. New Testament Commentary: Peter and Jude. Grand Rapids, MI: Baker Book House, 1987, p. 19.

20. NBC News' "Meet the Press." "Transcript for July 24: Fred Thompson, Dick Durbin, David Gregory, William Safire, Stuart Taylor and Nina Totenberg." 24 July 2005. <http://msnbc.msn.com/id/8658626>

21. Jeffrey, Terence. "Dick Durbin's Evolving Standard of Decency." Townhall.com. 27 July 2005. <http://www.townhall.com/columnists/terencejeffrey/tj20050727. shtml>.

22. Geisler, p. 58.

23. Hinman, Lawrence W. "St. Thomas Aquinas 'The Summa Theologica' Part II, Question 40" University of San Diego. <http://ethics.acusd.edu/Books/Texts/ Aquinas/JustWar.html>.

24. Ferraro, Vincent. "Principles of the Just War." Mt. Holyoke College. 2004. <http://www.mtholyoke.edu/acad/intrel/pol116/justwar.htm>.

25. Torres, Katherine. "UN Still Hamstrung on Defining Terror." United Press International. 8 July 2005. <http://washingtontimes.com/upi/20050706-064557-8630r.htm>.

26. Snodgrass, Klyne. Between Two Truths: Living with Biblical Tensions. Grand Rapids, MI: Zondervan Publishing House, 1990, p. 179.

The best artist has that thought alone
Which is contained within the marble shell;
The sculptor's hand can only break the spell
To free the figures slumbering in the stone.

Michelangelo Buonarroti

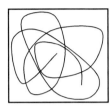

CHAPTER TEN

# Nudity and Sexuality in Art

### Is the following book excerpt pornographic?

There were two women, daughters of the same mother. They became prostitutes in Egypt, engaging in prostitution from their youth. In that land their breasts were fondled and their virgin bosoms caressed. The older was named Oholah, and her sister was Oholibah. They were mine and gave birth to sons and daughters.

Oholah engaged in prostitution while she was still mine; and she lusted after her lovers, the Assyrians—warriors clothed in blue, governors and commanders, all of them handsome young men, and mounted horsemen. She gave herself as a prostitute to all the elite of the Assyrians and defiled herself with all the idols of everyone she lusted after. She did not give up the prostitution she began in Egypt, when during her youth men slept with her, caressed her virgin bosom and poured out their lust upon her.

Therefore I handed her over to her lovers, the Assyrians, for whom she lusted. They stripped her naked, took away her sons and daughters and killed her with the sword. She became a byword among women, and punishment was inflicted on her.

Her sister Oholibah saw this, yet in her lust and prostitution she was more depraved than her sister. She too lusted after the Assyrians—governors and commanders, warriors in full dress, mounted horsemen, all handsome young men. I saw that she too defiled herself; both of them went the same way.

But she carried her prostitution still further. She saw men portrayed on a wall, figures of Chaldeans portrayed in red, with belts around their waists and flowing turbans on their heads; all of them looked like Babylonian chariot officers, natives of Chaldea. As soon as she saw them, she lusted after them and sent messengers to them in Chaldea. Then the Babylonians came to her, to the bed of love, and in their lust they defiled her. After she had been defiled by them, she turned away from them in disgust. When she carried on her prostitution openly and exposed her nakedness, I turned away from her in disgust, just as I had turned away from her sister. Yet she became more and more promiscuous as she recalled the days of her youth, when she was a prostitute in Egypt. There she lusted after her lovers, whose penis' were like those of donkeys and whose semen was like that of horses. So you longed for the lewdness of your youth, when in Egypt your bosom was caressed and your young breasts fondled.

Is this pornographic literature? I have asked this question of various Christians, and in every case, the answer I receive is "Yes." However, I hope you said "No" because God wrote this parable to describe Judah's unfaithfulness to Him in Ezekiel 23:1-21. God's position on nudity and sexuality confounds many Christians to the point some

Christians will call God's written artwork pornographic. What is the place for nudity and sexuality in art as far as a Christian is concerned?

## Reformation Inclination

During the Renaissance and the Reformation eras, the subject of the place of nudity and sexuality in art would not have engendered much debate. The Christian community of those times regarded the arts (including nudity and sexuality) as an expression of human creativity. The supreme purpose of art was to bring glory to God. Christians viewed human creativity as a reflection of the image of our creative God. However, in our era, this attitude has changed. We have been greatly influenced by the unbiblical prudishness of the Victorian Era and confuse the ideas of the Victorian Era with biblical principles. "The arts, cultural endeavors, enjoyment of beauty, enjoyment of creativity—both God's creativity in nature around us and man's creativity—these creative gifts have in our century and day and age been relegated to the bottom drawer of Christian consciousness, despised outright as unspiritual or un-Christian,"[1] even wrongly labeled pornographic in some cases. In this chapter we will investigate aesthetics, which sets standards for artwork and tries to determine art's meaning in human experience.

## Justice Department Bust

Some people in our culture, particularly Christians, view nude artworks as immoral. Former Attorney General John Ashcroft's staff, evidently without his knowledge, spent $8,650 for blue curtains to drape over a nude statue entitled the Spirit of Justice. The bare-breasted statue graced the background of Mr. Ashcroft's news conferences. A January 23, 2002 intra-Justice Department e-mail said the purpose of the drapes was to hide the statue.[2]  Is this statue immoral?  Is Michelangelo's statue of <u>David</u> immoral?  Should we purchase pants to hide his private parts?

Unfortunately, the purpose of the arts in Christian circles today often is not to bring glory to God, but a morose utilitarian concept that says the only use for art by Christians is to promote the gospel and enhance worship services.  However, this was not true of the Renaissance and Reformation artists, many of whom were Christians and created artworks containing nudity and portraying sexuality:

> To fit into the patterns of evangelism, artists have often compromised, and so prostituted their art. But Handel, with his <u>Messiah,</u> Bach with his <u>St. Matthew's Passion,</u> Rembrandt with his <u>Denial of St. Peter</u> . . . were not evangelizing nor making tools for evangelism; they worked to the glory of God. They did not compromise their art. They were not devising tools for religious propaganda or holy advertisement.[3]

This utilitarian concept has led Christians to believe there is secular art and Christian art.  Christians talk about Christian music and secular music.  Music is neither secular nor sacred.  Music is.  There are no biblical parameters or principles to regulate music.  What distinguishes music is the lyrics.  You may add lyrics that convey a Christian message or an evil message, but you can use the same music to get either message across. The message does not "Christianize" the music. Franky Schaeffer indicated that the idea of secular and Christian art is a false, unbiblical modern-day dichotomy. The Bible does not see things as spiritual and secular. "The true division in the Christian life . . . is that line we call sin . . . everything else comes under the heading of our Christian life. Either Christ has redeemed the whole man . . . or He has redeemed none of them."[4]

H. R. Rookmaaker, the late professor of art history at the Free University of Amsterdam, summarized the issue succinctly, "Here I must say emphatically: art must never be used to show the validity of Christianity. Rather, the validity of art should be shown through Christianity."[5]

Therefore, we must eschew the unbiblical idea that if art has no "Christian" value, it is worthless or meaningless. The late Francis Schaeffer, philosopher and founder of L'Abri Fellowship said, "A work of art has value in itself . . . for many Christians this is unthinkable. Art . . . is something to be enjoyed. The Bible says that the art in the tabernacle and the temple was for beauty."[6] This is the position that is taken against all nudity in art—it is sinful and evil because it is dirty and has no "Christian" value.

If that is our opinion of artwork, a re-evaluation of our standards for judging art is necessary before a conclusion concerning the validity of nudity in art can be reached. Rookmaaker said, "Christian art is nothing special. It is sound, healthy, good art. It is art that is in line with the

God-given structures of art, one which has a loving and free view on reality, one which is good and true. In a way there is no specifically Christian art. One can distinguish only good art and bad art, art which is sound and good from art which is false or weird in its insight into reality."[7] Art is only good or bad; it is not secular or sacred.

## Art Critic (not to be confused with Art Carney)
A Brit, a Frenchman and a Russian were viewing a painting of Adam and Eve frolicking in the Garden of Eden. "Look at their reserve, their calm," muses the Brit. "They must be British."

"Nonsense," the Frenchman disagrees. "They are naked, and so beautiful. Clearly, they are French."

"No clothes, no shelter," the Russian points out, "they have only an apple to eat, and they are being told this is paradise. They are Russian."[8]

What makes good art? Francis Schaeffer described four standards for judging art: technical excellence (for example, in painting, consider the use of color, form, balance, and the lines), validity (that deals with motivation, that is, invalid motivation that stems from a desire to make money or please an audience, or a valid, serious expression of what the artist wants to do), intellectual content (that deals with the artist's work as a body—does it express his world view?), and the integration of content and vehicle (evaluating if the style correlates with the message).[9]

The work of art should first be judged by these four standards. If each one is positive, then the issue of nudity in a work of art must be evaluated in terms of the Scriptures, the intent of the author, and its cultural background.

## The Naked Truth

The Bible has much to say concerning nudity in the arts. Philippians 4:8 tells us to think on the things that are pure—things that do not show a lack of love for others. "Purity in art means helping those who read or listen or see to have pure thoughts. It does not titillate, does not play on people's wrong desires, it does not seduce. It helps man see the good and the beautiful. It shows iniquity, it protests, but in a protest of love against the unjust and debased and evil."[10] Renaissance art mainly used nudity to depict the heroic human, a symbol of human greatness expressed in the philosophy of humanism. Michelangelo's David is an excellent example. For Rembrandt, the nude depicted humans in their weakness. None of his artworks were pornographic, "neither by intention nor in the way it influences the onlooker. In fact, lightly covered figures are often much more erotic."[11]

Sexuality is a gift from God, and is therefore not inherently evil, sinful, impure, immoral, or dirty. We humans have all sinned sexually to some degree, but that does not make sexuality and nudity always wrong. The human body was created by our God and "can be beautiful, and this beauty is not a thing to be ashamed of."[12]

The Bible, a literary art form, contains many references to nudity and sexuality. It is irrational to say the Word of God is unbiblical, evil, or dirty. For example, references are made to sexual intercourse in marriage. Genesis 4:1 says, "Adam lay with his wife Eve, and she became pregnant and gave birth to Cain." Genesis 4:17 says, "Cain lay with his wife, and she became pregnant and gave birth to Enoch." God could have simply said Adam begat Cain, Cain begat Enoch, but God evidently wanted to emphasize the sexual activity of our progenitors.

## I Have a Headache

I Corinthians 7:2-5 says, "But since there is so much immorality, each man should have his own wife, and each woman her own husband. The husband should fulfill his marital duty to his wife, and likewise the wife to her husband. The wife's body does not belong to her alone but also to her husband. In the same way, the husband's body does not belong to him alone but also to his wife. Do not deprive each other except by mutual consent and for a time, so that you may devote yourselves to prayer. Then come together again so that Satan will not tempt you because of your lack of self-control." If you are married, when is the last time you used the excuse not to have intercourse saying, "Sorry dear, not tonight—I have to devote myself to prayer?" You cannot just use this as an excuse—the husband and wife must agree to do this. Devoting yourself to prayer is the only listed biblical reason to deny sexual intercourse to your spouse, and your spouse must agree to devote time to prayer as well for the reason to be biblical. There should be sensitivity to not asking your spouse to make love if he or she is sick or exhausted, but the Bible gives only one excuse. The Lord expects intercourse to be a regular part of marriage.

## Incest Unrest

2 Samuel 13:1-14 vividly describes the incestuous rape of King David's daughter Tamar by her half-brother Amnon, a son of David:

> In the course of time, Amnon son of David fell in love with Tamar, the beautiful sister of Absalom son of David. Amnon became frustrated to the point of illness on account of his sister Tamar, for she was a virgin, and it seemed impossible for him to do anything to her. Now Amnon had a friend named Jonadab son of Shimeah, David's brother. Jonadab was a very shrewd man. He asked Amnon, 'Why do you, the king's son, look so haggard morning after morning? Will not you tell me?'

> Amnon said to him, 'I am in love with Tamar, my brother Absalom's sister.' 'Go to bed and pretend to be ill,' Jonadab said. 'When your father comes to see you, say to him, 'I would like my sister Tamar to come and give me something to eat. Let her prepare the food in my sight so I may watch her and then eat it from her hand.'

> So Amnon lay down and pretended to be ill. When the king came to see him, Amnon said to him, 'I would like my sister Tamar to come and make some special bread in my sight, so I may eat from her hand.'

> David sent word to Tamar at the palace: 'Go to the house of your brother Amnon and prepare some food for him.' So Tamar went to the house of her

brother Amnon, who was lying down. She took some dough, kneaded it made the bread in his sight and baked it. Then she took the pan and served him the bread, but he refused to eat.

'Send everyone out of here,' Amnon said. So everyone left him. Then Amnon said to Tamar, 'Bring the food here into my bedroom so I may eat from your hand.' And Tamar took the bread she had prepared and brought it to her brother Amnon in his bedroom. But when she took it to him to eat, he grabbed her and said, 'Come to bed with me, my sister.'

'Do not, my brother!' she said to him. 'Do not force me. Such a thing should not be done in Israel! Do not do this wicked thing. What about me? Where could I get rid of my disgrace? And what about you? You would be like one of the wicked fools in Israel. Please speak to the king; he will not keep me from being married to you.' But he refused to listen to her, and since he was stronger than she, he raped her.

Then Amnon hated her with intense hatred. In fact, he hated her more than he had loved her. Amnon said to her, 'Get up and get out!' 'No!' she said to him. 'Sending me away would be a greater wrong than what you have already done to me.'

But he refused to listen to her. He called his personal servant and said, 'Get this woman out of

> here and bolt the door after her.' So his servant
> put her out and bolted the door after her. She was
> wearing a richly ornamented robe, for this was the
> kind of garment the virgin daughters of the king
> wore. Tamar put ashes on her head and tore the
> ornamented robe she was wearing. She put her
> hand on her head and went away, weeping aloud
> as she went.

Tamar's brother Absalom murdered Amnon for this rape
and usurped the throne from his father David because
David ignored the rape. To alienate himself from his
father and to alienate the Jewish people from King David,
Ahithophel (interestingly, the grandfather of Bathsheba)
advises Absalom to, '"Lie with your father's concubines
whom he left to take care of the palace. Then all Israel
will hear that you have made yourself a stench in your
father's nostrils, and the hands of everyone with you will
be strengthened.' So they pitched a tent for Absalom on
the roof, and he lay with his father's concubines in the
sight of all Israel." God is not reticent to talk about rape
and incest.

## Sick Sodom

In Genesis 19:1-11, all the men and boys of Sodom
gathered outside Lot's home to homosexually rape his
two angelic visitors. Lot protested and offered to give
them his two virgin daughters to whom "you can do what
you like with them." What a dad. What kind of Father's
Day card would be appropriate for him? After escaping
from Sodom, Lot's daughters intoxicate their father and
rape him:

That night they got their father to drink wine, and the older daughter went in and lay with him. He was not aware of it when she lay down or when she got up. The next day the older daughter said to the younger, "Last night I lay with my father. Let's get him to drink wine again tonight, and you go in and lie with him so we can preserve our family line through our father." So they got their father to drink wine that night also, and the younger daughter went and lay with him. Again he was not aware of it when she lay down or when she got up.

So both of Lot's daughters became pregnant by their father. The older daughter had a son, and she named him Moab; he is the father of the Moabites of today. The younger daughter also had a son, and she named him Ben-Ammi; he is the father of the Ammonites of today (Genesis 19: 33-38).

Lot became the father of his own grandchildren when his daughters, whom Lot was willing to let be gang raped by the men and boys of Sodom, incestuously raped him.

A similar incident to the near rape in Sodom occurs in Judges 19:22-28:

While they were enjoying themselves, some of the wicked men of the city surrounded the house. Pounding on the door, they shouted to the old man who owned the house, "Bring out the man who came to your house so we can have sex with him."

The owner of the house went outside and said to them, "No, my friends, do not be so vile. Since this man is my guest, do not do this disgraceful thing. Look, here is my virgin daughter, and his concubine. I will bring them out to you now, and you can use them and do to them whatever you wish. But to this man, do not do such a disgraceful thing."

But the men would not listen to him. So the man took his concubine and sent her outside to them, and they raped her and abused her throughout the night, and at dawn they let her go. At daybreak the woman went back to the house where her master was staying, fell down at the door and lay there until daylight.

When her master got up in the morning and opened the door of the house and stepped out to continue on his way, there lay his concubine, fallen in the doorway of the house, with her hands on the threshold.

The men of the city raped her all night until she died. God does not flinch or hesitate to write these graphic details. (God also wanted us to know, recorded in verse 29, "When he [the man whose concubine was murdered] reached home, he took a knife and cut up his concubine, limb by limb, into twelve parts and sent them into all the areas of Israel." God is not averse to describing detailed violence, either.)

## Eunuchs Need not Apply

The Scriptures reference human sexual organs.

Deuteronomy 23:1 says, "No one who has been emasculated (had their testicles destroyed or removed) by crushing or cutting may enter the assembly of the LORD." God compares Israel to a naked woman in Ezekiel 16:7, "I made you grow like a plant of the field. You grew up and developed and became the most beautiful of jewels. Your breasts were formed and your hair grew, you who were naked and bare." Song of Solomon 4:5 adds, "Your two breasts are like two fawns, like twin fawns of a gazelle that browse among the lilies" (If your path crossed these fawns, you would stare at them and want to pet them, which is Solomon's point about his wife's breasts). It cannot be sinful to discuss sexual organs.

## The Greatest Love Song Ever Written

The Scriptures are even more explicit than what I have described so far. Foreplay is described in a non-titillating way. Song of Solomon contains long sections describing foreplay by a husband and wife. When is the last time you heard a sermon on these passages describing marital lovemaking? Solomon is pleased his wife is a virgin on their wedding night (4:12), "You are a garden locked up, my sister, my bride; you are a spring enclosed, a sealed fountain." He remarks that her vagina, her garden, is lubricated for sexual intercourse (4:15), "You are a garden fountain, a well of flowing water streaming down from Lebanon." She encourages winds, which bring more moisture, to blow on her "garden," and also invites her husband to engage in oral sex and sexual intercourse (4:16), "Awake, north wind, and come, south wind! Blow on my garden, so its fragrance may spread abroad. Let my lover come into his garden and taste its choice fruits." Solomon summarizes their seminal sexual experience (5:1), "I have come into my garden, my sister, my bride; I have gathered my myrrh with my spice. I have eaten my honeycomb and my honey; I have drunk my wine and my milk." She describes performing oral sex on him, (2:3) "Like an apple tree among the trees of the forest is my lover among the young men. I delight to sit in his shade, and his fruit is sweet to my taste."[13] She does a striptease dance for him (7:1), "curves" (NASB) means a swaying motion, or dancing. Solomon is eager to caress his wife's breasts, which he likes engorged (7:7-8), "Your stature is like that of the palm, and your breasts like clusters of fruit. I said, 'I will climb the palm tree; I will take hold of its fruit.' May your breasts be like the clusters of the vine, the fragrance of your breath like apples, and your mouth like the best wine." Solomon had more to say on this subject in Proverbs 5:19, "May your fountain be blessed, and may you rejoice in the wife of your youth. A loving doe, a graceful deer—may her breasts satisfy you always, may you ever be captivated by her love." These references are sexual but not pornographic.

## What If?

What would the Christian community do to a Christian who wrote stories that talked frankly about sexual intercourse, incestuous rape, homosexual gang rape that included small boys, gang rape with the permission of the girls' believing father, gang rape and murder, caressing female breasts, growth of pubic hair, foreplay, striptease dancing, vaginal lubrication due to sexual arousal, and oral sex?

Christians carry a Book to church every week containing these stories and references. God is not embarrassed to talk about these issues and has no problem with us talking about them either because they are not titillating. These passages present an interesting, though perhaps unanswerable, question. If God had decided to give His revelation in paintings or video instead of literature, what would these passages look like?

The Scriptures have no problem with presenting nudity and sexuality. Even though immoral acts are detailed, they tell the truth about the incidents and are not pornographic, which fits Rookmaaker's qualifications for nudity in art. Nudity in the arts, when its intention is not to create erotic ideas, lustful thoughts or fantasies, or pornographic titillation is neither anti-biblical nor anti-Christian.

## I Know it When I See it

How do we distinguish between a valid nude art form and pornography? We can distinguish between two types of sexually explicit materials. One category is sex education material and fine arts. The people who created these mediums did not intend to arouse people sexually (the Bible being one example), even though that could occur. The other type is pornography, either "soft" pornography, where the intention of the creator of these materials is to arouse erotic ideas, sexual fantasies, and lustful thoughts in the viewer, "hard core" pornography, which abandon reality constraints. The purpose of hard core pornography is to violate all standards of decency, deny human dignity, emphasize the obscene, and arouse lust.[14]

The distinction between art forms and pornography is the intention of the artist. If the objective of the artwork is sexual arousal, it is pornography, whether soft core or hard core. There is a vast difference between sexual pictures and words tastefully presented, as in the Bible and in marriage manuals that seek to educate, and crude obscenities aimed at promoting lust.[15] The latter attempt to legitimize pedophilia, homosexuality, bestiality, casual sex, adultery, and multiple sexual partners, all of which are immoral.[16]

The question of nudity in the arts is really an outgrowth of a person's worldview. If you reject all nudity and sexual references, you have a misunderstanding of the human body's relationship to sin. You probably see the human body as sinful or shameful, a position your Creator does not share. Your views are shaped by the philosophies of Plato, not the Word of God. If you lust after nudity in the arts, you have a sin problem. You have found that sexual materials supply a replacement for God in your life and provide meaning you are not finding in Him. You are esteeming great value to pornography, just like the pornographers do who argue pornography has therapeutic and social value that must be regarded as constitutionally-protected free speech.

A good example of the evil this can cause is represented in Fouquet's The Red Virgin.

> The girl was shown with one breast exposed. . . . Was this the Madonna about to feed her baby? No . . . the girl was the king's mistress . . . Prior to this time,

> Mary was considered very high and holy . . . But now not only was the king's mistress painted as Mary with all the holiness removed, but the meaning, too, was being destroyed . . . gradually the threat spread to all of knowledge and life. All meaning to all individual things or all particulars was removed. Things were being viewed as autonomous, and there was nothing to which to relate them or give them meaning.[17]

Foquet and others who share his worldview try to remove God from providing meaning for life. Pornography has taken His place for many. However, this does not mean Christians must reject non-pornographic sexual material, or we would have to reject our Bible.

## Paint Stripper

The problem arises as to a Christian's personal involvement in nude art forms. I believe the answer to this is found in the cultural attitudes of those around you. Our society has associated all nudity with sexual arousal regardless of the intention of the artist. "Nudity in films and on the stage, permissiveness in books and in fashion and in advertising, all this is partly a reaction against Victorian prudishness (itself an unhealthy view of sex), partly a sign of increasing lawlessness as all conventions and norms are thrown out."[18]

For example, a Christian who would pose nude for a painting or sculpture in our culture would undoubtedly be accused of immorality from believer and nonbeliever alike, even though the intention of the artist or model was not to arouse lust in others.  "In our society a woman is not expected to show her body without clothes . . . modesty in fact is a moral quality, and its expression is different in different cultures and society."[19]  For many, breast-feeding a baby is considered a provocative move on the part of the mother.  Gabrielle Redfern, a Miami Beach, Florida resident, caused a stir when she breast-fed her child at a Miami Beach Commission meeting.  Joe Fontana complained, "It is distracting.  Why inside?  Why not step outside to do it?"[20]

Our culture is not only perverted in its acceptance of pornography, but it is also perverted in its view of sexual purity and innocence.  Many Christians have not helped the situation by promoting an unbiblical view of sexuality and the human body.  In fact, their views have made God a pornographer.

> Purity is a norm, but not an easy rule that can be applied indiscriminately.  We have to exercise our human judgment, with all our understanding, wisdom, and prudence.  For to the artist, purity is an intention.  It might be appropriate to use the nude in his art, whether it is in literature or in the visual arts, and even to speak of intercourse with completely pure motives . . . In all this it is vital to realize that it is not what goes into us that makes us impure, but what is already within us, or goes out of us, as Jesus showed so trenchantly (Matthew 15:11).[21]

Our goal is to use critical thinking skills to determine the intention of the artist.  Nudity and sexuality have a place in art.  We can visit and enjoy art museums.

A controversy in Venice, California, highlights my point about Americans view of nudity in art. The Los Angeles City council voted to accept a donation of a metal, nude statue, sans head and arms, and to erect it in a popular traffic circle near the beach. Religious and social conservatives and feminists have objected to the statue (the latter because they see the statue a symbol of violence against and objectification of women). Members of the Venice Foursquare Gospel Church gathered in April 2005 to pray the statue be cancelled while "a parade of real women on the nearby beach regularly flaunt their own torsos in string bikinis."[22] The editorial begins insightfully, "The College of Cardinals elected an ultraconservative pope earlier this week under a ceiling replete with genitals, breasts and buttocks that apparently gave no offense. Good thing Michelangelo painted his Sistine Chapel masterpieces in Rome and not Venice — California, that is."[23] Americans are bewildered about trying to understand art.

## Conclusion

Nudity in the arts, when its intention is not to create erotic ideas, lustful thoughts, or fantasies, or pornographic titillation is neither anti-biblical nor anti-Christian. The Bible does not teach all sexuality is evil or dirty.

In the next chapter we will turn our attention away from ethics and aesthetics to a debated theological question— can we reconcile the seeming paradox between God's sovereignty and our free will?

## For Review and Discussion

- When you read first the opening five paragraphs of this chapter from Ezekiel 23:1-21, did you believe it was pornography? Why, or why not?

- Why was nudity and sexuality in art not a problem during the Renaissance and Reformation eras? What did nudity in art mean to them?

- The Justice Department draped the Spirit of Justice statue to cover its breasts. Should they have done this? Explain your answer.

- Is Michelangelo's David immoral? Explain your answer.

- Explain your view of whether there is Christian art.

- How can the Bible contain explicit sexual remarks yet not be pornography.

- How would you teach the Song of Solomon to an audience of men, women, and children?

- Do you agree with John Court's three distinctions about sexually explicit material? Explain your answer.

- What is your view of a Christian posing nude for an artwork?

- Explain when, if ever, nudity and sexuality are appropriate in artwork.

# ENDNOTES

1.  Schaeffer, Franky. Addicted to Mediocrity. Westchester. IL: Crossway Books, 1981, p. 16.

2.  Burger, Timothy. "E-mails Bare Cover Up." New York Daily News. 17 July 2002. <http://www.nydailynews.com/front/story/3695p-3303c.html>.

3.  Rookmaaker, H. R. Art Needs No Justification Downer's Grove, IL: InterVarsity Press, 1978, p. 30.

4.  Schaeffer, p. 27.

5.  Rookmaaker, H. R. Modern Art and the Death of a Culture. London: InterVarsity Press, 1970, p. 228.

6.  Schaeffer, Francis A. Art and the Bible. Downer's Grove, IL: InterVarsity Press, 1979, p. 33.

7.  Rookmaaker 1970, p. 28.

8.  Fryc, Karen. "Paint & Art Jokes, Quotes, Humour and Fun Pictures." Little Monkey Murals. <http://www.littlemonkeymurals.com/ArtJokes.htm>.

9.  Schaeffer 1979, pp. 41-47.

10. Rookmaaker 1970, p. 239.

11. Ibid, p. 239.

12. Ibid, p. 239.

13.   Dillow, Joseph C. <u>Solomon on Sex: A Biblical Guide to Married Love</u>. Nashville: Thomas Nelson Publishers, 1977, p. 31.

14.   Court, John H.  Pornography: <u>A Christian Critique</u> Downer's Grove, IL:    InterVarsity Press, 1980, pp. 46-47.

15.   Court, p. 46.

16.   Ibid, p. 22.

17.   Schaeffer, Francis A.  <u>How Should We Then Live?</u> Old Tappan, NJ: Fleming H. Revell, Company, 1976, p. 71.

18.   Rookmaaker 1970, p. 240.

19.   Ibid, p. 240.

20.   "16 Breast-Feed in Protest at Public Meeting." Associated Press.  21 April 2005.  <http://www.foxnews.com/story/0,2933,154196,00.html>.

21.   Rookmaaker 1970, pp. 240-241.

22.   Editorial. "As a Protest, What a Bust." Los Angeles Times.  21 April 2005.  <http://www.latimes.com/news/opinion/la-ed-statue21apr21,0,6292667.story>.

23.   Ibid.

I shall be telling this with a sigh
Somewhere ages and ages hence:
Two roads diverged in a wood, and I --
I took the one less traveled by,
And that has made all the difference.

Robert Frost


What is to be, will be.
And what isn't to be sometimes happens.

L. M. Montgomery

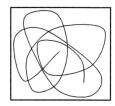

CHAPTER ELEVEN

# Logic, the Sovereignty of God, and Free Will

## Come On, Sevens

A paradigm shift is a change from one way of thinking about the world to another way of viewing it.[1] Paradigm shifts can cause considerable consternation. A "shift in meaning and significance can cause chaos in the attempt to achieve continuity of meaning and significance because human beings do not always shift in the same way or to the same degree."[2]

The paradigm shift in the understanding of nature from Newtonian, or classical physics to German physicist Werner Heisenberg's quantum, or modern physics has called into question some people's understanding of God. The first person to realize this was Albert Einstein. Others followed. Quantum physics is worth our time and study because it gives us insights that will aid our understanding of God. It is an apt metaphor to help us understand the alleged conflict between the sovereignty of God and the free will of man.

Heisenberg's 1925 theory caused chaos. Following the lead of German physicist Max Planck, Heisenberg decided not to concentrate on what atoms were, but instead concentrate on what atoms did. Scientists pre-Heisenberg believed atoms were miniature solar systems that operated in fixed patterns. At our visual level of reality, the universe appears to be mostly calm and orderly. However, Heisenberg discovered that at the sub-atomic realm, things are chaotic.

A quantum is the smallest known particle of energy. The problem associated with the quanta is that they are uncertain and unpredictable; thus Heisenberg's theory is called the Uncertainty Principle. A quantum energy particle will travel from point A to point B, but you cannot predict what path it will take to get there. Paul Davies illustrated this:

> The image on a television screen is produced by myriads of light impulses emitted when electrons fired from a gun at the back of the set strike the fluorescent screen. The picture you perceive is reasonably sharp because the number of electrons involved is enormous, and by the law of averages, the cumulative effects of many electrons is [sic] predictable. However, any particular electron, with its inbuilt unpredictability, could go anywhere on the screen. The arrival of an electron at a place, and the fragment of picture that it produces, is uncertain. According to Bohr's philosophy, bullets from an ordinary gun follow a precise path to the target, but electrons from an electron gun simply turn up at the target. And however good your aim, no bull's-eye is guaranteed. The event 'electron at place x on the television screen' cannot be considered as *caused*

[author's italics] by the gun, or anything else. For there is no known reason why the electron should go to point x rather than some other place.[3]

To borrow a line from the Wizard of Oz, "We're not in Kansas anymore." The sub-atomic world is unpredictable. There has been speculation that time travel would be possible through wormholes connecting black holes in space. However, Stephen Hsu and Roman Buniy of the University of Oregon argued if wormholes are governed by quantum mechanics, they "would likely transport their payloads to an undesired time and place."[4]

According to Stephen Hawking, Werner Heisenberg:

> . . . pointed out that you could not measure both the position, and the speed, of a particle exactly. To see where a particle is, one has to shine light on it. But by Planck's work, one cannot use an arbitrarily small amount of light. One has to use at least one quantum. This will disturb the particle, and change its speed in a way that cannot be predicted. To measure the position of the particle accurately, you will have to use light with a short wave length, like ultra violet, x-rays, or gamma rays. But again, by Planck's work, quanta of these forms of light have higher energies than those of visible light. So they will disturb the speed of the particle more. It is a no win situation: the more accurately you try to measure the position of the particle, the less accurately you can know the speed, and vice versa. This is summed up in the Uncertainty Principle that Heisenberg formulated; the uncertainty in the position of a particle, times

the uncertainty in its speed, is always greater than
a quantity called Planck's constant, divided by the
mass of the particle.[4]

You are in good company if this seems incomprehensible
and impossible. Albert Einstein concurred. A physicist
and one-time friend of Einstein's, Niels Bohr, said,
"Anyone who is not shocked by quantum physics has
not understood it."[5]    One reason Einstein rejected
quantum theory was theological (Einstein was Jewish),
based on his deterministic world view.    "Determinism
is the philosophical belief that every event or action is
the inevitable result of preceding events and actions.
Thus, in principle at least, every event or action can be
completely predicted in advance, or in retrospect."[6]
Einstein believed God determined every event in human
history. Einstein said, "God does not play dice with the
universe."[7] The evidence, however, indicates that Einstein
was wrong.   "Hundreds of different experiments seem
to verify (quantum physics) correctness."[8]   By applying
quantum physics, the laser, the electron microscope, the
transistor, the superconductor, and nuclear power have
been developed.[9]  God plays dice.

Einstein lost credibility as a scientist among his colleagues
because of his failure to grasp the new paradigm. His
earlier work on relativity was esteemed (which ironically
created a new paradigm when he rejected Newton's
concept of absolute space), but colleagues ridiculed his
later work trying to disprove quantum physics. As often is
the case, he could not see the new scientific paradigm.[10]
His deterministic bias blinded him to the truth of quantum
physics.

## Is it a Crap Shoot?

What are the theological implications of God playing dice? Some see parallels between quantum physics and Zen Buddhism. Davies believed the message is that there can be effects without causes,[11] but as Schilling rightly said, quantum physics at least causes probabilities.[12] Heinz Pagels in <u>The Cosmic Code: Philosophy as the Language of Nature</u>, said, "Even God can give you only the odds for some event to occur, not certainty."[13] Ian Barbour, in his 1966 <u>Issues in Science and Religion</u>, added to Pagels thought. He said, "The future is not simply unknown, it is 'not decided,' but it is not completely 'open,' since the present determines the range of future possibilities."[14] Benjamin Reist's conclusion was, "The future is not yet decided for the living God, as well as for us."[15] It is my conclusion that all these scientists and philosophers have missed the theological implication of quantum physics. Their assertions do not mesh with Scripture, and based on the Coherence Theory of truth, I reject them. This new paradigm that says uncertainty leads to certainty (the quantum particle does eventually arrive at point B after leaving point A) provides a metaphor to help us understand the alleged paradox between the sovereignty of God and the free will of man.

## God is Sovereign

God's sovereignty means He completely controls everything. Arthur Pink said God must be sovereign, "So that none can defeat His counsels, thwart His purpose, or resist His will."[16] God said in Isaiah 46:10-11, "I make known the end from the beginning, from ancient times, what is still to come. I say: My purpose will stand, and I will do all that I please. From the east I summon a bird of prey; from a far-off land, a man to fulfill my purpose. What I have said, that will I bring about; what I have planned, that will I do." God declares He is sovereign and demonstrates it in His actions.

## Humans have Free Will

Free will means that humans have the right to make un-coerced choices. People can choose to do what they want, even sin. God gives us the right to make choices.

## Illuminating the Illusionary Illogicality

Free will and God's sovereignty seem paradoxical. Yet if God in His sovereignty chooses to limit His control by offering choices to humans, He remains sovereign. For example, I can control what my children eat, but still give them choices. I can offer them a choice between vanilla or chocolate ice cream. I control that they are eating ice cream instead of cake; they choose the flavor they prefer. God sets limited choices before us. What is occurring now determines the array of future choices. For example, you cannot work in New York City, live in Hong Kong, and fly back and forth on a daily basis. Wherever I live, there are a limited number of jobs I am qualified to do that have positions available when I am job searching; there are a limited number of houses I can afford and in which no one is living; and there are a limited number of people who are looking for friends who have the same interests I have. God and the circumstances of life in which He places us limit our choices.

In <u>Knowledge of the Holy</u>, A.W. Tozer attempts to reconcile the seemingly contradictory beliefs of God's sovereignty and man's free will:

> An ocean liner leaves New York bound for Liverpool. Its destination has been determined by proper authorities. Nothing can change it. This is at least a faint picture of sovereignty. On board the liner are scores of passengers. These are not in chains, neither are their activities determined for them by decree. They are completely free to move about as they will. They eat, sleep, play, lounge about on the deck, read, talk, altogether as they please; but all the while the great liner is carrying them steadily onward toward a predetermined port. Both freedom and sovereignty are present here, and they do not contradict. So it is, I believe, with man's freedom and the sovereignty of God. The mighty liner of God's sovereign design keeps its steady course over the sea of history.[17]

God limits our choices to the ocean liner. We can only choose what is available on our ship and we do not have access to other vessels.

By His foreknowledge, God knows all possible choices we could make, actual and potential. He has more information about what we could potentially do (and the potential consequences of those actions, followed by the potential choices we could make next, ad infinitum) than what we actually do, since what we could possibly do is immeasurable. God weeds out the choices available to us. For example, Jesus knew if the miracles performed in Capernaum had been done in Sodom, that city would not have been destroyed and would have still been in existence in Jesus' day (Matthew 11:23). God knew Cain would get over his depression and not murder his brother Abel if he repented and confessed his sin of unbelief and jealousy (Genesis 4:7). God knows the future and can limit our choices.

## Hellacious Choice

The Lord defends people's right to believe what they want. Reflecting on this, G. K. Chesterton said, "Hell is a monument to human freedom." James W. Sire said, "Hell is God's tribute to the freedom He gave us to choose whom we would serve."[18] When the rich young ruler turned and walked away, deciding not to follow Jesus, the Lord did not run after him. Jesus did not change His requirements for being a disciple so the young man would follow Him. Jesus did not force the rich ruler to follow Him. Jesus gave the man a choice, even though what the ruler decided was a bad one. Jesus let the man walk away, eventually into Hell.

## God's Got Gargantuan Goals

The Bible declares that God has sovereign goals and plans. He works all things according to the counsel of His own will (Ephesians 1:11). The book of Revelation, chapters 20 and 21, declares God's Kingdom will come. God chose people to salvation before the foundation of the world and those He chose come to faith in Christ (Ephesians 1:4). Yet in the midst of His sovereignty, God gives choices to His creatures. His foreknowledge knows what decisions we will make before we make them. God can intervene in limiting future decisions by limiting our options to get

the course of affairs headed back in the direction He desires. A good illustration of this is the prophet Jonah. God
wanted Jonah to travel east to the city of Nineveh; Jonah
headed west by ship, exercising his choice to disobey
God. Then God limited Jonah's next available choices.
The Lord sent a violent storm and the ships' crew tossed
Jonah overboard to stop the wrath of God. God appointed
a giant fish to swallow Jonah (Jonah 1:17). The reluctant
prophet changed his mind and went to Nineveh as God
wanted. Jonah still made the choice, but God limited His
options to "Live or die, your choice."

Another illustration of God limiting choices to control our
decisions is Jesus' birth in Bethlehem. Mary and Joseph
lived ninety miles north of Bethlehem in Nazareth (Luke
2:4). To get them to Bethlehem, which is where God
had prophesied 700 years earlier the Messiah would be
born (Micah 5:2), the Lord arranged that Caesar Augus-
tus would make everyone in the empire go to the city of
their ancestors and register for a tax. Mary and Joseph's
ancestors lived in Bethlehem. They traveled to the little
town of Bethlehem, and while there, Mary gave birth to
the Everlasting Light, the Christ Child (Luke 2:1-7). God's
desires were accomplished by limiting Joseph and Mary's
options—go to Bethlehem or face the ire of the emperor,
even though Mary and Joseph did not see God's specific
involvement in the circumstances of their lives.

Just like not all electrons reach the television screen, not
all of God's interventions will be successful, though, because of human's ability to sin. Jonah could have chosen
to drown; Joseph and Mary could have chosen to defy the

emperor. There are times when God's interventions are thwarted by human sin. You have done it often; I even more. God's dealings with the Jews in Amos 4:6-11 provide an excellent example of this:

> I gave you empty stomachs in every city and lack of bread in every town, yet you have not returned to Me, declares the LORD. I also withheld rain from you when the harvest was still three months away. I sent rain on one town, but withheld it from another. One field had rain; another had none and dried up. People staggered from town to town for water but did not get enough to drink, yet you have not returned to me, declares the LORD.

> Many times I struck your gardens and vineyards, I struck them with blight and mildew. Locusts devoured your fig and olive trees, yet you have not returned to me, declares the LORD.

> I sent plagues among you as I did to Egypt. I killed your young men with the sword, along with your captured horses. I filled your nostrils with the stench of your camps, yet you have not returned to me, declares the LORD.

> I overthrew some of you as I overthrew Sodom and Gomorrah. You were like a burning stick snatched from the fire, yet you have not returned to me, declares the LORD.

God did everything He could to get Israel to repent and

return to worshiping Him. Israel in her rebellion refused and the Lord's desires were thwarted. Does this passage in Amos describe God as a failure?

If you believe in determinism, or that humans do not have free will, then you must conclude God is a failure. If God is a failure, He is not a perfect God and is therefore unable to save us. However, if God in His sovereignty decides to allow humans free will that can reject His requests for repentance, He remains sovereign. God is not a cosmic chess master, playing both sides of the board, making all his moves and all ours    too. . .God is a person who takes immense risks,"[19] notably allowing our free will.

Salvation is an excellent example that human sin and free will can thwart God's desires. 2 Peter 3:9 says God is, "not wanting anyone to perish, but everyone to come to repentance." For the majority of humans, coming to repentance and not perishing does not occur. *Many* find the broad way that leads to destruction; *few* find the narrow way that leads to life (Matthew 7:13-14). God would like everyone to say yes to salvation, but human sin and free will thwart His gracious plan.

The cross is also an excellent example that God's interventions can be successful, even in the midst of human sin. The apostle Peter says in Acts 2:22-24, "Men of Israel, listen to these words: Jesus the Nazarene, a man attested to you by God with miracles and wonders and signs which God performed through Him in your midst, just as you yourselves know—this Man, delivered up by the predetermined plan and foreknowledge of God, you nailed to a cross by the hands of godless men and put Him to death. And God raised Him up again, putting an end to the agony of death, since it was impossible for Him to be held in its power." Men had their free choice—"you nailed to a cross," but God's will was done—"God raised Him up again."

From human perspective, all of life seems random. Like the audience members who cannot see the stagehands at a theater, we cannot see what God is doing behind the scenery. We are free to make the choices God presents to us and are morally accountable for those decisions, but God is operating in the background limiting those choices so His will is done on Earth. If we do not do what He wants, God has the option to limit the next choices we make, but we can still not do what He wants, with consequences.

God can override human decisions. Joseph told his brothers in Genesis 50:20, while reflecting on them selling him into slavery, "You intended to harm me, but God intended it for good to accomplish what is now being done, the saving of many lives." Joseph's brothers exercised their free will, un-coerced; God sovereignly did as He pleased in response to use the situation to bring glory to His Name.

## It Just So Happened
There is a randomness built into our day-to-day affairs. The Bible makes it clear some things "just happen." Ruth 2:1-4 says:

> Now Naomi had a relative on her husband's side, from the clan of Elimelech, a man of standing,

whose name was Boaz. And Ruth the Moabitess said to Naomi, "Let me go to the fields and pick up the leftover grain behind anyone in whose eyes I find favor."

Naomi said to her, "Go ahead, my daughter." So she went out and began to glean in the fields behind the harvesters. As it turned out, she found herself working in a field belonging to Boaz, who was from the clan of Elimelech. Just then Boaz arrived from Bethlehem and greeted the harvesters, "The LORD be with you!"

Ruth, unknown to her, just happened to be working in the field of Boaz, a relative of her dead husband. Since Naomi, her mother-in-law, had no more sons, the law (Deuteronomy 25:5-10) stated that a relative of the deceased could marry the widow and raise children in the dead man's name, which was known as being a kinsman-redeemer. Boaz falls in love with Ruth, marries her, and they have a child named Obed. Obed had a child named Jesse. One of Jesse's sons was David, King of Israel. From the line of David came Jesus Christ. All of this from Ruth randomly choosing a field in which to pick grain after the harvest.

In 1 Kings 22:34 we read, "Now a certain man drew his bow at random and struck the king of Israel in a joint of the armor. So he (the king) said to the driver of his chariot, 'Turn around, and take me out of the fight; for I am severely wounded.'" The archer was not aiming at King Ahab; he just aimlessly, "at random," released an arrow from his bow (my argument would be weakened if the king's name was Random, but it was Ahab).

Jesus tells us there is randomness in life.  He says in Luke 13:1-5, "Now on the same occasion there were some present who reported to Him about the Galileans, whose blood Pilate had mingled with their sacrifices.  And He answered and said to them, 'Do you suppose that these Galileans were greater sinners than all other Galileans, because they suffered this fate?  I tell you, no, but unless you repent, you will all likewise perish.  Or do you suppose that those eighteen on whom the tower in Siloam fell and killed them, were worse culprits than all the men who live in Jerusalem?  I tell you, no.'"  Jesus' implication is that these people just happened to be at the wrong place at the wrong time.  God was not punishing them.  They were victims of Pilate's hatred for the Jews and someone's poor craftsmanship.

For example, God does not target people with natural disasters; natural disasters "just happen."  People who live in "tornado alley" in Mid-America, near rivers vulnerable to flooding, and near beaches susceptible to tsunamis and hurricanes are rolling the dice that these events will not affect them.  These people, by their own free will, chose to live in these dangerous areas and may be killed because of the choices they have made, not because God singled them out for destruction.  People who normally have little interest in God get their shorts twisted in a knot when natural disasters occur.  "How could a loving God let this happen?"  "Theodicy" is the technical theological term for this question.  Daniel Schorr, Senior News Analyst for National Public Radio, disdaining President Bush for saying Intelligent Design could be an option in schools, opined about Hurricane Katrina.  "If this was a result of intelligent design, the Designer has something to answer for."[20] If Schorr and others bothered to study science they would find natural "disasters" have a long-term positive affect on the environment. Besides, people know these horrific disasters can occur and choose to move to these places regardless; they rolled the dice. God did not make them move there. It is no more God's fault people get killed in these circumstances than He is responsible for someone getting killed who stands in the middle of the road and gets hit by a speeding bicycle. Decisions have consequences.

What about human tragedies? Should God do something to stop them? On March 12, 2005, Terry Ratzmann walked into the Living Church of God, meeting in a suburban Milwaukee hotel and fired twenty-two bullets from a 9mm pistol, killing seven, injuring four others, then committed suicide. An uncle of one the injured said, "I wanted to know where God was when this happened. He was supposed to be everywhere. He could have at least been there."[21] God was there; He neither intervened in Ratzmnn's free will nor turned the bullets into paper. It just happened as a result of sin.

Even the new pope, Benedict XVI, struggles with God's decisions. Speaking at the Auscwitz WWII German death camp he asked, "In a place like this, words fail; in the end, there can be only a dread silence, a silence which itself is a heartfelt cry to God: Why, Lord, did you remain silent? How could you tolerate all this?"[22]

Quantum physics is a model for events just happening arbitrarily. Just like the electrons in the television are random, yet arrive at the right destination, so our free will does not thwart God's ultimate desires. God rolls dice and allows us to make choices that may even be contrary to His plan. By His power, foreknowledge, and ability to limit our future choices, His will is done in Heaven and on Earth (Matthew 6:9). The electron gun is involved in the electron's arrival at the right place on the television screen, but does not completely determine it.[23] In a similar manner, God is involved in our lives, but gives us choices.

Romans 1:20 tells us that God's attributes and divine nature can be seen in His creation. In quantum physics we see His sovereignty as it relates to human free will. No one need see randomness as incompatible with the character of God. The Lord has built randomness into the subatomic and visible world, and by giving us free will, has built randomness into our lives.

## Conclusion
Those who debate the sovereignty of God versus the free will of man usually pick one side as being more important than the other (some covenant theologians deny free will even exists since Adam). However, the doctrine of God's sovereignty is not more important than the doctrine of free will. Both are completely true and reconcilable, using quantum physics as a metaphor.

Between determinism and free will, I choose free will.

Referring to matter disappearing into black holes, Stephen Hawking said, "Thus it seems Einstein was doubly wrong when he said, 'God does not play dice.' Not only does

God definitely play dice, but He sometimes confuses us by throwing them where they cannot be seen."[24] Choose what you like when you make a decision; God has sovereignly provided your choices. Choose well; God is watching and willing to limit your next choice.

Use, do not lose, your mind. Honor God with your thinking and decisions. Be a critical thinker. Change your world.

## For Review and Discussion

- Explain a paradigm shift.

- Explain how quantum particles move.

- What made Einstein a determinist? Explain whether you agree with him.

- Explain God's sovereignty.

- Explain free will.

- Explain the difference between what God actually knows and what He potentially knows. How is this different than what humans know?

- Explain God limiting our choices.

- Explain why Christ's death on the cross was not a defeat for God's sovereignty.

- Do you agree events "just happen?" Explain your answer.

- Does the government giving aid to disaster victims to rebuild their homes after floods and hurricanes destroy them encourage unwise behavior? Explain your answer.

- Summarize how quantum physics is a metaphor for the sovereignty of God and the free will of humans.

## ENDNOTES

1.     See Kuhn, Thomas S. The Structure of Scientific Revolutions. Chicago: The University of Chicago Press, 1962, p. 10.

2.     From Dr. Wayne Faust's class notes, Oxford Graduate School, p. 2.

3.     Davies, Paul. God and the New Physics. London: J. M. Dent & Sons, Ltd., 1983, p. 103.

4.     Rincon, Paul. "Wormhole 'No Use' for Time Travel." BBC News. 23 May 2005. <http://news.bbc.co.uk/1/hi/sci/tech/4564477.stm>.

5.     Hawking, Stephen. "Does God Play Dice?" Hawking: Public Lectures. <http://www.hawking.org.uk/lectures/ dice.html>.

6.      Trump, Matthew A. "The Philosophy of
        Determinism." University of Texas at Austin.
        14 August 1998. <http://order.ph.utexas.edu/
        chaos/determinism.html>.

7.      Einstein, Albert. "God." Quote DB. <http://www.
        quotedb.com/quotes/878>.

8.      DeYoung, Donald B. Astronomy and the Bible.
        Grand Rapids: Baker Book House,  1988, p. 122.

9.      Davies, p. 101.

10.     Kuhn, p. 56.

11.     Davies, p. 102.

12.     Quoted in Reist, Benjamin A. Processive
        Revelation. Louisville: Westminster/John  Knox
        Press, 1992, p. 40.

13.     Ibid, p. 41.

14.     Ibid, p. 42.

15.     Ibid, p. 43.

16.     Pink, Arthur W. The Sovereignty of God.  Grand
        Rapids, MI: Baker Book House, 1982, p. 19.

17.   Keathley, Hampton."The Ocean Liner."Bible.
      2005.<http://www.bible.org/illus.asp?topic_
      id=1464>.

18.   Sire, James W. The Universe Next Door: A Basic
      Worldview Catalog, 3rd ed. Downers Grove, IL:
      InterVarsity Press, 1997, 35.

19.   Eldredge, John. Wild at Heart: Discovering the
      Secret of a Man's Soul. Nashville: Nelson Books,
      2001, 30.

20.   Schorr, Daniel. "'Intelligent Design' and Hard
      Times." 31 August 2005.
      <http://www.npr.org/templates/story/story.
      php?storyId=4826756 >.

21.   Williams, Julie and Ryan Nakashima. "Church
      Shooter Upset Over Sermon." Associated Press.
      <http://apnews.excite.com/ article/20050313/
      D88QC5200.html>.

22.   Simpson, Victor L. "Pope: How Could God
      "Tolerate' Holocaust?" MyWay  28 May 2006.
      <http://apnews.myway.com/article/20060528/
      D8HT21CO0.html>.

23.   Davies, p. 104.

24.   Hawking.

# About the Author
## Dr. Brian J. Shelley

**Continuing Education Dean**
**Central Pennsylvania College**
**Lancaster**

**Served as a Sr. Pastor for twenty years**

**Graduate Degrees**

**Oxford Graduate School (1997)**
**Doctor of Philosophy**

**Moody Graduate School (1992)**
**Master of Arts**

Have You Lost Your Mind?
Honoring God With Your Thinking and Decisions

Published by

GlobalEdAdvancePress
37321-7635 USA

**ISBN 978-0-9801674-1-2**

Printed in the United States
202915BV00002B/70-120/P